Curriculum and Pedagogy in Inclusive Education

While activists, politicians and policy-makers grapple with the big picture, teachers and learners are making inclusion happen in their day-to-day lives. This unique text shows the importance and reality of curriculum and pedagogy in developing inclusive practice in a range of settings.

Bringing together an exemplary collection of key articles, this Reader provides ways of thinking about inclusive curricula and pedagogy as starting points for possible action, as well as

- illustrating how teachers can get education right or wrong for diverse learners depending on the pedagogical decisions they make;
- discussing the role of the ordinary, special and inclusive pedagogy;
- showing examples of teaching that elicits genuine participation and active learning;
- providing case studies and lessons from learners about what makes good teaching for them.

Curriculum and Pedagogy in Inclusive Education will be inspirational reading for anyone with an interest in making inclusion happen.

Melanie Nind was formerly a Senior Lecturer in Inclusive and Special Education at the Centre for Curriculum and Teaching Studies, The Open University, but is now Reader in Education at the University of Southampton.

Jonathan Rix, Katy Simmons and **Kieron Sheehy** are all lecturers in Inclusive and Special Education at the Centre for Curriculum and Teaching Studies, The Open University.

Companion Volumes

The companion volumes in this series are:

Ethics and Research in Inclusive Education
Values into practice
Edited by Kieron Sheehy, Melanie Nind, Jonathan Rix and Katy Simmons

Policy and Power in Inclusive Education
Values into practice
Edited by Jonathan Rix, Katy Simmons, Melanie Nind and Kieron Sheehy

This Reader is part of a course: *Researching Inclusive Education Values into Practice*, that is itself part of the Open University MA programme.

The Open University MA in Education

The Open University MA in Education is now firmly established as the most popular postgraduate research degree for education professionals in Europe, with over 3,500 students registering each year. The MA in Education is designed particularly for those with experience of teaching, the advisory service, educational administration, or allied fields.

Structure of the MA

The MA is a modular degree, and students are therefore free to select from arrange of options the programme which best fits in with their interests and professional goals. Specialist lines in management, applied linguistics and lifelong learning are also available. Successful study in the MA programme entitles students to apply for entry into the Open University Doctorate in Education Programme.

Open University supported learning

The MA in Education programme provides great flexibility. Students study at their own pace, in their own time, anywhere in the European Union. They receive specially prepared study materials, supported by tutorials, thus offering the opportunity to work with other students. The University also offers many undergraduate courses. Within the area of Inclusive Education there is an Undergraduate second level course *Inclusive Education: Learning from each other.*

The Doctorate in Education

The Doctorate in Education is a part-time doctoral degree, combining taught course, research methods and a dissertation designed to meet the needs of professionals in education and related areas who are seeking to extend and deepen their knowledge and understanding of contemporary educational issues.

How to apply

If you would like to register for this programme, or simply find out more information about available course, please write for the *Professional Development in Education* prospectus to the Course Reservation Centre, PO Box 724, The Open University, Walton Hall, Milton Keynes MK7 6ZW, UK (Telephone +44 (0) 1908 653231). Alternatively, you may visit the Open University website http://www.open.ac.uk. where you can learn more about the wide range of courses offered at all levels by The Open University.

Curriculum and Pedagogy in Inclusive Education

Values into practice

Edited by
Melanie Nind, Jonathan Rix,
Kieron Sheehy and
Katy Simmons

RoutledgeFalmer
Taylor & Francis Group

LONDON AND NEW YORK

The Open
University

First published 2005
by RoutledgeFalmer
2 Park Square, Milton Park, Abingdon, Oxon OX14 4RN

Simultaneously published in the USA and Canada
by RoutledgeFalmer
270 Madison Ave, New York, NY 10016

RoutledgeFalmer is an imprint of the Taylor & Francis Group

© 2005 Compilation, original and editorial matter,
The Open University

Typeset in Bembo by
Newgen Imaging Systems (P) Ltd, Chennai, India
Printed and bound in Great Britain by
TJ International Ltd, Padstow, Cornwall

British Library Cataloguing in Publication Data
A catalogue record for this book is available
from the British Library

Library of Congress Cataloging in Publication Data
A catalog record for this book has been requested

ISBN 0–415–35207–X (hbk)
ISBN 0–415–35208–8 (pbk)

Contents

Acknowledgements

The following chapters are reproduced with the permission of Taylor & Francis Group (www.tandf.co.uk/journals):

Chapter 3
The need for a new model
Santiago Molina Y. Garcia and John Alban-Metcalfe

European Journal of Special Needs Education, 13, 2, 170–179

Chapter 4
Students' experiences of ability grouping: disaffection, polarisation and the construction of failure
Jo Boaler, Dylan Wiliam and Margaret Brown

British Educational Research Journal (2000), 26, 5, 431–648

Chapter 5
The education of black children: why do some schools do better than others?
Maud Blair

In Majors, R. (ed), *Educating Our Black Children: New directions and Radical Approaches*, RoutledgeFalmer *(2001), 28–44*

Chapter 6
Exclusive tendencies: concepts, consciousness and curriculum in the project of inclusion
Peter Clough

International Journal of Inclusive Education (1999), 3, 1, 63–73

Chapter 8
Research case studies in teaching, learning and inclusion
Adrienne Alton-Lee, Christine Rietveld, Lena Klenner,
Ngaio Dalton, Cathy Diggins and Shane Town

International Journal of Inclusive Education (2000), 4, 3, 179–210

Chapter 12
Inclusive practice in English secondary schools: lessons learned
Lani Florian and Martyn Rouse

Cambridge Journal of Education (2001), 31, 3, 399–412

Chapter 17
One teacher and a class of school students: the culture of the mathematics classroom and its construction
Corinne Angier and Hilary Povey

Educational Review (1999), 51, 2, 147–160

The following chapter is reproduced with the permission of Sage Publications Ltd:

Chapter 2
Common or specialized pedagogy?
Jenny Corbett and Brahm Norwich

From 'Learners with special educational needs.' Corbett and Norwich in Mortimore, P. (ed) *Understanding Pedagogy and its Impact on Learning.* Paul Chapman *(1999), 115–136*

The following chapter is reproduced with the permission of Blackwell Publishing Ltd:

Chapter 11
Towards an inclusive school culture: the affective curriculum
Gerda Hanko

British Journal of Special Education (2003), 30, 3, 125–131

The following chapter is reproduced with the permission of Kluwer Academic Publishers:

Chapter 14
An inclusive pedagogy in mathematics education
Claudie Solar

Educational Studies in Mathematics (1995), 28, 311–333

The following chapter is reproduced with the permission of PRO-ED:

Chapter 13
The evolution of secondary inclusion
Jacqueline Thousand and Richard L. Rosenberg

Remedial and Special Education (1997) 18, 5, 270–285

The following chapter is reproduced with the permission of the National Disability Authority:

Chapter 18
Living and Learning: the school experience of some young people with disabilities
Máirín Kenny, Eileen McNeela and Michael Shevlin

From Shevlin, M. and Rose, R. (eds) *Encouraging voices: respecting the rights of young people who have been marginalized. (2003)* Dublin: National Disability Authority, *138–158*

The following chapters are reproduced with the permission of the authors:

Chapter 7
Pedagogy, observation and the construction of learning disabilities
Carol A. Christensen and Carolyn D. Baker

Pedagogy, Culture and Society (2002), 10, 1, 73–93

Chapter 9
Learning 'how' and learning 'why': watching teachers in Asia move towards more inclusive styles of work
Janet C. Holdsworth

ISEC 2000 conference paper
http://www.isec2000.org.uk/abstracts/papers_h/holdsworth_1.htm

Chapter 1

Introduction
Models and practice in inclusive curricula

Melanie Nind

Why focus on curriculum and pedagogy?

The catalogues of the educational publishing houses are bursting with titles about inclusive education: inclusion at home and internationally, theories of inclusion, inclusive policy and inclusive provision. On closer scrutiny, we find that very little of this literature actually focuses on curriculum and pedagogy in inclusive classrooms. Indeed, the UK educational literature generally is remarkable for its lack of emphasis on pedagogy (Simon, 1981). In this volume, we attempt to go some way toward filling this gap, for as Peter Clough argues in Chapter 6, 'in the end, it is teachers who mediate policy through their activities in and out of the classroom, through their participation in the realisation of the curriculum'. The chapters collected together here all have something constructive to offer to teachers who, in mediating policy and realising the curriculum, are actively seeking to promote inclusion.

Problematising the curriculum

Debates about a curriculum for inclusion, particularly in England and Wales, have tended to be dominated by the issue of whether one curriculum can fit all. While there is evidence that certain groups of learners, such as children with Down's syndrome and children with specific learning difficulties, have distinctive group characteristics, evidence that effective teaching for such distinctive groups of pupils is different from effective teaching for other pupils is weak (Corbett and Norwich, Chapter 2, this volume; Hornby *et al.*, 1997; Norwich and Lewis, 2001). It does not necessarily follow that particular pupils, notably those with special needs for whom the case if most often made, need a different curriculum from other learners. The need for a different, special curriculum for special pupils, has in the past, been assumed and this premise has partly underpinned the growth of special schools in the UK. Schools for pupils with 'severe learning difficulties' were notable for their very particular developmental or skills-based curricula. In contrast, there has been no systematic attempt to develop 'MLD pedagogy' or an 'MLD curriculum' (Norwich and Lewis, 2001) for pupils whose learning difficulties were deemed 'moderate'. For them, a watered down ordinary curriculum with a greater emphasis on core and practical subjects was seen as sufficiently special.

The arrival of the National Curriculum in England and Wales put an end somewhat to any blossoming of more specialised curricula, though not to the development and popularity of specialised pedagogies, such as the instrumental enrichment of Reuven Feuerstein; the conductive education of the Peto Institute; behaviour modification and so on, which have continued to spread. Nor did the arrival of the National Curriculum put an end to debate about what kind of curriculum was needed. Instead it suffocated the debate somewhat into being dominated by an either-or approach – is either the National Curriculum or the old special curriculum more appropriate? This has sometimes ventured into how can we combine the two, or do one and call it the other (as discussed by Grove and Peacy (1999) and Byers (1999)), but less often has the debate become about creating new curricula or thinking about the curriculum more creatively and inclusively.

Much of the either-or debate comes back to how we think about children with special educational needs, as essentially the same, as in Warnock's (DES, 1978) ideas of sharing the same educational aims, or as very different and therefore as needing very different curricula. The two contrasting positions are typified by Thomas and Loxley's (2001) advocacy of shared needs and Aird's (2001) assertion of difference:

> Children who are slower to learn – for whatever reason – need the same in order to learn as any other child . . . our humanity tells us they need: interest, confidence, freedom from worry, a warm and patient teacher.
>
> (Thomas and Loxley, 2001, p. 26)

> The needs of some disabled children are radically different from those of the average child. These different needs must be given proper status.
>
> (Aird, 2001, p. 10)

As Corbett and Norwich's chapter illustrates, the drive towards inclusive education places in high profile this tension between characteristics that all learners share and characteristics that distinguish them. For some (such as Hornby and Kidd, 2001) the answer is to transplant special techniques into the mainstream setting. For others, it is to re-discover the competence of ordinary teachers at meeting learning challenges. Ainscow (1997), for example, maintains, that rather than 'transplant special education thinking' (p. 3) into ordinary schools we must look to the best practice of ordinary teachers as a starting point. Hart (1996) has similarly made a convincing case that it is better for ordinary teachers to have self-belief about 'their own power to take positive action in response to concerns about children's learning' (p. x) than to be restrained by special education thinking. Making the best of ordinary teaching can avoid 'individualizing the "problem" ', or 'disconnecting it' from the context in which it arises (p. x).

Booth (1992) has argued that special schools exist because of the inadequacies of mainstream schools in supporting the learning of all. Would Aird be asserting the special nature of some children if the mainstream curriculum were better or more inclusive? Thomas and Loxley (2001) argue that it is only the legacy of special education and myths generated by it that lead us to believe ordinary good teaching (and by implication the curriculum) is not enough. They argue, it is not special techniques that are needed but just the amount of help that is given and the sensitivity with which it is given that differs for some learners.

Mittler (2000) argues that inclusive pedagogy cannot be something additional bolted on to existing poor pedagogy; the starting place must be good pedagogy, which can become good pedagogy for more diverse learners. If we adopt the position that good teaching is good teaching for all does this also mean a good curriculum is a good curriculum for all? This would lead to a common curriculum and teaching approach, but not necessarily to the curriculum and approach we are most familiar with.

The importance of pedagogy and curriculum to the inclusion project becomes more evident when we remember that inclusion and exclusion take place in the context of the curriculum. Difficulties in learning are not noticed in a vacuum, but arise because students fail to meet the requirements of a given curriculum. This can be seen as a result of a mismatch between the learner and the learning opportunities (Booth, 1992). Clough (1998, p. 7) has argued that failure to learn is failure to teach or curriculum failure: 'a child who fails is one for whom a successful teaching method and curriculum has not been found or maximized'. This might lead us to join the never-ending search for ever-more special approaches, or to question the very way in which such failure has been built in to the system. Early in the life of the National Curriculum, for example, Swann (1992) argued that its structure and national assessment framework invited or built in failure.

A central difference between concepts of inclusion and earlier notions of integration is that, in inclusion, it is recognised that schools have to undergo change to become a good fit with the diverse learners they serve rather than pupils having to fit with unchanged curriculum and organisation (Barton, 1995; Rouse and Florian, 1997). Some schools are trying to do this by tinkering at the edges of their provision whilst others are looking at a more radical reappraisal of all they do. The chapters in this volume show a range of such responses, with Thousand and Rosenberg's chapter (Chapter 13) illustrating a particularly fresh approach to thinking about the curriculum.

Ways of thinking about inclusive curricula

While not always central to the inclusion literature, moves towards more inclusive curriculum and pedagogy are unfolding all the time. Ways of working through some of the tensions are being grappled with by teachers with and without the support of others (as shown by Kellett in Chapter 15, Rix in Chapter 10 and Florian and Rouse in Chapter 12). This often takes the form of some kind of action research, trying things out, evaluating progress, re-thinking and trying again. Starting points for such action are both the context in which people are working and the ideas they have. This introductory chapter provides an overview of some of the ways of thinking that influence positive action toward developing inclusive curriculum and pedagogy.

One approach to thinking about much of the practice discussed in this volume is that of a third way. That is, there is mainstream curriculum and pedagogy, there is special curriculum and pedagogy and third and different from both of these is inclusive curriculum and pedagogy. To what extent and in what ways this third inclusive approach combines elements of mainstream and special practice will depend on people's starting points and what it is they envisage they are working towards. Ways of thinking about and creating inclusive practice, which I expand on later, include differentiation, transformation, building connections, letting the child lead and focusing on interactions and processes.

1 *A simplistic linear response: differentiation.* Perhaps the most established response to making learning accessible for a diverse range of abilities and learning styles is differentiation. Traditional notions of differentiation as a means of sorting pupils into more and less able and providing them with experiences matched accordingly have obvious limitations. The chapter by Boaler, William and Brown (Chapter 4) illustrates the problems with this model. Other commonly seen approaches are differentiation by outcome, in which pupils are expected to learn different things from a shared experience, and differentiation by classroom organisation, in which a variety of organisational methods are used to realise the curriculum in different ways (McNamara and Moreton, 1997). Thus some children will be learning to work with others, while others are learning to apply design concepts, and teaching is organised so that children will learn from talk as well as reading and writing. Carefully structured peer tutoring can be seen as a form of differentiation and has been shown to be effective in inclusive classrooms (Fuchs *et al.*, 1997; Mortweet *et al.*, 1999). This might point action researchers towards taking up the challenge of exploring whether there is mileage in thinking about a differentiated curriculum in its most elastic and creative manifestation.

2 *A transformative response: learning without limits.* One of the problems with differentiation is idea that we have to adapt the curriculum for pupils of different abilities and hence the unproblematised acceptance of notions of fixed or inherent ability. The notion of fixed ability does not, however, go unchallenged. Hart (2003) and colleagues in the *Learning without Limits* project have sought to develop inclusive approaches that do not rely on this limiting concept. They propose an alternative to ability-based pedagogy underpinned by a more optimistic view of human educability. This addresses the need to cater for diversity within classrooms without assuming that students can legitimately be grouped into the 'more able', 'average' and 'less able'.

A core principle in this is transformability – working to *transform* both current patterns of interaction and future possibilities for learning – by opening up opportunities that might otherwise have remained closed, and by taking concerted action to release learning from limits that might otherwise constrain future development.

This core principle influences all curriculum decisions. It involves recognising young people as active agents who make sense of their day-to-day experience in their own terms and who act accordingly. The job of the teacher and the inclusive curriculum is to connect teachers' power and learners' power in *co-agency*; to connect with and harness young people's own power to make a difference to their own future lives. Curriculum activities need to enable everyone to participate and succeed, and rather than having different tasks for different groups according to their perceived levels of achievement, common tasks are presented in ways that make them open, accessible and engaging for everybody. An example is double-sided worksheets with the same task presented in different ways on either side and trusting the students to choose which side they want to do. In this way of thinking there is a strong ethic of everybody - what 'everybody' must have the opportunity to do, learn and experience and choices based on what will make for better learning for everybody and not just better for 'some people'.

One approach to reading the chapters in this volume is to question the ways in which the curriculum and pedagogy described fulfil the brief of making learning better for everybody and the extent to which they can be transformative.

3 *A social/emotional response: a curriculum that connects.*   Another way of thinking about inclusive practice is to focus on the need for the curriculum to make connections with learners' perspectives - to start from, and value, what learners bring rather than just assume that learners will adjust to school objectives, priorities, teaching styles and curriculum.

> We need to de-centre and see the world through their [learners'] eyes so that we can make the curriculum and the learning experience relevant and meaningful.
>
> (Collins *et al.*, 2001, p. 75)

Hart (1996, p. 17) argues that we need to 'build up "territories of information" about each child, that is, knowledge about the child's cultural and experiential world, activities, expertise and interests outside of school' and that this must inform the curriculum. Slee (1999, p. 200) sees this as a 'pedagogy of recognition' whereby diverse learners can recognise their own experiences and identities in the curriculum. Corbett and Norwich (in Chapter 2) see this 'connective pedagogy' as a way of working that connects with individual learners and their way of learning that in turn connects them with the curriculum and wider community. bell hooks (1994) goes further with her concept of 'engaged pedagogy' whereby 'everyone's presence is acknowledged' and students' lived experiences are not just included but become central to the curriculum, generating the excitement needed for meaningful learning. In this approach to inclusive practice the curriculum should be a coalition between the learner's world and the teacher's, thus preventing learners being seen as 'other' to the educational norm – a sense which can easily be internalised so that education becomes something that other people do (Stuart and Thompson, 1995).

Blair, in Chapter 5, argues the importance of valuing learners and genuinely listening versus the consequences of not doing so. Hanko, in Chapter 11, develops this theme in more directly, focusing on the social and emotional aspects of the curriculum. Similarly, the chapters in the final part each illustrate ways in which we might work with pupils' perspectives in constructing meaningful curricula.

4 *An early years response: a curriculum organised by the child.*   Again, dealing with the issue of connections Blenkin and Kelly's objection to the National Curriculum for young children is that it is a curriculum that is organised by others and does not relate to the everyday, commonsense knowledge and learning of learners:

> a curriculum divided into subjects is, potentially, the most alienating form of curriculum for young children because it formalizes experience too soon and, in doing so, makes it distant from the everyday, commonsense knowledge and learning that the young child is familiar with and responsive to.
>
> (Blenkin and Kelly, 1993, p. 58)

For children under three, an appropriate curriculum framework is the activities and experiences provided by educators; the activities devised by the children themselves; all the language and communication they are involved with and which is around them; and all their sensory stimuli (Rouse and Griffin, 1992, cited by Owens, 1997). Relationships with significant responsive adults and developmentally appropriate learning experiences are central tenets for the curriculum in the early years and we can think about these as central to an inclusive curriculum too.

Lloyd (1997, p. 177) points out that in the early curriculum 'the starting point is what the child can do rather than what she or he cannot do'. Adults are 'enablers, responsible for structuring and managing a challenging and stimulating learning environment which emphasizes opportunities for creativity and play, as well as a rich variety of personal interactions' and this is highly 'compatible with an inclusive view of education'.

The chapters by Rix and Kellett (Chapters 10 and 15, respectively) show how creative, responsive teachers can use reflective practice to make their teaching more sensory, appealing or meaningful and more connected to learners' starting points, whatever their age.

5 *A dynamic response: an interactive curriculum.*   If inclusive education means that schools need to fit with pupils, rather than just vice versa, this shifts attention to how the curriculum and pupils interact – what goes on between them in an ongoing, moment-by-moment process. From an interactive perspective making changes in order to reach out to all learners is not a one-off event, but a dynamic, transformative process in which feedback from pupils is continually sought and used to enhance the curriculum. An interactive curriculum, Kellett and Nind (2003) argue, is shaped by pupils themselves as they share and negotiate power. It is inclusive in the way it teaches and embodies empowerment, democracy and citizenship.

Christensen and Baker's chapter (Chapter 7) shows this dynamic, interactive element of inclusive curricula and pedagogy as the authors show that how we teach affects how well our students do and how we see them. Holdsworth's chapter (Chapter 9) illustrates how teachers can interact with the resources they have, including their own learning and what the children bring, to open up opportunities.

6 *A dynamic response: a process-based curriculum.*   Another dynamic response to the challenge of making the curriculum inclusive is to think about it in terms of processes rather than content. The curriculum would therefore be planned holistically, seeing the social environment and (national curriculum) subjects as 'contexts of experience' in which all pupils can engage in personally relevant work. Focusing in processes enables the construction of meaningful involvement in subjects for pupils with profound learning difficulties, for example, as they are engaged less in

Subject-related processes	Learning to learn processes	General processes
Related to scientific, mathematical, musical, etc. domains	Related to empowering the learner for further learning – not domain-specific	The kinds of processes we need to rehearse on a daily basis in school, but which need not necessarily lead us into further learning or be related to subject domains
e.g. *Scientific* • sorting • classifying • testing • observing • comparing	e.g. • attending • collaborating • interpreting others' thoughts and feelings • exploring • trying out	e.g. • choosing • listening • watching • manipulating • writing • waiting
Mathematical • counting • measuring • sequencing	• remembering • anticipating • enjoying together	
Musical • rhythm • tempo • responding to pitch		

The framework was prompted by observing a science lesson in which the pupils did not do anything related to science concepts but a lot of conforming to school rules and rehearsing the skills they had been involved with all morning.

Many processes could appear in more than one category. The important part is thinking about the meaningfulness of the lesson for the individual and group.

A lesson plan e.g. science: materials and their properties with a wet and dry goods stimulus could involve the following processes: observing, comparing, sorting, predicting, exploring, manipulating, communicating preferences, joint focus, turn-taking, sharing proximity . . . These would be available to all and targeted for some. Significantly, whether the focus is on subject processes or individual learning to learn priorities, the learning is embedded rather than added-on.

Figure 1.1 A process-based framework adapted from Kellett and Nind (2003, p. 134).

learning *about* the subject than learning *through* the subject (Ouvry and Saunders, 1996). One framework in which both learning about and through the subject is planned for is described by Nind and Cochrane (2002) and Kellett and Nind (2003). With an emphasis on curriculum processes rather than content, the framework encourages a balance between subject-related processes, general processes and learning to learn processes. A lesson, therefore, might be planned to support pupils working on the science processes of testing, observing and comparing, the general processes of listening, watching and waiting and the learning to learn processes of attending, exploring and anticipating as illustrated in Figure 1.1.

Another process-based approach is evident in Solar's chapter (Chapter 14) in which we see an emphasis on non-discriminatory classroom practice and processes of challenging stereotypes in and through the curriculum.

Conclusion: creative responding

A final way of thinking about inclusive curriculum and pedagogy, or perhaps a concept that incorporates all the other responses discussed, is that of responding to meet the challenge creatively and collaboratively. I have referred to this elsewhere as adopting an inclusive mindset (Open University, 2004). Conversations about what makes for inclusive practice (I must acknowledge personal communications with Dawn Male, Steve Cochrane and Georgina Glenny, for instance) has often led to the conclusion that it is a 'can-do attitude' that makes all the difference. Inclusive pedagogy and curricula emerge largely from a position that this can and must be do-able. This is not to pass the buck to teachers and say 'get on with it'. Rather, it is to acknowledge that much of the inclusive practice going on daily in classrooms is happening because of teachers' reflective practice, collaborative problem-solving and creative activity, which bring to fruition the kind of classrooms and learning they believe in. I suggest that how this happens in practice is explored in many of the chapters in this volume.

References

Ainscow, M. (1997) 'Towards inclusive schooling', *British Journal of Special Education*, 24(1), pp. 3–6.

Aird, R. (2001) *The Education and Care of Children with Severe, Profound and Multiple Learning Difficulties*. London: David Fulton.

Barton, L. (1995) 'The politics of education for all', *Support for Learning*, 10(4), pp. 156–160.

Blenkin, G.M. and Kelly, A.V. (1993) 'Never mind the quality feel the breadth and balance', in Campbell, R.J. (ed.) *Breadth and Balance in the Primary Curriculum*. London: Falmer Press.

Booth, T. (1992) *Learning for All: Unit 1/2 Making Connections*. The Open University.

Byers, R. (1999) 'Experience and achievement: initiatives in curriculum development for pupils with severe and profound and multiple learning difficulties', *British Journal of Special Education*, 26(4), pp. 184–188.

Clough, P. (1998) 'Introduction: what's special about inclusion', in Clough, P. (ed.) *Managing Inclusive Education: From Policy to Experience*. London: Paul Chapman.

Collins, J., Harkin, J. and Nind, M. (2001) *Manifesto for Learning*. London: Continuum.

DES (1978) Special Educational Needs (The Warnock Report). London: HMSO.

Fuchs, D., Fuchs, L.S., Mathes, P.G. and Simmons, D.C. (1997) 'Peer-assisted learning strategies: making classrooms more responsive to diversity', *American Educational Research Journal*, 34(1), pp. 174–206.

Grove, N. and Peacey, N. (1999) 'Teaching subjects to pupils with profound and multiple learning difficulties: considerations for the new Framework', *British Journal of Special Education*, 26(2), pp. 83–86.

Hart, S. (1996) *Beyond Special Needs: Enhancing Children's Learning Through Innovative Thinking*. London: Paul Chapman.

Hart, S. (2003) 'Learning without limits', in Nind, M., Sheehy, K. and Simmons, K. (eds) *Inclusive Education: Learners and Leaning Contexts*. London: David Fulton. hooks, b. (1994) *Teaching to Transgress*. London: Routledge

Hornby, G. and Kidd, R. (2001) 'Transfer from special to mainstream – ten years later', *British Journal of Special Education*, 28(1), pp. 10–17.

Hornby, G., Atkinson, M. and Howard, J. (1997) *Controversial Issues in Special Education*. London: David Fulton.

Kellett, M. and Nind, M. (2003) *Implementing Intensive Interaction in Schools*. London: David Fulton.

Lloyd, C. (1997) 'Inclusive education for children with special educational needs in the early years', in Wolfendale, S. (ed) *Meeting Special Needs in the Early Years: Directions in Policy and Practice*. London: David Fulton.

McNamara, S. and Morcton, G. (1997) *Understanding Differentiation: A Teachers Guide*, London: David Fulton.

Mittler, P. (2000) *Working Towards Inclusive Education: Social Contexts*. London: David Fulton.

Mortweet, S.L. Utley, C.A., Walker, D., Dawson, H.L., Delquadri, J.C., Reddy, S.S., Greenwood, C.R., Hamilton, S. and Ledford, D. (1999) 'Classwide peer tutoring: teaching students with mild mental retardation in inclusive classrooms, *Exceptional Children*, 65(4), pp. 525–536.

Nind, M. and Cochrane, S. (2002) 'Inclusive curricula? Pupils on the margins of special schools'. *International Journal of Inclusive Education*, 6(2), 185–198.

Norwich, B. and Lewis, A. (2001) 'Mapping a pedagogy for special educational needs', *British Educational Research Journal*, 27(3), pp. 313–329.

Open University (2004) *E243 Inclusive Education: Learning from Each Other*, Book 5 *Making it Happen*, Unit 13 Inside Classrooms.

Ouvry, C. and Sanders, S. (1996) 'Pupils with profound and multiple learning difficulties', in Ashdown, R., Carpenter, B. and Bovair, K. (eds) *Enabling Access: Effective Teaching and Learning for Pupils with Learning Difficulties*. London: David Fulton Publishers.

Owens, P. (1997) *Early Childhood Education and Care*. London: Trentham.

Rouse, M. and Florian, L. (1997) 'Inclusive education in the market place', *International Journal of Inclusive Education*, 1(4), pp. 323–336.

Simon, B. (1981) 'Why no pedagogy in England?', in Simon, B. and Taylor, W. (eds) *Education in the Eighties*. London: Batsford.

Slee, R. (1999) 'Policies and practices? Inclusive education and its effects on schooling', in Daniels, H. and Garner, P. (eds) *Inclusive Education: Supporting Inclusion in Education Systems*. London: Kogan Page.

Stuart, M. and Thomson, A. (eds) (1995) *Engaging with Difference: The 'Other' in Adult Education*. Leicester: National Organisation for Learning.

Swann, W. (1992) 'Hardening the hierarchies: the National Curriculum as a system of classification', in Booth, T., Swann, W., Masterton, M. and Potts, P. (eds) *Curricula for Diversity in Education*. London: Routledge/OU.

Thomas, G. and Loxley, A. (2001) *Deconstructing Special Education and Constructing Inclusion*. Buckingham: Open University Press.

Part I

The problem and potential of pedagogy

Chapter 2

Common or specialized pedagogy?

Jenny Corbett and Brahm Norwich

The term pedagogy, with its classical Greek origin, evokes something special and technical, perhaps even esoteric. That interest in teaching and teaching methods has been renewed recently under the label of pedagogy says much about the recycling of issues in the field of education and in the study of education. It also reveals the determining impact of the wider social context on education. In discussing pedagogy and special educational needs (SEN) in this chapter we need to address how pedagogy relates to other aspects of the educational process. What is the relationship between pedagogy and the curriculum, another term with esoteric connotations? One perspective is that the curriculum is about what is to be learned, the content of learning and its organization into different areas and fields of learning for different stages and ages of learners. Curriculum questions relate at one end to wider philosophical questions about the aims of education and what is worth learning and why.

At the other end, curriculum questions are intimately connected with questions about ways of promoting learning, questions to do with ways and means, the how of teaching or what has come to be called pedagogy. But the relationship between curriculum and pedagogy is more inter-connected than this analysis indicates. There are different models of the curriculum which imply different assumptions about the nature and origins of what is to be learned, its specification and about the relationships between teachers and learners (Skilbeck, 1984). Curriculum is not simply about what is to be learned, so that pedagogy is not simply about how to teach this content. Some models of curriculum, which are sometimes known as process or constructivist models, assume that the content of learning cannot be specified in advance and therefore cannot be used to determine independently the best way of promoting learning. In a process model of the curriculum, the very ways of promoting learning come to define the content of learning, and therefore the curriculum.

In this chapter, we discuss pedagogic issues relating to learners with SEN from this perspective of the inter-connections between pedagogy and curriculum. But as we will argue, pedagogic practices are also intimately connected with issues to do with the organization and grouping of learners in schools and classrooms. This point can be illustrated briefly by noting how the ability composition of a class and the numbers of learners in it can affect the kinds of teaching and classroom management methods used. One of our main points in this chapter is that pedagogic issues relevant to learners with SEN illustrate sharply these general points about inter-connections. Our second main point is that the SEN focus highlights a critically important aspect of general pedagogic questions that pedagogy is centrally about the relevance of teaching to difference and diversity. An interest in teaching methods has been a central focus in the education of learners with SEN from the origins of special education in specialist kinds of teaching approaches and materials. So, there is a sense in which the current interest in pedagogy is nothing new in the field of special needs education. It could be said that special educators have always been developing and testing out new teaching approaches and materials, as those with difficulties and disabilities are so clearly dependent on the quality of teaching.

The current general interest in pedagogic practice derives from wider social and economic policies to raise educational standards. Much has been written about the global pressures to increase the skill levels of the population better to equip countries to compete in the global economy. This policy interest tends to bias the focus on pedagogy to general technical teaching prescriptions, such as the National Literacy framework (DfEE, 1998).

These prescriptions do not necessarily take account of the diversity of learners and the inter-connections between pedagogy, curriculum and the organization of education provision. What is under consideration here is the concept of effectiveness in teaching, which is associated with the renewed interest in pedagogy and has arisen as part of the movement seeking greater school effectiveness and improvement. We will be arguing that concepts of effective teaching need to take account of diversity. If we adopt and adapt the kind of inclusive language used in the SEN Green Paper (DfEE, 1997) *Excellence for All*, we would say that 'pedagogy is for all'.

We will be focusing our discussion on those with disabilities and difficulties in learning because the field of SEN has traditionally been associated with this kind of exceptionality. But we are aware that there are many issues relating to provision and pedagogy which are common between this area of exceptionality and the areas of high ability and English as a second language.

[. . .]

Is pedagogy for SEN different or more of the same?

In adopting an inclusive position on pedagogy, we have to consider one of the continuing debates about providing for individual needs. Is teaching for pupils who have difficulties in learning *additional teaching of the same kind* as for those without difficulties or is it teaching which is *different in kind*? It may, of course, be that sometimes it is more of the same and sometimes a different kind of teaching. But either way we need to know when it is one or the other. There are special educators who deny that there is any need for different kinds of teaching, just the extension and refinement of similar kinds of teaching (e.g. Solity and Bull, 1987).

This position denies that some children, the one-in-five assumed to have SEN, are different from other children in their learning needs. Support for this is derived from research studies which fail to show differences in learning characteristics between groups identified in terms of whether they are identified and labelled as having a learning difficulty or not (Solity, 1993). What is at issue here is the wider and more general question of whether different teaching methods or pedagogies are more suited to some children and not others across the full range of abilities and attainments. This question has been studied in terms of aptitude – treatment interactions particularly in the USA (Corno and Snow, 1986). Research studies have examined whether more or less structured kinds of teaching result in greater learning gains for children differing in general characteristics, such as verbal abilities. Though there are continuing uncertainties, a general conclusion from these US studies has been that greater mediation in teaching and teacher direction was more suited to lower ability learners in a range of curriculum subject areas. These studies have relevance to SEN pedagogy questions, particularly in relation to pupils with Moderate Learning Difficulties (MLD), who merge into the group of lower ability learners. However, this type of study does not provide a research justification for different pedagogy between those with MLD labels and those designated as low attainers without a SEN designation. The implication of these aptitude-interaction studies is whether there should be differences in pedagogies between above average and below average learners.

[. . .]

Access to special educational provision is not dependent on demonstrating that differential pedagogies are needed. This is a very important point which underlies much of the uncertainty surrounding SEN resource allocation. There are two distinct though related levels of referring to education provision. The higher level relates to provision in terms of resources, placement and general curriculum and teaching approaches. This is the level where decisions are made about additional or different provision at one of the stages of the SEN Code of Practice including the stage of Statementing. The lower level relates to decisions about what and how to teach a particular individual child in a particular context. The two levels are distinct in the sense that the higher level decisions are about access and entitlement based on summative assessments, while the lower level decisions are about the planning of teaching based on formative assessments. But, though they are not easily related in practice, ideally decisions about access and entitlement to additional resources should follow decisions about individual pedagogic needs.

The Government's recent involvement in advising teachers on teaching methods has assumed a commonality of teaching methods across special and mainstream contexts. This is stated most starkly in the Green Paper in relation to pupils with specific learning difficulties (SpLD):

> As teachers become more adept at tackling reading difficulties, children with SpLd (such as dyslexia) should in all but exceptional circumstances be catered for in mainstream schools without a statement. What is more, class-based strategies which help children with SpLD can help children with literacy difficulties caused by other factors.
>
> (DfEE, 1997, section 15–16, p. 14)

Although this is a logical position to take given the Green Paper's generally inclusive stance, it leaves unaddressed questions about the nature of pedagogy for pupils with difficulties in learning. To address these questions we propose a conceptual framework (Table 2.1) for understanding the relationships between educational needs and pedagogies which is relevant to pedagogic differentiation in SEN and in teaching generally.

A child with SEN might just need more of the same kind of pedagogy as others without SEN. So, pedagogic needs might be common to all pupils irrespective of social, ethnic, gender and disability, reflecting that they all have *common* educational needs. For example, in teaching reading to all children, some might need a different balance between phonological and whole word methods than others. These pedagogic differences can be seen as part of a common repertoire of pedagogic practices. This would be the view favoured by those supporting a strong inclusive position to the education of pupils with difficulties and disabilities (Solity and Bull, 1987; Ainscow, 1995).

But there are differences between children which might call for different styles of pedagogy. We believe that you cannot rule out in principle that some pupils with significant difficulties in learning can share certain distinctive characteristics and might respond better to *specific* kinds of pedagogy. Therefore, specific kinds of pedagogies are relevant to significant difficulties in learning. For example, children with significant difficulties in phonological skills might benefit from intensive phonological training which is different from the phonological emphasis given as part of the

Table 2.1 Different kinds of educational needs and pedagogies

Educational needs	Pedagogies
1 *Common to all*	1 *Common to all*
	What is common to all drawing on a common variety of different teaching styles
2 *Specific or distinct*	2 *Specific to some, not others*
What is common to some but not others	Specific to kinds of significant difficulties in learning
3 *Individual*	3 *Individual*
What is unique to individual and different from all others	Reflecting person's individuality

common pedagogic style. But, these specific kinds of pedagogies might not replace the common ones. It is not a question of needing common pedagogies or different ones. It may be that a child needs the common kinds of pedagogy *and* additionally some specific kinds. Common and specific needs may be complementary needs. However, this may require more teaching time to combine the methods.

Common and specific pedagogies, however, may not take full account of pedagogically relevant differences between individuals who share certain distinctive learning characteristics. Pupils with difficulties in learning may need some pedagogic methods which suit their unique individual needs. Common, specific and unique individual needs are not alternatives but may be complementary to each other. Pedagogy, therefore, also needs to be considered in terms of the relationships and balances between practices which are common to all, specific to some and not others and unique to individuals.

Historical perspectives

It is also important to assess the impact of any pedagogy in relation to its stage of historical development. It is salutary to recall that special schools for children with severe and multiple disabilities were a relatively recent addition to the educational system. Those children deemed to have IQ scores below 50 were regarded as ineducable and unable to learn. Their physical and emotional needs were catered for by social and health service providers.

It is in this context that a pedagogy for children with severe and complex learning disabilities developed. It had grown out of work done by psychologists in the back wards of long-stay hospitals who found that institutionalized adults who had been labelled as 'idiots' and assumed to be unable to learn any social skills could be trained to do tasks for themselves. These might involve such mundane actions as putting a coat on and off, eating with a knife and fork, opening a door or selecting a drink out of two alternatives. The significant attitude underlying these teaching approaches, which set specific learning outcomes, is that all human beings, whatever the severity of their disability, have the capacity to learn and adapt.

[. . .]

Traditional methods of teaching deaf children to communicate have developed out of a social attitude that has denigrated any form of communication other than speech. Attempts by deaf children to use the natural language of signing used to be punished and they were forced to try to speak even though the severity of their hearing loss might have made this an almost impossible task.

The teaching of deaf children illustrates important aspects of the politics of pedagogy. Teaching or learning signing becomes a crucial element within the process of adopting a deaf cultural identity and a failure to induct a deaf child into their cultural heritage in this way is seen by many disability rights activists as a betrayal. The politics of pedagogy for deaf children comprises two learning landscapes, delineated by boundaries between mere integration on the one side and true inclusion on the other. A pedagogy which demands the exclusive use of speech is placing assimilation into the status quo as the dominant aim; a pedagogy which encourages the use of signing is validating the significance of a proud identity. These pedagogic practices must be understood as political acts if the wider significance of an inclusive ideology is to be properly understood.

Special educational needs has a strong historical association with the medical profession and the application of medical ideas to the identification and teaching of children with disabilities and difficulties. When government first made legislative provision for children with disabilities and difficulties at the end of the last century, medical officers played a central role in the identification and placement process. With the emergence of professional educational psychologists, particularly after the Second World War, this role was taken over by them. The intelligence tests introduced at the start of this century were designed to provide systematic evidence with which to identify children who were assumed to have intellectual impairments which prevented them from benefiting from mainstream school teaching. The identification process was in the medical tradition of defining areas of deficiency and applying this to teaching and learning. This focus on individual deficits in functioning has come to be associated with 'the medical model'. One of the longstanding criticisms of the medical model from an educational perspective has been that it is negative in focusing on what the child cannot do; not on what she or he can do and learn.

Much of the criticism of the medical model can be understood to derive from professional rivalries between health and educational professionals. The focus on deficits does not in itself define an exclusively medical perspective and set of assumptions, especially as the deficits talked about in education are functional ones relating to performances. These are different from the deficits identified in the medical diagnostic process which searches for underlying biological and other causes of these functional deficits. Nor does a medical approach assume necessarily that all functional deficits are unalterable. Psychologists who took over the key professional responsibilities for identification by the mid-1970s continued the deficit focus of assessment, but did so in terms of psychological processes presumed to underlie school learning and attainment. This interest in underlying psychological deficits was developed in a series of tests of perceptual, memory and linguistic processes presumed to be necessary for school learning and progress, such as the Illinois Test of Psycholinguistic Abilities (Kirk and Kirk, 1971) and the Frostig Test of Visual Perception (Frostig and Horne, 1964). The focus on underlying deficits was meant to be positive in that once the profile of perceptual and memory deficits was identified, a programme of remedial teaching could be designed to restore these processes. The pedagogic implication of these approaches was that specific groups of children – those with mild and specific learning difficulties – needed to receive special teaching programmes in settings separate from mainstream classes and focused on remediating these general underlying deficits. In practice, this tradition of remedial teaching came into disrepute for several reasons. First, there was scant evidence that any gains in underlying perceptual and memory functioning transferred to improved learning of basic educational skills relevant to the curriculum

(Ysseldyke, 1973; Solity, 1993). Second, there were doubts about the validity of the psychological deficit constructs and risks of stigmatizing children through false identification of these underlying deficits. Third, the specialist remedial programmes kept these children separate from their peers in mainstream classes and schools.

This tradition of special education teaching assumed that certain children have specific educational needs which require distinct pedagogies. It ignored those educational needs which are common to all and those which are unique to individuals. With the growth of interest during the 1970s in the rights of children with disabilities to be in mainstream schools and the criticisms of the relevance of deficit categories to planning teaching programmes for them, there was a sharp move away from deficit-focused approaches in SEN teaching. Behavioural analytic models were proposed as offering a pedagogic alternative which focused on performances in particular contexts. Underlying processes and deficits were swept away in a refocusing on the conditions and consequences of learning specific tasks. The behavioural framework did not depend on pedagogic approaches derived from general categories of difficulties. Each child's difficulties in learning were to be analysed in individual terms, with the focus on what individual teaching was needed.

The concept of SEN was introduced by the Warnock Committee (DES, 1978) during this period and was strongly influenced by this focus on individual learning performance. Statements of SEN were designed to identify a child's individual needs in terms of goals and objectives and the provision required to meet these needs. In this way, behavioural objectives were introduced as a positive teaching approach which was not side-tracked into futile and stigmatizing efforts to remediate deficits (Ainscow and Tweddle, 1978).

The basic principles of using behavioural objectives in teaching have been and continue to be very influential in special needs education. They have been adopted and adapted in government guidance on provision in the form of Individual Educational Plans (IEPs) for the wider group of those with special educational needs in the SEN Code of Practice. These principles imply that the assessment of the individual learner's attainment is relative to some common curriculum goal, such as literacy or numeracy. Learning is assumed to be cumulative and progressive, so the next step is identified towards the goal and this is defined in specific performance outcome terms. Optimal teaching methods are then adopted relevant to the specific learning objective based on what is known about the individual learner and appropriate approaches. Learning progress is monitored with the collection of performance data which is used to inform and guide the teaching and learning.

Many of these principles have been adopted in the moves by recent governments to raise educational standards generally through systematic school development planning, in regulations over target setting for schools and in guidance for teaching literacy and numeracy. These similarities between the principles of general school improvement and objectives teaching approaches in special education reflect the adoption of a more technical approach to education. It is an approach which appears to become more or less dominant depending on changing social, economic and political circumstances. Since the 1960s, its adoption came first in special education through the influence of empirically based behavioural psychology and subsequently in mainstream schools through school effectiveness research and technically based management approaches. We conjecture that these performance planning and outcome principles are adopted when social and political conditions call for greater control of educational outcomes. This would explain how they were adopted first within special education, which had been for many decades a backwater in education until the advent of the movement supporting greater rights for the disabled from the 1960s. The political need to raise standards in the general school system was subsequent to this in the 1980s, in response to what were seen to be serious skill gaps in Western societies.

Pedagogies can become punitive, destructive and ineffective, however, if they overlook individual identity to focus only on the disability rather than the person. Again, just as any good teacher tries to treat their students with respect, so the pedagogy has to be used appropriately. Any form of behaviour modification programme is potentially abusive and controlling. It involves an unequal power relation and is using methods which are designed to instil patterns of learned behaviour. Whilst it may be presented as a negotiated process entered into with the agreement of the learner, there is an implicit reliance that both sides accept responsibility for making necessary changes to the learning patterns or behaviour patterns of one of them. Behaviour contracts might be viewed as primarily concerned with the well being of the school community as a whole and with maintaining order, rather than with individual needs.

[. . .]

Current range of pedagogic practices: issues and examples

In special schools

In a recent research study, Adams (1998) examines the pedagogy of special schools which teach children with moderate or severe learning disabilities. She found that the essential element of a pedagogy for children with moderate learning disabilities was control. Much of the teaching was dull and repetitive rote learning with group tasks set and scant signs of differentiation. There was nothing special about it. The blandness of approach was such that could commonly be found in those mainstream classrooms where pedagogic practice lacked imagination. She concluded her evaluation of this pedagogy with these reflections:

> What emerged most strongly from the analysis of learning activities was the difficulty which teachers perceived in dealing with the learning needs of this group of pupils. The challenging behaviours which the class had demonstrated early in the academic year had led to formal structures, rules and regulations for the classroom. Managing behaviour remained foremost in the minds of

teachers and in many lessons this influenced the styles of teaching and learning . . . A mistrust of collaboration, which was thought to lead to pupils being off task, to chatter and to disruption, meant that pupils spent much time working individually on similar tasks, not on individualised work.

(pp. 182–183)

The latter comment is particularly revealing. It illustrates the fallacy of assuming that working individually is in any way special. Recent emphasis upon the importance of IEPs in all mainstream schools, including the secondary sector, suggests that individual work is particularly appropriate for children with learning disabilities. However, many secondary teachers find this extremely difficult to support and antipathetic to their commitment to group learning.

In contrast, Adams found that the pedagogy for severe learning disabilities was generally thoughtful and child-centred. It recognized individual differences and sought to connect with the specific interests and understanding of each child. She observed that teachers managed classrooms to facilitate learning and that

This resulted in a great degree of fluidity in the environment with pupils moving around the classroom for differing activities . . . With help almost always close at hand there were few occasions when pupils were not occupied, so that the atmosphere was at once informal and calm.

(Ibid., p. 208)

She noted in particular that this style of classroom management helped to avoid incidents of challenging behaviour from children whose past record had been one of emotional volatility. In adopting a pedagogy which relates to the child as an individual and then helps to include them in classroom activities, such teaching promotes personal growth and dignity through high levels of empathetic awareness.

It is clear from research like this that current pedagogic practices in special schools vary considerably in quality. There have been recent expressions of concern about the quality of provision and teaching in special schools for children with emotional and behaviour difficulties from OFSTED school inspectors (Cole *et al.*, 1998). The introduction of the National Curriculum has connected curriculum and teaching in special schools with mainstream schools within a common framework and challenged special schools teachers to find ways of applying the national framework while adapting it to the needs of pupils in their schools.

In mainstream schools

With more than 50 per cent of children having Statements of SEN in mainstream schools in England, any discussion of pedagogy and SEN needs to consider pedagogic practices in ordinary primary and secondary schools (Norwich, 1997). This proportion represents about 1.4 per cent of all pupils in the English school system. But these are children with significant SEN, who represent only about one-tenth of all children considered to have a difficulty in learning at some stage in their school careers, about 1 in 5 of all children.

[. . .]

Individual Education Plans have become the main pedagogic requirement within ordinary schools for developing individual teaching for children with SEN. IEPs are short records of the child's strengths and difficulties, parental views and the views of the child where appropriate. They also include learning targets, relevant teaching strategies, staff involvement and how progress is to be monitored and assessed. IEPs are meant to set targets for a period of between one and two terms in specific terms which makes assessment of progress possible.

IEPs were partly introduced as a system of accountability and a way of ensuring that schools were providing adequate pedagogy for those with less significant SEN who did not need a Statement. The paperwork involved in formulating and regular reviewing of IEPs has been greeted by many teachers as a bureaucratic nightmare, especially in larger schools (Cooper, 1996). However, IEPs have also been seen in a more positive light as a constructive way of planning individual teaching.

The influence of behavioural objectives in teaching, an approach based on performance planning and outcome principles, is evident in the form and use of IEPs. A generic kind of planning is assumed irrespective of the area or kind of learning. Planning is considered to be about setting specific single learning objectives for which specific strategies are selected. There is no place for teaching which has multiple and related objectives which call for inter-connected strategies. Neither is there a place for general teaching strategies where there are open-ended objectives. The IEP format may be relevant to the learning of certain basic educational skills, but there are difficulties when a single approach is applied to other areas, such as in personal and social development, creative and problem-solving areas of learning.

IEPs have also been criticized for their potential to separate out and stigmatize those who have them. In so doing their operation can be seen to bolster a mainstream system which is insensitive to individual needs if there is no feedback and connection with general curriculum planning and teaching. IEPs are often thought to be for planning individual teaching on a one-to-one basis. However, this is not necessarily so. The setting of individual targets does not require separate or withdrawal individual teaching strategies. It may be considered preferable to arrange teaching to be done in group settings as part of regular class learning activities.

It has also been suggested that all children could have records of their individual educational needs. There are already examples of schools which undertake some individual targeting with all their pupils with a focus on specific pedagogies. The advantage of applying this system to all children means that those with SEN would not need to be treated differently. The risk with this kind of individual planning is that it could become excessively wasteful of precious time needed for learning activities. Also, there might still be the need for more detailed individual planning for those with greater difficulties in learning. But, whether there are individual learning plans for some or for all, individual planning cannot be separated from curriculum planning and teaching which is sensitive to individual needs. No individual planning process can cover the range and depth of planning involved in providing a broad and balanced curriculum. IEPs are not meant to be a substitute for a curriculum and pedagogy which is suitable for the diversity of learners. What is needed is a combination of appropriate curriculum differentiation which takes place at a school or department level and individual planning which supplements this by fine-tuning and focusing the priority areas for teaching a children with SEN. This is a combination of top down systemic curriculum planning which builds flexibility into teaching approaches and bottom up individual assessment and planning. This point relates back to the earlier discussion in the introduction about the need to see the inter-connections between pedagogy and curriculum.

As we have said in our introduction, pedagogy cannot be isolated from its organizational and policy context. Meeting the needs of the minority with difficulties is connected to meeting needs of the majority through differentiated curriculum and pedagogic practices. It also connects with the grouping and place-ment of pupils both within and between schools. The move towards greater placements of those with Statements in ordinary schools has been associated with two types of organizational arrangement. One has been the additional resourcing of particular schools which specialize in some area or areas of SEN. The other type of arrangement is the placement of individual children with Statements in main-stream class with the support of specialist teaching and/or learning assistant sup-port. This might involve some withdrawal teaching for individuals or small groups during regular class time or outside class time. It will be clear that the kinds of teaching used for the range of significant SEN now met by teachers in ordinary schools depend on the particular organizational and grouping arrangements. The kind of teaching required by a child with a significant SEN will depend on whether her or his mainstream class is ability grouped or not, on whether there is withdrawal teaching or not, how such teaching relates to the mainstream class teaching programmes and whether there are other children with significant SEN in the class. Figure 2.1 shows how pedagogy cannot be isolated from the policy and organizational context. It is a summary of the relationships between school spe-cialization, learner diversity, differentiation practices and pedagogy just discussed.

Different curriculum goals and their relationship to different kinds of pedagogic adaptations

This framework set out in Table 2.2 is one way of making sense of the pedagogic implications of the central distinction we have proposed between common and dis-tinct educational needs, which we link with the distinction between curriculum goals for all and specialized and additional curriculum goals for some. Where cur-riculum goals are common for all then adaptations accept learners' strengths and difficulties. Following the analysis set out in the Warnock Report 1978, it is com-monly considered that there are three broad kinds of adaptations which are relevant to different kinds of disabilities and impairments: for sensory and motor impairments

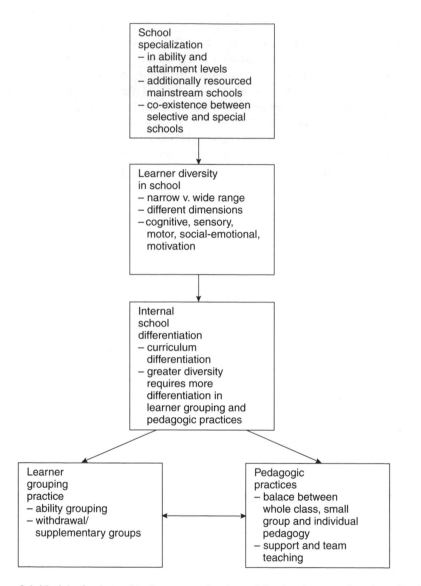

Figure 2.1 Model of relationship between school specialization, learner diversity, school differentiation and pedagogic practices.

there are adaptations to instructional presentations and response modes; for cognitive learning disabilities there are adaptations to the level of learning objectives; and for emotional and behaviour difficulties there are adaptations to social and emotional climate and interactions in teaching and learning. Where there is more than one kind of impairment or disability then there would be combinations of

Table 2.2 Framework of relationships between different curriculum goals and pedagogic adaptations

Curriculum goals	Common to all	Specialized goals for some
Pedagogic adaptations	*Which accept learner's strengths and difficulties* 1 Adapt instructional pre-sentation and learner response modes (sensory and motor impairments) 2 Adapt level of learning objectives (cognitive learning disabilities) 3 Adapt social–emotional climate and interactions of teaching–learning (emotional and behavioural adjustment difficulties)	*Which focus on learner's difficulties to circumvent or reduce them* 1 Learn alternative communication or mobility access (e.g. sign system, spatial/building orientation, braille) 2 Lessen deficit/impairment (e.g. instrumental enrichment for intellec-tual impairments (Feuerstein); self-control programmes (for conditions like ADHD)) 3 Restore function (e.g. Reading Recovery)

Source: Based on Norwich, 1990.

adaptations. By contrast, where curriculum goals are specialized for some, adaptations focus on difficulties in order either to reduce them or circumvent them. When circumventing them alternative communication or mobility access systems are taught, for example, sign systems, spatial and building orientation strategies and braille. When aiming to reduce difficulties, teaching aims to reinstate functions, such as intellectual functioning with specialized programmes such as Instrumental Enrichment (Feuerstein, 1980) and self-control functioning through cognitive-behavioural programmes for children with attentional and activity difficulties. There are also specialized programmes which aim to restore function not just to improve functioning in area of difficulties, such as Reading Recovery (Clay, 1985).

Pedagogic practices for a more inclusive school system

Booth and Ainscow (1998) have recently explored the area of pedagogic practices which support inclusion by presenting field work from several different cultural settings. This international perspective is interesting as it takes the ideology of inclusion into many real-life settings to see how teachers translate ideology into practice. Their concluding reflections are particularly challenging in saying that

> The examination of the nature of perspectives permits an understanding of the way research in this field has been constrained by a particular history of special education, dominated by a particular medical and psychological view

of why students experience difficulties in schools, and how they might be resolved. We suggest that a perspective which fully utilises the fertility of the concepts of 'inclusion' and 'exclusion' allows a break from such a history and the creation of a new one.

(p. 246)

A phrase which refers to 'the fertility of the concepts' can be seen to epitomize that degree of introspective theorizing which Clark *et al.* (1998) acknowledge can be constricting in the development of pedagogic initiatives relating to inclusion.

Perhaps an appropriate analogy for the current state of pedagogic practices for inclusion is that they are sandwiched between two opposing forces, different in flavour and texture and coming from completely different origins, but complementary. The top layer (and most conspicuously high-profile) is the theory of inclusion which relates to ethics, civil rights and conceptions of social justice. It is essentially about values and sets out idealized systems and relationships unsullied by practical realities. This is where critics of inclusive ideologists condemn their ideas as utopian and unrealistic. The under-layer of this sandwich is the voice of practitioners, administrators and policy-makers, embedded in day-to-day responsiveness and coping strategies. Their lives have been made more difficult in recent years by increased demands from external evaluators and it is not surprising if they resist any potentially stressful new elements to challenge their pedagogy. Inclusive practices, such as mixed ability teaching, team teaching and collaborative learning, for example, can seem intolerable to them, when they measure these in the context of league tables and SATs. In between the philosophical ideals and the daily practice, it is all too easy to lose sight of what kind of pedagogy is inclusive to all learners.

In their recent analysis of special education theorizing, Clark *et al.* (1998, p. 162) suggest that in some models of special education it is assumed that there are 'no really-existing 'special needs' which necessarily cause problems for educators and call for some carefully-worked-out response'. This seems to be a denial of the very tangible difficulties which many children do experience and a rejection of the specific pedagogies which we have discussed as having been developed as a response to their apparent disabilities and difficulties in learning. This kind of statement may be intended as a powerful challenge and can be a painful provocation to teachers working with children with disabilities and difficulties. These teachers often feel that they have devoted their careers to developing and enhancing distinct pedagogies which they have felt was beneficial to children they were deeply committed to supporting.

Teachers working in the special school sector learn to develop a caring pedagogy which is essentially founded upon their insights into the nuances of each individual child's behaviour patterns and means of communicating (Corbett, 1992, 1997). Whether this differs significantly from what might be expected of any good teacher is the critical factor to consider when addressing an inclusive pedagogy. In tracing the historical developments which led to a special needs pedagogy, a key assumption was that it was possible to help most people learn new skills and that behaviour patterns could change. This is an inclusive attitude in that it does not exclude some learners as being unable to learn and develop.

The pedagogy of itself is not the problem; adopting pedagogical practices which have been successful in the special school sector can be a valuable means of supporting inclusion. Task analysis and the creation of manageable steps towards achieving skills in literacy and numeracy can be seen in many aspects of differentiated mainstream practice and what is termed 'precision teaching' or 'objectives teaching' (e.g. Kessissoglou and Farrell, 1995; Cornwall, 1997; Sinclair, 1997). The widespread popularity of systems like the use of Circle Time and Behaviour Contracts in primary and secondary schools also illustrates the successful transfer of pedagogy from the special to the mainstream sector (e.g. Curry, 1997; Myers, 1998).

Clark *et al.* (1998) say that both special education and concepts of special needs are products of particular social processes rather than descriptions of the reality of children's characteristics or rational responses to those characteristics. But the social processes which foster a special pedagogy can be positive as well as negative: positive, in assisting a learner to acquire meaningful and transferable knowledge and relevant and self-determining actions and dispositions, and negative, in focusing on isolated facts and skills and short-term behaviours to suit others' needs.

For a pedagogy to enhance the quality of inclusive practices in the mainstream, there has to be an accurate evaluation of just what an inclusive pedagogy means in practice. There is a major dilemma in trying to promote inclusive values and maintaining a commitment to genuine individual learning and development in practical contexts. One way of dealing with the mismatching is to assess the process by which the teacher relates to the learner and then the learner is brought into a wider social inclusion. This could be seen as having two key aspects: the first, to connect with the individuals; the second, to connect them with the wider community of the classroom, school, recreation or housing. These two aspects are not one-off processes but ongoing expressions of responsiveness, which require imaginative, lateral thinking and high levels of flexibility.

'Connection' is an apt way of describing a pedagogy relevant to inclusion for it captures the central role of the teacher in the process, what we wish to call a connective pedagogy. Connecting in an inclusive learning environment presents challenges to the teacher. It is much easier to connect in selective settings of homogeneous, academically able and motivated learners. The level of empathy required to understand diverse learning styles is considerable. In their range of examples, Booth and Ainscow (1998) show how useful subjects like drama can be in opening up attitudes and helping disabled students to feel more included, deliberately introducing topics which include the outsider.

Assuming that inclusion refers to all learners, it is interesting to consider what connective pedagogy means for a wide range of individual differences. Beginning with a child who is deaf and blind, connection here cannot mean speaking to the child from any distance. It has to involve touch. To connect with this learner, the teacher needs to help the child feel safe and secure in the familiarity of daily rituals.

This may be done through massage, stroking and feeling familiar textures. To gain some sense of time and space, the routine may include feeling a different texture at the beginning of each school day. In this way, the teacher can first connect on a one-to-one level and then connect the child into their surroundings through using all the senses as appropriate and allowing the child to use them as a communication or enabling tool in making contact with objects in their daily lives (Park, 1997, 1998). Children who have profound and multiple disabilities may respond to the connection of mother–infant interaction, leading them into a wider exploration of their environment, through play and reflecting back to them their own sounds and gestures (Watson and Fisher, 1997).

In contrast, making connection with a child who shows emotional and behavioural difficulties involves recognizing her or his experience of the world. The teacher has to act as a link for them into social behaviours that are acceptable in a school setting, whilst validating their identity and way of perceiving themselves and others. It should be clear that inclusion and connection relate to many varied differences among school students, not just those traditionally seen as 'special needs'. It has a special relevance to that level of connection which can help children from different ethnic minorities feel included and validated. It also includes that connection which helps young people discovering their sexuality is outside the norm to feel that their identity is valued and their experience of difference is given equal respect as is their desire to be part of the school community.

These two aspects of connection, if operating successfully, will promote respect for individual identity and participation in group activities in differing ways which are comfortable for those involved. But, for connection to be enduring, what is individually comfortable needs to be respected. Forced social participation, even if subtle, threatens respect for the individual and runs counter to valuing individuality. Similarly, some forms of individual connection can isolate the child from the wider social context which runs counter to inclusive values. So, if these two aspects of connection are taken into account, then casualties are less likely in mainstream practices. Where disabled young people are placed in classrooms and playgrounds without this degree of connection, they are more likely to suffer from isolation, bullying and an inappropriate curriculum with inadequate pedagogic responses. This is an example of locational integration (DES, 1978) with all its inherent weaknesses. A connective pedagogy is costly in time, effort, concentration, consistency, continuity and funding. However, it becomes easier with familiarity and practice. Connective pedagogy will incorporate some of the best of 'special needs' teaching. But it does not ignore differences; it celebrates rather than pathologizes the disabled child. And in connecting the specific learner to the group, it is an anti-discriminatory pedagogy which seeks to educate all of the learners in how to be more responsive and understanding of the individual differences in any of them.

[. . .]

References

Adams, J. (1998) *A Special Environment? Learning in the MLD and SLD Classroom*, PhD thesis, University of Northumbria at Newcastle.

Ainscow, M. (1995) Education for all: making it happen, *Support for Learning*, 10(4): 147–157.

Ainscow, M. and Tweddle, D. (1978) *Preventing Classroom Failure: An Objectives Approach*, London: Wiley.

Booth, T. and Ainscow, M. (eds) (1998) *From Them To Us: An International Study of Inclusion in Education*, London: Routledge.

Clark, C., Dyson, A. and Millward, A. (1998) *Theorising Special Education*, London: Routledge.

Clay, M. (1985) *The Early Detection of Reading Difficulties*, London: Heinemann.

Cole, T., Visser, J. and Upton, G. (1998) *Effective Schooling for Pupils with Emotional and Behavioural Difficulties*, London: David Fulton.

Cooper, P. (1996) Are individual educational plans a waste of paper? *British Journal of Special Education*, 23(3): 115–119.

Corbett, J. (1992) Careful teaching: researching a special career, *British Educational Research Journal* 18(2): 235–243.

Corbett, J. (1997) Teaching special needs: 'tell me where it hurts', *Disability and Society*, 12(3): 417–425.

Corno, L. and Snow, R.E. (1986) Adapting teaching to individual differences among learners, in M. Wittrock (ed.) *Handbook of Research in Teaching*, New York: Macmillan.

Cornwall, J. (1997) *Access to Learning for Pupils with Disabilities*, London: David Fulton.

Curry, M. (1997) Providing emotional support through circle-time: a case study, *Support for Learning*, 12(3): 126–129.

DES (1978) *Special Educational Needs: Report of the Committee of Enquiry into the Education of Handicapped Children and Young People (The Warnock Report)*, London: HMSO.

DfEE (1997) *Special Educational Needs: Excellence for All* (Green Paper).

DfEE (1998) *The National Literacy Strategy: Framework For Teaching*.

Feuerstein, R. (1980) *Instrumental Enrichment: An Intervention Program for Cognitive Modifiability*, Philadelphia: University Park Press.

Frostig, M. and Horne, D. (1964) *The Frostig Programme for the Development of Visual Perception*, Chicago: Follett.

Kessissoglou, S. and Farrell, P. (1995) Whatever happened to precision teaching? *British Journal of Special Education*, 22(2): 60–63.

Kirk, S.A. and Kirk, W.D. (1971) *Psycholinguistic Learning Disabilities*, Chicago: University of Illinois Press.

Myers, J. (1998) Inside the circle, *Special*, Spring: 34–35.

Norwich, B. (1990) *Reappraising special needs education*. London: Cassell Education Limited.

Norwich, B. (1997) *A trend towards inclusion: statistics on special school placements and pupils with statements in ordinary schools 1992–1996*, Bristol; CSIE.

Park, K. (1997) How do objects become objects of reference? *British Journal of Special Education*, 24(3): 108–113.

Park, K. (1998) Form and function in early communication, *The SLD Experience*, 21: 2–5.

Sinclair, L. (1997) Researching classroom practice in order to accommodate more able children, *Support for Learning*, 12(2): 81–82.

Skilbeck, M. (1984) *School-Based Curriculum Development*, London: Harper Education Series.

Solity, J. (1993) Assessing through teaching: a case of mistaken identity, *Division of Educational and Child Psychology*, 10(4): 27–47.

Solity, J. and Bull, S. (1987) *Special Needs: Bridging the Gap*, Buckingham: Open University Press.

Watson, J. and Fisher, A. (1997) Evaluating the effectiveness of intensive interaction teaching with pupils with profound and complex learning difficulties, *British Journal of Special Education*, 24(2): 80–87.

Yesseldyke, J.E. (1973) Diagnostic-prescriptive teaching: the search for aptitude treatment interactions, in L. Mann and D.A. Sabatino (eds), *The First Review of Special Education*, Philadelphia: JES Press.

Chapter 3

The need for a new model

Santiago Molina Y. Garcia and
John Alban-Metcalfe

Introduction

It is well known that the history of Special Education is characterized by the continuing invention of new terminology and nomenclature, much of which is designed to identify neutral terms and descriptions. The purpose is to remove pejorative connotations when applied to people for whom this kind of provision is made, and to the kind of provision itself and the models upon which such provision is based. With regard to the student body of children and young people, we have come a long way from the earlier denomination of 'abnormal children' to the most recent 'children and young people with special educational needs'; with regard to educational models, history is full of terminology ranging from the earlier 'special education', via 'mainstreaming', 'regular education' and 'integrated education', to the more recent 'inclusive education'.

In view of the amount of effort that has been put into getting the nomenclature right, the question is worth pondering: is the terminology used important in our continuing efforts to try to improve educational provision for such children and young people? Or, is the process of analysing and re-analysing the words and phrases we use more akin to Penelope's unknitting during the night what she had knitted during the day?

It seems to us that, if the criterion for success is *simply* to find the most apposite phrase in order to be politically (or otherwise) correct, the effort is hardly worthwhile. However, if the effort is focused on the logic of the 'experts', and the criterion is presenting ideas and practices in a clearer light, and if our models will lead us to have a more precise and informed understanding of the kind of education which will enable us to ensure a better match between educational provision and learner needs, then the ideational effort is fully justified.

It is not our intention to engage here in a critical review of all the semiological, pedagogical, sociological, economic, political and cultural implications of the terminology used at different times in relation to people with an 'impairment', 'disability' or 'handicap', valuable as such a task would be in elucidating the precise meaning of each and in understanding their relevance and appeal during different periods in the history of education. The objects of this chapter are much more modest;

we will concentrate on a critical evaluation of two taxonomic terms that have been popular during the last few years, namely 'integrated education' and 'inclusive education'. Consideration will then be given to the proposal of a new pedagogical alternative, 'interactive education', in order to stimulate informed debate about the most appropriate terminology to apply to the most suitable kind of provision for children and young people who have been identified as having some form of special need.

The ideational power of words

It is obviously the case that words condition both 'expert' and popular opinion at a certain moment in history, in turn, rebounding and affecting the current collective praxis; in this case, the words rebound on and affect educational provision. For this reason, we consider that, before a certain terminology is adopted, what it signifies and what it symbolizes need first to be analysed critically as a social phenomenon or construct. The purpose of this chapter is to do precisely that, albeit after the terminology in question has come into common usage.

[...]

Integration of pupils with special educational needs

If one searches for the meaning of the word 'integration' in a dictionary, one is referred to the verb 'integrate', for which the first definition is 'to join to something else so as to form a whole'; or the second: 'to form or to blend into a whole; unite' (*Longman's English Dictionary*). In either definition, the clear implication is that that which is now whole is composed of distinct parts, and that some parts were previously missing.

If applied to a system of education, the implication is that such a system comprises a whole, which is made up of two or more parts. The questions that this analysis raises include what are these parts? What is their defining character? One way of dividing and education system is in terms of those groups that contribute to, and participate in it, in an integrated way, namely the family, the teaching body and the pupil body. Obviously, the precise way in which these groups interact is limited by the culture (defined in a strictly anthropological sense).

However, as no one argues any longer that there should be different schools to cater for the needs of different families (unless the criterion is how rich you are!), it does not seem appropriate to argue for sending children and young people to different schools on the basis of certain personal characteristics. To impose either would seem (a) to be contrary to social justice and inconsistent with the Universal Declaration of Human Rights, and (b) to be logistically unachievable, given the ontological impossibility of establishing precise and unambiguous categories of pupils. Thus, if a school were to refuse entry to, say, pupils who have any kind of impairment, then the model that the school would be presenting would be that of a disintegrated or segregated social system, which could be represented as shown in Figure 3.1. Unfortunately, this model represents a de facto situation in the over

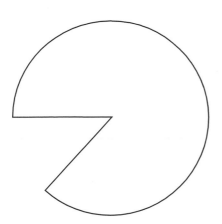

Figure 3.1 A segregated social system.

whelming majority of 'mainstream' schools in all European countries. The process of integration, therefore, is one of bringing together two distinct groups, whose nature has been defined by 'custom and practice'.

Anthropological study of the process of cultural integration, as occasioned when, as a consequence of some social phenomenon, two or more cultures are caused to collide, reveals that the processes of integration are neither as logical nor as precise as a semantic analysis of the term would suggest. This is because both social and cultural anthropology are replete with examples which show clearly that the process of integration is frequently hegemonic, with the dominant culture exercising a disproportionate amount of influence and power. It is regrettably the case that this kind of situation is mirrored precisely in the process of integrating pupils with special needs into mainstream schools: the dominant culture of the 'standard pupil' (where standard is measured in statistical terms) is imposed on the child or young person who has a disability, in both subtle and non-subtle ways, including in the imposition of a national curricula. Indeed, it has been argued (Gill, 1990) that the imposition of a national curriculum can be interpreted as being inconsistent with the UN Declaration of Human Rights. Schools are allowed to make 'curricular adaptations' in the form of modification and/or disapplication of the requirements of nationally imposed curricula for certain pupils, but the imperative to conform to the 'norm' is still present.

Inclusive education

This term, like 'integration', has come into common usage and has taken on a certain socio-educational meaning. It is our contention, first, that this term has come into being because, in spite of official and unofficial propaganda designed to achieve its promotion, the practice of integration is by no means widespread;

indeed there are moves in some member countries towards a retreat from earlier ideals, leading to greater segregation. Second, the concept of 'inclusive education' is imprecise to the point of not being open to relevant conceptual analysis. Thus, in reality, as the official statistics indicate quite clearly, of the 2 per cent identified in the Warnock Report as having severe and profound learning difficulties, or a severe hearing or visual impairment, only a small minority have been integrated into a 'mainstream' school. In other words, among this population, integration applies to a small proportion of an already small percentage of children and young people. This situation has been particularly true in secondary education. More recently, again according to official statistics, there is evidence of a move towards greater segregation of pupils who comprise this population. The adoption of the term 'inclusive education' may, then, be interpreted as a move to dress this retrenchment in acceptable, if not indeed politically correct, phraseology. Let us consider the basis of this supposition.

In looking up a dictionary definition of the term 'inclusion', the reader is again directed to the verbal form, 'to include', which is defined as 'to have as a part; contain in addition to other parts or to put in with something or someone else; take in or consider as part of a group'; or 'to contain, enclose; to take in or combine as part of a larger group' (*Longman's English Dictionary*). It is quite clear, first, that the term refers explicitly to physical situations (to introduce a part which is outside into the whole), or is merely quantitative (to introduce something smaller into something bigger); there is also the connotation of a dominant and a subordinate group. Second, applying this term to education in general, and special education in particular, what are evident are the political and social implications of introducing into a 'mainstream' school (the larger socio-educative sphere) pupils who were until recently in special schools (the smaller socio-educative sphere, both numerically and in terms of influence). The 'inclusion' nomenclature can be represented as in Figure 3.2.

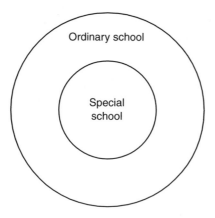

Figure 3.2 The 'inclusion' nomenclature.

An advantage that use of the term 'inclusive education' can be seen to have over 'integrated education' is that of ideological neutrality. But this only serves to meet the classical desire of any hegemonic society or group of presenting education as an entity that is ideologically neutral. In being neutral, however, the term lays itself open to the criticism levelled at the kind of social conformism characteristic of many post-modern and neoliberal societies. This is that, in an attempt to achieve neutrality, the concept of inclusion when applied to education has become blurred, thereby rendering itself inaccessible to socio-critical analysis. A practical example of adopting a politically neutral stance serves to illustrate the negative consequences it can have for pupils with special needs in terms of the application of educational policies.

From the moment that the term 'inclusive education' becomes central to educational thinking, the focus turns immediately on those aspects of education and educational provision shared by both 'normal' pupils and those with a disability (as if the latter were a homogeneous group!), at the expense of differences in the specific nature of each child or young person and her/his particular strengths and areas of weakness, and consequences that these differences have in terms of educational needs. Thus, the imperative of aiming for inclusion, and the corresponding aim to identify commonality at the expense of difference, are in grave danger of resulting in an anodyne concept of special needs. One of the virtues of categorizing pupils in terms of their special need is that it serves to provide some sort of guarantee that appropriate 'disability-related' specialist provision will be made, whereas an approach which is orientated towards identifying individual pupil's needs is open to the danger that one factor – perhaps the guiding factor – in assessing a pupil's needs may be the availability of resources (financial and other) to meet those needs (cf. Norwich, 1990).

Thus, there is evidence of wide within-country variations in the identification of pupils with special educational needs, and evidence in certain countries of drastic reductions in the services of specialized psychopedagogical staff (especially specialist support teachers). This new term 'inclusive education' can, therefore, be seen not to be quite as neutral as it first appears, or as some of its well-intentioned advocates would have us believe. On the contrary, it serves admirably the purpose of social 'demobilization', characteristic of post-modern and neoliberal societies. For these reasons, then, caution should be exercised before accepting it imitatively and without debate; serious and calm debate is called for, to which these brief ideas are intended to contribute.

Interactive education

In order to contribute to this debate, it is worth considering an alternative theoretical basis for analysing educational and special educational principles and provision. The originators of this approach, which was first developed in the 1980s, were a group of educational professionals, most of whom were members of the Centre pour la Recherché an Éducation Spécial et Attention Spécialisée (CRESAS) in

Paris, under the direction of Professor Mira Stambak. The stimulus for their proposal was collective reflection by the group members on the ineffectiveness of traditional pedagogy in its attempts to prevent educational failure and to achieve the kind of inclusion/integration of children with some form of impairment or disability into mainstream schools in a way that resulted in a positive and healthy experience for all pupils, teachers and families.

In light of the request for continuing debate, called for in conclusion to the previous section, the reader will hardly be surprised to read that an 'interactive education' or 'interactive pedagogy' approach is not being advocated as a pedagogical model that is either complete or even fully refined. On the contrary, because its conceptual configuration is based on reflection on concrete educational practice, using the principles and methodology of action-research, it can best be thought of being a developing model. Thus, what is said here must be understood as a purely provisional formulation, for discussion and debate here and elsewhere, and taken as a possible reference point for reflection and critical evaluation about specific examples of actual educational practice.

As noted before, the institutional ambit represented by the educational system implies the existence of other spheres, each with its own cultural characteristics, but with many similarities, if they are all spheres within the same society, the same geopolitical conjunction and the same moment in history. For this reason, an educational system that respects individual and collective human rights must subsume, and be subsumed by, other social subsystems in that society to form a coherent whole. At the same time, it must build its own socio-educational culture as the result of the integration of the particular cultures of the different social groups and the scope that different institutions afford, while respecting rigorously the specific and special needs of the social groups and the subject areas that must of necessity interact critically and creatively in a continuing ontogenetic process. For such a system, a system which respects cultural particularities and the needs of all constituent social groups, a system which recognizes and gives equal weighting to the needs of both the majority ('normal' pupils) and the minority (pupils with SEN), we suggest that the most appropriate term is 'interactive education', which can be represented as in Figure 3.3.

As the graphic representation in the figure suggests, the model implies the existence of only one type of school, which comprises all types of pupil; it has in mind that all pupils, as individual persons, have specific individual needs that should be respected equally with the individual needs of others, as equal members of society. At the same time, from a cultural point of view (in the strictly anthropological sense), the model also assumes that both common and different motivations and needs may exist among and between pupils belonging to the majority and the minority groups. This implies the necessity of both groups sharing space, time and curriculum components, and in parallel, the concomitant necessity of absolute respect for individualized space, time and curriculum components. In other words, what the 'interactive' model implies is the building of interactive knowledge and understanding from the nearest developmental zone; this, in turn, requires having

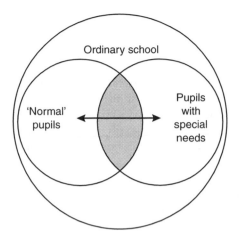

Figure 3.3 Interactive education.

in mind both what each pupil is able to do on her/his own, and what s/he is capable of doing with the help of other pupils or the teacher. In this way, curriculum development and design become vital variables for an individual, collective and cultural perspective on pupils. In our opinion, therefore, this model enjoys the advantages of positive aspects of integration and inclusion models while, at the same time, rejecting the negative. It is not possible within the confines of this chapter to consider more deeply the theoretical and practical implications of the 'interactive' model; for this reason, we shall limit ourselves to some basic principles.

The concept of learning

Learning is a process which comes about as a consequence of thinking. In this case, the subject-matter is cooperative and interdependent projects carried out by pupils with different abilities, previous knowledge and experience, motivations, levels of biological and psychological maturity, and capacity for making representations of their culture. It is also a process which can be optimally successful as a result of significant mediation by an adult, with whom the pupil can identify affectively.

Understanding of how children and young people learn and of how best to promote the learning process are inseparably related; for this reason, they serve mutually to support and explain each other – thinking deeply by the teacher can lead to ameliorating the learning needs of the pupil. For all that, in order to know and understand the nature of the learning that takes place, it is necessary to define carefully those situations in which learning can manifest itself. The learning process involves the use of the intellectual and social strategies of announcing, inviting discussion, defining a common project, persuading others to participate, convincing, solving problems, and transferring and generalizing knowledge. In other words, it involves the elaboration of flexible plans, which allow the pupil to assimilate the requirements of a given situation and to accommodate to different situations.

Pedagogical principles

Interactive education or interactive pedagogy (to give it its more universally European title) consists basically of supporting the ideas that pupils express in situations in which they are induced or encouraged to work cooperatively. It involves exchanging and comparing ideas in order to enable pupils to see the world from each others' perspective and so to motivate them into action and interaction.

Interactive pedagogy requires a social environment which takes into account the different facets of a pupil's personal make-up (sensory, intellectual, affective, social, spiritual, moral) and its diversity (in relation to personal experiences, culture, particular points of view), and also individual differences in the process of personal development. In order to cater for all these differences, the school must be an institution which provides space and time in which pupils are engaged together in healthy activities; through these shared activities, social, emotional and intellectual development is achieved.

Interactive pedagogy strives to establish a climate of self-confidence among children and young people, such that they will not be fearful of expressing their thoughts and feelings, and will come to celebrate the ways in which they are each different from one another, whatever the nature of their individual or socio-cultural characteristics. For this reason, what is essential is the existence of specialized psychopedagogical support within schools, for the enhancement of pupils' particular areas of strength and difference, in an atmosphere in which to be different does not cause one to be in any way marginalized, excluded or segregated.

Interactive pedagogy tries to establish a social environment within the school that is based on respect for, and assimilation of, individual and collective differences, in order to establish a common culture for the pupils and staff. In this way, no matter the diversity of origins, abilities or interests, intellectual and social exchange will always be possible, as will be the establishment of solid points of reference, for promotion of joint activities, and the development of shared projects.

Interactive pedagogy is critical in the selection of curricular prescriptions, while being respectful of the socio-political groups that are powerful at a given moment in history. At the same time, the official curriculum is only taken into account when the intellectual, social and affective development of each pupil can be guaranteed in a significant way. For all that, it is necessary that the curricular programme be always designed and implemented through a continuing process of action-research, structured in a spiral or defined in levels from epitomes, via conceptual nets which are built in a progressive and provisional way, to conceptual maps.

In interactive pedagogy, grouping of pupils is always heterogeneous and flexible not only because in practice a homogeneous group is impossible to achieve, but also as a matter of principle. In the conception of learning which is characteristic of interactive pedagogy, intellectual, social and affective development is only achievable as the result of cooperative interaction between, and thinking in common by, people of different ages, abilities, interests and cultural backgrounds.

Interactive pedagogy requires, therefore, a radical change in the criteria by which educational provision is evaluated, criteria which must be in accordance with the abilities, interests and cultural backgrounds of each pupil. For this reason, this kind of pedagogy cannot be evaluated on the basis of objectives imposed from outside; rather it must involve a process of formative, procedural and enlightening evaluation which, in turn, requires a serious and rigorous process of 'triangulation' when decisions are to be taken. Such decisions about each pupil's future have implications for, for example, course content and development, and if and when a pupil should progress from one class to another.

Provisional conclusions

After all that has been examined here, the reader may wonder whether a permanently continuing debate (so characteristic of Special Education), leading to the introduction from time to time of yet more terminology in relation to defining and redefining both individual pupils and systems of education, has any educational purpose or value. Our opinion has already been expressed: if our Penelopean endeavours were to fail to go beyond strictly academic limits and the pages of specialized journals, we would consider it a strange debate, and nothing more. However, such a debate has the potential to have extraordinary social implications when transferred and applied to the ambit of educational policies and practice. The conclusions could be used in support of existing policies or to justify cuts in the budgets destined for the education of children and young people with a disability or learning difficulty; they could even (heaven forbid!) be used to influence the thinking of teachers in such a way as to make them less critical, leading to a non-critical transfer to the classroom of what some would regard as the new technocratic dogma described as a 'national [and therefore, universally imposable] curriculum', which only allows permission for slight 'curricular adaptations'. Or – and this is our goal – they could lead to a real and fundamental improvement in the quality of education for all pupils.

Unfortunately, the former scenario appears to be the current reality, and it is precisely because of this that a fundamental analysis and critical debate of the terminology discussed here needs to be conducted. As already noted, the implications of what is happening currently are not concerned solely with the proper aims, objectives and philosophies of special educational provision; they are concerned with real, here-and-now, practical issues, such as the quantity and quality of specialized psychopedagogical support that is being made available.

However, as every nation has its own particular history and its own particular social, cultural and economic circumstances, so terminology and definitions which originate in any single country are open to the criticism that they may reflect social, cultural and economic constraints more than the needs of individuals to which they relate – particularly those individuals who are not seen as net generators of income, or indeed are not valued members of that society. It is perhaps, therefore, most appropriate that this kind of debate be conducted in a Pan-European forum, where, hopefully, a more objective, less partisan evaluation can take place, and a European approach be developed.

References

Gill, N. (1990). 'Are the rights of children being respected in the National Curriculum?', *Education*, 175, 407.

Norwich, B. (1990). *Reappraising Special Needs Education*. London: Cassell.

Chapter 4

Students' experiences of ability grouping

Disaffection, polarisation and the construction of failure

Jo Boaler, Dylan Wiliam and Margaret Brown

Introduction and background

In the UK there is a long tradition of grouping by 'ability' – a practice founded upon the idea that students have relatively fixed levels of ability and need to be taught accordingly. In the 1950s, almost all the schools in the UK were 'streamed' – a process by which students are segregated by 'ability' and taught in the same class for all subjects. A survey of junior schools in the mid-1960s (Jackson, 1964) found that 96 per cent of teachers taught to streamed ability groups. The same study also revealed the overrepresentation of working-class students in low streams and the tendency of schools to allocate teachers with less experience and fewer qualifications to such groups. This report contributed towards a growing awareness of the inadequacies of streamed systems, supported by a range of other research studies (most notably the longitudinal study carried out by Barker and Ferri, 1970) which highlighted the inequitable nature of such systems. Studies by Hargreaves (1967), Lacey (1970) and then Ball (1981) all linked practices of streaming and setting (whereby students are divided into different classes by 'ability' for individual subjects) to working-class underachievement.

The late 1970s and early 1980s witnessed a growing support for mixed-ability teaching, consistent with the more general public concern for educational equality that was pervasive at the time. But in the 1990s, concerns with educational equity have been eclipsed by discourses of 'academic success', particularly for the most 'able', which has meant that large numbers of schools have returned to the practices of ability-grouping (Office for Standards in Education (OFSTED), 1993). Indeed ability-grouping is now widespread in the UK, not only in secondary schools, but also in primary schools, with some children as young as 6 or 7 being taught mathematics and science (and occasionally other subjects) in different classrooms, by different teachers, following different curricula with different schemes of work. This phenomenon may also be linked directly to a number of pressures from government. The 1988 Education Reform Act (ERA) required schools to adopt a national curriculum and national assessment which was structured, differentiated and perceived by many schools to be constraining. Research into the effects of the

ERA on schools has shown that a number of teachers regard this curriculum as incompatible with mixed-ability teaching (Gewirtz et al., 1993). The creation of an educational 'market place' (Whitty et al., 1998) has also meant that schools are concerned to create images that are popular with local parents and 'setting' is known to be popular amongst parents, particularly the middle-class parents that schools want to attract (Ball et al., 1994). The White Paper Excellence in Schools (Department for Education and Employment (DfEE), 1997) revealed the new Labour Government's commitment to setting: 'unless a school can demonstrate that it is getting better than expected results through a different approach, we do make the presumption that setting should be the norm in secondary schools' (p. 38). In mathematics however, relatively few subject departments have needed to change back to ability-grouping as the majority have remained faithful to practices of selection, even when they have been the only subject department in their particular school to do so. An OFSTED survey in 1996 reported that 96 per cent of schools taught mathematics to 'setted' groups in the upper secondary years (Guardian, 1996). This has non-trivial implications for students' learning of mathematics. Despite this, our understanding of the impact of ability-grouping practices upon mathematics teachers' pedagogy and, concomitantly, students' understanding of mathematics, is limited.

[. . .]

This chapter reports upon interim data from a four-year longitudinal study monitoring the mathematical learning of students in six UK schools. It develops and expands themes arising from a study of two schools that offered 'traditional' and 'progressive' approaches to the teaching of mathematics (Boaler, 1997a,b,c). Although ability-grouping was not an initial focus of that study, it emerged as a significant factor for the students; one that influenced their ideas, their responses to mathematics, and their eventual achievement. One of the schools in that study taught to mixed-ability groups, the other to setted groups, and a combination of lesson observations, questionnaires, interviews and specially devised assessments revealed that students in the setted school were significantly disadvantaged by their placement in setted groups. A complete cohort of students was monitored in each school over a three-year period from the beginning of year 9 until the end of year 11 (ages 13–16).

[. . .]

Research design

The six schools in the present study have been chosen to provide a range of learning environments and contexts. All are regarded as providing a satisfactory or good standard of education in mathematics, as evidenced by the inspection reports of OFSTED, and all are partner schools with higher education institutions for initial teacher training. The schools are located in five different local education authorities, all in the Greater London area. Some of the school populations are mainly white, others mainly Asian, while others include students from a wide range of ethnic and cultural backgrounds. The General Certificate of Secondary Education

(GCSE) performance of the schools ranges from the upper quartile to the lower quartile, nationally, and the social class of the school populations ranges from mainly working class, through schools with nationally representative distributions of social class, to strongly middle class. One of the schools is an all-girls school and the other five are mixed.

All six schools teach mathematics to mixed-ability groups when students are in year 7 (age 11). One of the schools allocates students to 'setted' ability groups for mathematics at the beginning of year 8 (age 12), three others 'set' the students at the beginning of year 9 (age 13), and the other two schools continue teaching to mixed-ability groups. At the time of writing, the cohort of students in our study has completed the end of year 9, so that students in four of the six schools have been taught mathematics in setted groups for at least a year.

The data collection methods included 120 hours of observation of mathematics lessons within the schools, the administration of questionnaires relating to attitudes to and beliefs about mathematics at the end of both year 8 and year 9, and a total of 72 interviews with pairs of students towards the end of year 9.

The lesson observations were conducted throughout years 8 and 9, and evenly distributed across the schools, resulting in approximately 10 hours of observations per school per year; the detailed notes for each lesson observed were transcribed in full.

In May and June of both years 8 and 9, a questionnaire relating to attitudes and beliefs in mathematics was administered by members of the project team, in order to ensure confidentiality. The questionnaire included eight closed items, and two open items ('Describe your maths lessons' and 'How could your maths lessons be improved?') From approximately 1000 students in the cohort, a total of 943 questionnaires were completed in year 8, and 977 in year 9, with matched questionnaires for both years from 843 students.

During June and July of year 9, we also conducted six interviews in each school with pairs of students – a pair of boys and a pair of girls from each of the top, middle and one of the lower sets, and with students from a comparable range of attainment in the mixed-ability schools. Each interview lasted approximately 30 minutes, and followed an agreed protocol which identified 18 prompts. Students were chosen for interview by asking teachers of the selected classes (who were aware of the focus of the research) to nominate pairs of students who would be relaxed and happy to talk. Each interview was transcribed in full. We have also collected data on attainment, social class, gender and ethnicity although this is still being analysed.

The qualitative data from the open items in the questionnaire, the interview transcripts and the lesson observation notes were coded using open coding (Glaser and Strauss, 1967), from which the three themes to be discussed emerged.

Research results

When students moved from year 8 to year 9 in our study, it became clear from questionnaire, lesson observation and interview data that many students in the setted schools began to face negative repercussions as a result of the change from mixed-ability to setted teaching. Forty of the 48 students interviewed from setted groups wanted either to return to mixed-ability teaching or to change sets. The students reported that teaching practices emanating from setting arrangements had negatively affected both their learning of mathematics and their attitudes towards mathematics.

High sets, high expectations, high pressure

In Boaler's (1997b) study, at least one-third of the students taught in the highest set were disadvantaged by their placement in this group, because they could not cope with the fast pace of lessons and the pressure to work at a high level. The students that were most disaffected were able girls, apparently because able girls, more than any others, wanted to understand what they were doing – in depth – but the environment of set 1 classes did not allow them to do this.

We chose to observe set 1 lessons and interview set 1 students in this study to determine whether the environment of set 1 lessons in other schools was similar to those in Boaler's study and whether students were disadvantaged in similar ways. Early evidence suggests that this is the case. Every one of the eight girls interviewed from set 1 groups in our study wanted to move down into set 2 or lower. Six out of eight of the set 1 boys were also extremely unhappy, but they did not want to move into lower groups, presumably because they were more confident (although no more able) than the girls, and because of the status that they believed being in the top set conferred. Observations of set 1 lessons make such reactions easy to understand. In a range of top-set classes the teachers raced through examples on the board, speaking quickly, often interjecting their speech with phrases such as 'Come on we haven't got much time' and 'Just do this quickly'. Set 1 lessons were also more procedural than other – with teachers giving quick demonstrations of method without explanation, and without giving the students the opportunity to find out about the meaning of different methods or the situations in which they might be used. Some of the teachers also reprimanded students who said that they did not understand, adding comments such as 'You should be able to, you're in the top set'. The following are descriptions of 'top-set' lessons, from students in the four setted schools:

School E: mainly white, working-class school with low attainment

> If we can't answer the question or something, he'll say 'Oh yeah, you're not going to be in set 1 next year – you are the set 1 class you shouldn't be doing this, you should be doing this'.
>
> (Graham, School E, set 1)

> P: *He* likes being successful.
> G: He wants to turn up a number 1 set – but he's going too fast, you know, a bit over the top.
> P: He explains it as if we're maths teachers. He explains it like really complex kind of thing, and I don't get most of the stuff.
>
> (Paul and Graham, School E, set 1)

I want to get a good mark, but I don't want to be put in the top set again, it's too hard and I won't learn anything.

(Molly, School E, set 1)

School F: ethnically diverse, middle- and working-class school with average attainment

The teacher says 'You'd better do this, by like 5 minutes time' then you start to rush and just write anything.

(Lena, School F, set 1)

You don't even get time to think in the maths lessons.

(School F, girls, set 1)

I want to go down because they can do the same work but just at a slower pace, so they understand it better, but we just have to get it into our head the first time and that's it.

(Aisha, School F, set 1)

School A: mainly white, middle- and working-class school with average attainment

A: Sometimes they work too fast for me and I can't keep up with the rest of the class.

J: And all your other friends are in different groups so you can't really ask them for help, because you're the top set and you're supposed to know it all.

(Ayla and Josie, School A, girl, set 1)

S: Most of the difference is with the teachers, the way they treat you. They expect us to be like, just doing it straight away.

M: Like we're robots.

(Simon and Mitch, School A, set 1)

School C: mainly white, middle-class school with very high attainment

L: This year find it really hard and I haven't been doing as well as I wanted to be.

I [Interviewer]:   Did you enjoy it more last year? [in mixed-ability groups]

L: Yeah definitely, because it's a whole different process, you're doing different books, you're able to be taught more, you just feel that you're not being rushed all the time.

(Lena, School C, set 1)

I used to enjoy maths, but I don't enjoy it any more because I don't understand it. I don't understand what I'm doing. So if I was to move down I probably would enjoy it. I think I am working at a pace that is just too fast for me.

(Andrea, School C, set 1)

[. . .]

In questionnaires, students in the six schools were asked, 'Do you enjoy maths lessons?' Students in top sets were the most negative in the entire sample, with 43 per cent of set 1 students choosing 'never' or 'not very often', compared with an average of 36 per cent of students in other sets and 32 per cent of students in mixed-ability classes. Students were also asked whether it was more important 'to remember work done before or think hard' when answering mathematics questions. The set 1 groups had the highest proportion of students who though remembering was more important than thinking. In the set 1 classes, 68 per cent of students prioritised memory over thought, compared to 56 per cent of students in the other setted groups and 51 per cent of students in mixed-ability groups.

Low sets, low expectations and limited opportunities

Students in low sets at the four schools appear to be experiencing the reverse of the students in high sets, with repercussions that are, if anything, even more severe and damaging. Indeed, the most worrying reports of the implications of the setting process for students in our sample came from students in lower groups. These students reported a wide range of negative experiences, substantiated by observations of lessons. These included a frequent change of teachers, the allocation of non-mathematics teachers to low sets and a continuous diet of low-level work that the students found too easy. Examples (in which a new paragraph denotes a change of speaker) include:

> It's just our group who keeps changing teachers.
> I: Why?
> Cause they don't think they have to bother with us. I know that sounds really mean and unrealistic, but they just think they don't have to bother with us, cause we're group 5. They get say a teacher who knows nothing about maths, and they'll give them us, a PE teacher or something. They think they can send anyone down to us. They always do that. They think they can give us anybody.
> (Lynne, School E, set 5)

> R: We come in and sir tells us to be quiet and gives us some work and then he does them on the board and then that's basically it.
> J: Even though we're second from bottom group, I think it would be much better if we didn't have the help with it.
> R: Because he thinks we're really low.
> J: Really stupid or something.
> (Ramesh and Jack, School A, set 6)

Students were particularly concerned about the low level of their work and talked at length about teachers ignoring their pleas for more difficult work, making students who had finished the work in the first 5 minutes of the lesson sit and wait with nothing to do for the remaining 55 minutes. In some cases students were told things like, 'You can't have finished, you're set 5' (School E, set 5 girl). In some

lower-set lessons the students were not given any mathematics questions to answer –
only worked solutions to copy off the board.

> L: We come in, sit down, and there's like work on the board and he just says
>   copy it. I think it's all too easy.
> R: It's far too easy.
> I: What happens if it's too easy? Do they make it any harder?
> M: No we just have to carry on. We just have to do it. If you refuse to do it
>   he'll just give you a detention. It's just so easy.
> R: Last year it was harder. Much harder.
>
> (Lee and Ray, School E, set 5)

> C: He just writes down the answers for us from the board, and we say to
>   him, we say we can do it, but he just writes them down anyway.
> I: So what are you meant to do?
> C: Just have to copy them down. That's what we say to him, 'cause a lot of
>   people get frustrated from just copying off the board all the time.
>
> (Carol, School A, set 6)

> L: We do baby work off the board.
> N: Yeah it's just like what we already know, you know 1 add 1.
> L: Say it's three times something equals nine.
> N: It's easy and it's boring.
>
> (Lynne and Nelly, school E, set 5)

In questionnaires, 27 per cent of students taught in the lower sets in the setted
schools reported that work was too easy, compared with 7 per cent of students in
the upper sets and 14 per cent of students in the schools using mixed-ability teaching in year 9. Students in lower groups were upset and annoyed about the low level
of the work they were given; in addition to finding lessons boring, they knew that
their opportunities for learning were being minimised:

> Sir treats us like we're babies, puts us down, makes us copy stuff off the board,
> puts up all the answers like we don't know anything.

> And we're not going to learn from that, 'cause we've got to think for ourselves.

> Once or twice someone has said something and he's shouted at us, he's said,
> 'Well you're the bottom group, you've got to learn it', but you're not going to
> learn from copying off the board.
>
> (School A, set 6, girls)

The students' reports were consistent with our observations of low-set lessons, in
which students were given answers to exercises a few minutes after starting them
or required to copy work off the board for the majority or all of lessons. In
response to the questionnaire item 'how long would you be prepared to spend on

a maths question before giving up?' 32 per cent of students in the lower sets chose the lowest option – 'less than 2 minutes' – compared with 7 per cent of students in sets in the top half and 22 per cent of students in mixed-ability groups.

[. . .]

All four schools that use ability-grouping have told us that the system is flexible and that students will change groups if they are inappropriately placed, but the students in low groups believed there to be little hope of moving to higher groups. They believed that they were trapped within a vicious circle – to move up they needed good end of year test results, comparable with students in higher groups, but they could not attain good results because they were not taught the work that was assessed in the tests.

> R: In our class it was very easy and as soon as we got into the SATs, it was just like we hadn't done it.
> L: I want to be brainy, I want to go up, but I won't go up if this work is too easy.
>
> (Lee and Ray, School E, set 5)

In the same way as the 'top-set' teachers had fixed ideas about the high level and pace of work students should have been able to do, the teachers of the lower sets had fixed ideas about the low level of work appropriate for 'bottom-set' students. The students reported that teachers continued with these ideas, even when students asked them for more difficult work:

> N: I say 'Oh, I've done this before already'.
> L: And he says 'Well you can do it again'. He's nothing like 'Oh, I'll set you with some harder work or nothing'.
>
> (Nelly and Lynn, School E, set 5)

Restricted pedagogy and pace

In mixed-ability classes, teachers have to cater for a range of students whose previous attainment varies considerably. Most teachers respond to this challenge by providing work that is differentiated either by providing different tasks for different students within the same class ('differentiation by task'), or by giving all students a task that can be attempted in a variety of ways and at a variety of different levels ('differentiation by outcome'). Teachers often let students work 'at their own pace' through differentiated books or worksheets. In setted classes, students are brought together because they are believed to be of similar 'ability'. Yet, setted lessons are often conducted as though students are not only similar, but *identical* – in terms of ability, preferred learning style and pace of working. In the setted lessons we have observed, students have been given identical work, whether or not they have found it easy or difficult, and they have all been required to complete it at the same speed. This aspect of setted lessons has distinguished them from the mixed-ability lessons we have observed, even when the 'setted' lessons were taught by the same teachers. The restrictions on pace and level of work that are imposed in setted lessons have also been a considerable source of disaffection, both for students who find the pace of lessons too fast and for those who find it too slow.

In interviews, students talked at length about the restrictions imposed upon their pace of working since changing to setted groups, describing the ways in which they were required to work at the same speed as each other. Students reported that if they worked slower than others they would often miss out on work as teachers moved the class on before they were finished:

> D: People who are slow they don't never get the chance to finish because she starts correcting them on the board already.
>
> S: You don't finish the module.
>
> (David and Scott, School A, set 4)

Students also described the ways in which teachers used a small proportion of the students as reference points for the speed of the class (cf. Dahllöf, 1971), and the detrimental effect this could have on their learning:

> A: Sometimes you can do it fast, and at the end, you don't really know it.
>
> L: But if she knows some people have finished, then she tells the class, 'OK you've got even less time to do the work'. She's like, 'Look at these five people, they have finished, hurry up!'
>
> (Aisha and Lena, School F, set 1)

Students also reported that if they worked quickly they were disadvantaged as teachers made them wait for the rest of the class:

> D: Now we are sort of, people can be really far behind and people can be in front. Because it is sort of set, and we have these questions, say 'C', we have to all start.
>
> I: So you all start at the same, you all start at C?
>
> S: Yeah but then the people who work fast have to wait for the people at the end to catch up.
>
> D: Because I finished, nearly before half the class and I had a lesson to do nothing.
>
> (David and Scott, School A, set 4)

Again, the students linked these restrictions to the norms generated within setted groups:

> C: Last year it was OK but when we finished our work or anything miss would give us harder work to do. But in this year when you finish it you just got to sit there and do nothing.
>
> L: Yeah because in sets you all have to stay at one stage.
>
> (Craig and Liam, School F, set 3)

Such problems were not caused by teachers simply imposing an inappropriate pace upon their groups – some students found lessons too fast whilst other students in the same groups found the same lessons too slow. The two boys in school F, quoted here, described the problem well – in mixed-ability classes students would be given work that was chosen for them, if they finished the work, teachers would give them harder work; in setted lessons 'you all have to stay at the same stage'. Being able to teach the whole class as a single unit is the main reason that teachers put students into 'ability' groups, and it was also one of the main sources of the students' disaffection. The students also described an interesting phenomenon – that some teachers seemed to hold ideas about the pace at which a class should work that were independent of the capabilities of the students who were in that set. For example,

> If you're slow she's a bit harsh really. I don't think she really can understand the fact that some people aren't as fast as others. Because if you say that I don't understand the work – she'll just say something like 'You're in the middle set, you had to get here somehow, so you've got to do middle set work'.
>
> (David, School A, set 4)

The teachers of the top sets also exemplified this phenomenon with the frequent remarks they made to students in the vein of

> You are the set 1 class, you shouldn't be finding this difficult.
>
> (Peter, School E, set 1)

It seems that the placing of students into 'ability' groups creates a set of expectations for teachers that overrides their awareness of individual capabilities. This is a particularly interesting finding given that the main argument that the Prime Minister, Tony Blair, and other government ministers have given for supporting setting is that children need work that is at an appropriate pace and level for their particular 'ability'.

But the process of ability-grouping did not only appear to initiate restrictions on the pace and level of work available to students. It also impacted upon the teacher's choice of pedagogy. Teachers in the four schools in our study that used ability-grouping responded to the move to setted teaching by adopting a more prescriptive pedagogy to the same teachers who offered worksheets, investigations and practical activities to students in mixed-ability groups concentrated upon chalk-board teaching and textbook work when teaching groups with a narrower range of attainment. This is not surprising given that one of the main reasons mathematics teachers support setting is that it allows them to 'class teach' to their classes, but it has important implications for the learning of students. When students were asked in their questionnaires to *describe their maths lessons*, the forms of pedagogy favoured by teachers in the schools using ability-grouping were clearly quite different from those in the schools using mixed-ability teaching. We coded a significant number of students' responses to this question as 'lack of involvement' because students wrote such comments as 'lessons go on and on' or 'maths lessons are all the same'. Some 12 per cent of responses from students in setted groups reflected a lack of involvement, compared with 4 per cent of responses from students in mixed-ability groups. An additional 12 per cent of students from setted groups described their lessons as 'working through books', compared with 2 per cent of students in mixed-ability groups, whilst 8 per cent of setted students volunteered that the 'Teacher talks at the board', compared with 1 per cent of mixed-ability students. Only 15 per cent of students in setted groups described their mathematics lessons as either 'OK', 'fun', 'good' or 'enjoyable', compared with 34 per cent of mixed-ability students.

In a separate open question, students were asked how mathematics lessons could be improved. This also produced differences between the students, with 19 per cent of students taught in sets saying that there should be more open work, more variety, more group work, maths games or opportunity to think, compared to 9 per cent of mixed-ability students. Eight per cent of setted students said that lessons should be slower or faster, compared to 4 per cent of mixed-ability students, and 4 per cent of setted students explicitly requested that they return to mixed-ability teaching.

The influence of ability-grouping upon teachers' pedagogy also emerged from the students' comments in interview. The following comments came from students across the spectrum of setted groups:

I: What are maths lessons like?
J: Rubbish – we just do work out of a book.
I: How does that compare with other lessons in years 7 and 8?
M: They were better. We did more fun work.

                                                    (Janet and Molly, School E, set 1)

I: What would be your ideal maths lesson?
L: I would like work that is more different. Also when you can work through a chapter, but more fun.
N: It would have to be a bit more different.
L: Could do a chapter for 2 weeks, then the next 2 weeks do something else, an investigation or something – the kind of stuff we used to do.

                                                    (Nelly and Lynn, School E, set 5)

R: Last year it was better, 'cause of the work. It was harder. In year 8 we did wall charts, bar charts etc., but we don't do anything like that. It's just from the board.
L: I really liked it in year 7, because we used to like do it from the books. Like at the end of the year we used to play games. But like this year it's just been like work from the board.

                                                    (Ray and Lee, School E, set 5)

D: In year 8, sir did a lot more investigations, now you just copy off the board so you don't have to be that clever.

S: Before, we did investigations, like *Mystic Rose*, it was different to book-work,' cause books is just really short questions but those were ones sir set for himself, or posters and that, that didn't give you the answers.

(David and Scott, school A, set 4)

In year 7 maths was good. We done much more stuff, like cutting out stuff, sticking in, worksheets and all stuff like that. Now, every day is copying off the board and just doing the next page, then the next page and it gets really boring.

(Carol, School A, set 6)

The change in teaching approach that appeared to be initiated by setted teaching could simply reflect the increase in students' age and progression towards GCSE, but similar changes did not take place in the mixed-ability schools. The implications of such changes for students' learning of mathematics are discussed next.

Discussion

The students interviewed from our setted schools create an image of setted mathematics lessons that reflects disaffection and polarisation, which is broadly substantiated by our observations of lessons and by questionnaire data. It seems that when students were taught in mixed-ability groups, their mathematics teachers gave them work that was at an appropriate level and pace. When the students were divided into ability groups, students in high sets came to be regarded as 'mini-mathematicians' who could work through high-level work at a sustained fast pace, whereas students in low sets came to be regarded as failures who could cope only with low-level work – or worse – copying off the board. This suggests that students are *constructed* as successes or failures by the set in which they are placed as well as the extent to which they conform to the expectations the teachers have of their set. In particular, within top sets, students are constructed as successes and failures according to the extent to which they can cope with the highly procedural approaches adopted by teachers of those sets. Other notions of success in mathematics, such as those which emphasise depth of understanding, which are arguably much closer to the concerns of professional mathematicians (Buxton, 1981; Burton, 1997) are ruled out.

The requirement to work at an inappropriate pace is a source of real anxiety for many students, particularly girls, and is not confined to top sets:

M: I get really depressed about it, and I don't want to ask, but then again like it really depressed me, the fact that everyone in the class is like really far ahead and I just don't understand.

L: Yeah' cause like especially when everyone else understands it and you think 'Oh my God I'm the only one in the class that doesn't understand it'.

(Maggie and Linda, School C, set 3)

These students were not talking about minor feelings and peripheral details but issues that go directly to the heart of their experiences, and which have a profound impact both on their attitudes towards, and their achievement in, mathematics.

The major advantage that is claimed for ability-grouping practices is that they allow teachers to pitch work at a more appropriate level for their students. However, while ability grouping practices can *reduce* the range of attainment in a class, within even the narrowest setting system, there will be considerable variations in attainment. Some of this will be due to the inevitable unreliability of mechanisms of allocating students to particular sets, but even if the average attainment of students in a set is reasonably similar, this will mask considerable variation in different aspects of mathematics and in different topics, as the students were well aware. Indeed, the students held strong beliefs that individuals have different strengths and weaknesses and that it is helpful to learn from each other and to learn to be supportive of each other:

> C: I prefer groups when we're all mixed up. There's the clever and the dumb and the dumb learn from the clever and sometimes the clever they'll be learning from the people who don't know as much. Because some things the clever are good at and some things the not so educated are good at.
>
> L: Classes should have a mixture of everyone. And then everyone could learn from everyone, because it's not like the dumb ones don't know anything, they do know it, but the atmosphere around them in lessons means they can't work.
>
> C: And they just say to themselves – what's the point?
>
> (Craig and Liam, School F, set 3)

Perhaps the most surprising finding is that setting was not perceived as accomplishing the one thing that it was designed to do – to allow teachers to match the work set to the strengths and weaknesses of individual students. When the students were asked if work they were given was at 'the right sort of level', the proportion of those taught in mixed-ability groups who said that the work set was 'usually about right' for them was actually marginally higher (81 per cent) than that for those taught in sets (77 per cent).

[. . .]

As we have noted, many of the disadvantages of setting that we have described are contingent rather than necessary features of ability-grouping, but we believe that they are widespread, pervasive and difficult to avoid. The adoption of ability-grouping appears to signal to teachers that it is appropriate to use different pedagogical strategies from those that they use with mixed-ability classes. The best teachers are allocated to the ablest students, despite the evidence that high-quality teaching is more beneficial for lower-attaining students (Black and William, 1998, p. 42). Curriculum differentiation is polarised, with the top sets being ascribed qualities as mathematicians, not as a result of their individual qualities, but simply by virtue of their location in a top set. In order to ensure that the entire curriculum is covered, presumably to suit the needs of the highest-attaining students within the top set, the pace of coverage is both increased and applied to the whole class as a unit, and teachers seem to make increased use of 'transmission' pedagogies. For some students, who are able to assimilate the new material as it is covered, the experience may be satisfactory, but for the remainder, the effect is to proceduralise the curriculum until it becomes a huge task of memorisation. The curriculum polarisation results in a situation in which upward movement between sets is technically possible, but is unlikely to be successful, because a student moving up will not have covered the same material as the class he is joining. Finally, because of the perversities of the examination arrangements for mathematics GCSE, the set in which a student is taught determines the tier for which a student is entered, and thereby, the maximum grade the student can achieve. For most students, this decision will have been made 3 years or more before the examination is taken.

[. . .]

Conclusion

The traditional British concern with ensuring that *some* of the ablest students reach the highest possible standards appears to have resulted in a situation in which the majority of students achieve well below their potential. As one student poignantly remarked:

> Obviously we're not the cleverest, we're group 5, but still – it's still maths, we're still in year 9, we've still got to learn.
>
> (Lynn, School E, set 5)

References

Ball, S.J. (1981) *Beachside Comprehensive* (Cambridge, Cambridge University Press).

Ball, S.J., Bowe, R. and Gewirtz, S. (1994) Competitive schooling: values, ethics and cultural engineering, *Journal of Curriculum and Supervision*, 9, pp. 350–367.

Barker Lunn, J.C. and Ferri, E. (1970) *Streaming in the Primary School: A Longitudinal Study of Children in Streamed and Non-streamed Junior Schools* (Slough, National Foundation for Educational Research).

Black, P.J. and William, D. (1998) Assessment and classroom learning, *Assessment in Education*, 5, pp. 7–73.

Boaler, J. (1997a) Setting, social class and survival of the quickest. *British Educational Research Journal*, 23, pp. 575–595.

Boaler J. (1997b) When even the winners are losers: evaluating the experiences of 'top set' students, *Journal of Curriculum Studies*, 29, pp. 165–182.

Boaler, J. (1997c) *Experiencing School Mathematics: Teaching Styles, Sex and Setting* (Buckingham, Open University Press).

Burton, L. (1997) *Mathematics – Communities of Practice?* paper presented at *Meeting of the Research into Social Perspectives on Mathematics Education Group* held at University of

London Institute of Education 11 December (Birmingham, University of Birmingham School of Education).

Buxton, L. (1981) *Do You Panic about Maths? Coping with Maths Anxiety* (London, Heinemann).

Dahllöf, U. (1971) *Ability Grouping, Content Validity and Curriculum Process Analysis* (New York, Teachers College Press).

Department for Education and Employment (1997) *Excellence in Schools* (London, The Stationery Office).

Gewirtz, S., Balls, S.J. and Bowe, R. (1993) Values and ethics in the education market place: the case of Northwark Park, *International Studies in Sociology of Education*, 3, pp. 233–254.

Glaser, B.G. and Strauss, A.L. (1967) *The Discovery of Grounded Theory: Strategies for Qualitative Research* (New York, Aldine).

Guardian (1996) Blair rejects mixed ability teaching, 8 June, p. 7.

Hargreaves, D.H. (1967) *Social Relations in a Secondary School* (London, Routledge and Kegan Paul).

Jackson, B. (1964) *Streaming: An Education System in Miniature* (London, Routledge and Kegan Paul).

Lacey, C. (1970) *Hightown Grammar: The School as a Social System* (Manchester, Manchester University Press).

Office for Standards in Education (1993) *Mathematics Key Stages 1, 2, 3 and 4, fourth year 1992–93: A Report from the Office of Her Majesty's Chief Inspector of Schools* (London, Her Majesty's Stationery Office).

Whitty, G., Power, S. and Halpin, D. (1998) *Devolution and Choice in Education* (Buckingham, Open University Press).

Chapter 5

The education of black children

Why do some schools do better than others?

Maud Blair

Introduction

The literature on the schooling and education of black[1] children in Britain is extensive. With few exceptions (Channer, 1996; Nehaul, 1996; Blair and Bowne, 1998), most of what has been written has focused on issues of underachievement, over-representation in suspensions and expulsions, early drop-out rates in the USA, etc. This focus on the negative is not at all surprising. Black parents over the years have campaigned for better education for their children, have run their own supplementary schools to improve their children's chances, have tried to influence policy and practice in schools and have generally been vocal and active in their attempts to challenge discriminatory and unfair practices faced by black children and to reverse the continuing high levels of under-performance of black children in public examinations. Writers on the subject have tried to share their understandings of the nature and causes of these disadvantages, but despite the research, the community campaigns, the efforts of multiculturalists and antiracists, little seems to have changed over the decades and black and other minority children continue on aggregate to underperform in standardised tests compared to their white peers (Gillborn and Gipps, 1996).

A number of theories have been put forward to explain this situation. One explanation, the cultural dissonance explanation (Driver, 1979), holds that white teachers[2] do not understand the cultures of black children and therefore misinterpret their behaviour and impose sanctions more frequently or more harshly on black children leading to conflict and disaffection with school. Black children in a white racist society are deemed, therefore, to suffer from low self-esteem, especially if the curriculum either does not reflect their cultures and interests or these are represented negatively in curriculum materials (Green, 1982). Another theory, closely allied to cultural dissonance, is that teachers do not understand the learning styles of black children and therefore the teaching and learning experiences of black young people are negatively affected. For black children to succeed, it is argued, it becomes necessary for them to reject their own black identities and think and act white (Fordham and Ogbu, 1986; Fordham, 1996). There is also the argument that black children are aware that the job market does not operate in their favour and so they see little point in putting a lot of effort into academic work (Ogbu, 1988). Others have sought explanations in the children themselves, arguing that certain 'racial' groups are intellectually inferior to others (Jensen, 1969; Eysenck, 1971; Herrnstein and Murray, 1994) or that black children behave more badly and are therefore justifiably placed in lower academic sets (Foster, 1990). But the explanation that has been widely put forward both in Britain and in the USA is that racism – structural, institutional and individual – has been the main cause of the negative experiences of schooling of black and other minority children. In Britain, researchers have pointed to the disproportionate levels of reprimands and disciplinary measures that are routinely taken against black children in the classroom (Mortimore *et al.*, 1988; Tizzard *et al.*, 1988; Gillborn, 1990; Wright, 1992; Connolly, 1995), and in particular the unfair and unjust manner in which black students are disciplined.

> Perhaps even more significant than the frequency of criticism and controlling statements which Afro-Caribbean pupils received was the fact that they were often singled out for criticism even though several pupils of different ethnic origins were engaged in the same behaviour. ... In sum, Afro-Caribbean pupils were not only criticised more often than their white peers, but the same behaviour in a white pupil might not bring about criticism at all.
>
> (Gillborn, 1990, p. 30)

That black children were more likely to be placed into lower sets and streams was also observed (Wright, 1987; Foster, 1990). Although Foster argued that black students deserved their placement in lower sets because of their higher incidence of poor and disruptive behaviour, the evidence in favour of the racism and discrimination explanation has been overwhelming.

Some writers, however, have also argued for a more complex understanding of the political and social positioning of black children in schools (Rattansi, 1992; Scott-Jones, 1996) and of black males in particular (Noguera, 1997). Referring to the (damaging) effects of discrimination on black students which some writers have highlighted, Scott-Jones declares that

> There is no recognition (by some researchers) of the possibility of a range of reactions to discrimination on the part of students. There is no acknowledgment of the possibility that some students respond to discrimination with an increased determination to do well in school.
>
> (Scott-Jones, 1996)

Scott-Jones further argues that the way schools are organised may not be suitable for adolescents, especially those transferring from elementary to middle/secondary school. Others have pointed to the way that schools neglect the role of peer group pressure on adolescents as well as the importance of taking account of the adolescent's natural desire for independence at a time of confusing emotional and physical changes associated with growing up (Measor and Woods, 1984; Hargreaves *et al.*, 1996; Cullingford and Morrison, 1997).

The factors which exist to complicate and confound our understanding of the educational experience of black students, therefore, are many and varied. In an attempt to answer the question posed in the title of this chapter, I will argue that there are essentially three major factors which allow some secondary schools in Britain to succeed with black students where others have failed. The first is an understanding by the adults in the school of the *political and social concerns* of their students, and the willingness and courage to address these, however uncomfortable or difficult. Teachers need to know and understand their students individually in order to assist their daily interactions and cater for them as individuals, and also as members of groups in order to be familiar with some of the wider issues that affect students as members of the wider society. The second is adult understanding of and empathy with the *needs and concerns of adolescents*. There is a need for teachers to be in tune with the particular age-group of students they teach in order to cater appropriately for them. The third is the school's willingness to *work with parents as genuine partners* in the pursuit of a socially and academically rewarding experience for students. In their attempts to understand their students as individuals, teachers need to form *meaningful* partnerships with parents, partnerships which recognise that parents are the primary carers of children, and, especially where the teachers are white, that there are issues which affect minority ethnic group students' lives which they cannot grasp unless they deliberately seek that knowledge. Parents are well placed to provide that information.

The focus on black students in this chapter comes from the belief that if a school is willing to honestly address the issues that beset minority ethnic groups (for example black or Gypsy Traveller students) it is more likely to embrace the issues that exist for dominant groups, whereas schools that take a 'colour-blind' approach are more likely to interpret students' needs as meaning white students' needs, an approach which not only misses the diversity and complexity of students' lives, but also marginalises them (Blair *et al.*, 1998). Instead of creating a warm and welcoming environment for black and minority ethnic group students and their parents, 'colourblind' schools are more likely to develop a 'racially hot' environment marked not only by resentment and conflict but by disaffection and more likely than not, 'underachievement'. Education in such schools is for black communities, no longer, as Noguera states, '...the most viable path to social mobility, (but) serves as a primary agent for reproducing their marginality' (1997, p. 220). In order to illustrate my theories, I draw on research evidence from a study carried out by the Open University for the Department for Education and Employment (DfEE). Most of the examples are drawn from one of the 18 schools which were involved in the study.

A school that is successful for black students? Like finding a needle in a haystack

School effectiveness has been defined in the literature in measurable terms to mean success in standardised test scores, and more precisely in secondary schools in Britain, to mean acquiring grades A★ to C. In seeking schools where students performed well in standardised tests, we began in our study by drawing on the Office for Standards in Education (OFSTED) lists of the General Certificate of Secondary Education (GCSE) results and highlighted those schools which not only performed well in the league tables, but also had a workable figure of a minimum of 10 per cent of black students. The study also covered Bangladeshi and Pakistani students, but this chapter focuses entirely on black students largely because the school from which I draw my examples had less than 2 per cent students of South Asian origin. The issues for these groups of students (important though they are regardless of the numbers in the school) also differ in some important respects from those of black students, though my general theories outlined here apply to all students whatever their ethnic group.

Having selected schools which appeared on the OFSTED lists to be academically successful, we visited these schools in order to ascertain the level of success of the black (and South Asian) students. It was not so surprising to us to discover that schools which seemed on the face of it to be successful, were in fact only successful for some of their students. There is an assumption in the literature that an effective school is likely to combine a number of important factors. These are that the school has strong leadership, is well-organised, the staff are united and share a vision, there is a positive ethos, and that there are high expectations of students (Nuttall and Goldstein, 1989; Smith and Tomlinson, 1989; Reynolds and Cuttance, 1992). Smith and Tomlinson (1989) concluded that a school which was 'effective' was likely to be effective for all its students, including minority ethnic group students. However, many so-called 'effective' schools operate in a 'colour-blind' manner which assumes that all students have the same needs and are affected by the same issues. One school in our study, which would qualify as 'effective' by these criteria, provides an interesting example. A brief look at the ethos and the question of academic success serves to illustrate the point.

In relation to the school ethos, the level of negativity that existed in this school amongst the black students, and amongst the black boys in particular, indicated that their concerns were either not known or not heeded. The students were so pleased to be able to talk about what schooling was like for them that a group of them asked for a further interview after school because, after my one hour with them in which they gave several examples of racism, especially by specific members of staff, one boy declared that I had not 'heard the half of it'. This state of affairs was not confined to this one school alone but existed for nearly all the black boys interviewed and a significant number of the girls in all the schools, with the exception of the one, Northern Catholic School, from which I draw my examples of 'success'.

Academically, black girls in the school given in the example here appeared, on the face of it, to perform as well and sometimes better than their white male and female peers. However, even this was deceptive. When the category 'black girls' was further broken down into the different ethnic groups (African, African-Caribbean, 'mixed-race'), we found that a school which seemed successful for all black girls was in fact only successful for African and dual ethnicity ('mixed-race') girls. African-Caribbean girls did not do well.

[. . .]

There were therefore no schools in our study which could be said to be equally successful for all their students, least of all for the black students. We decided therefore, that rather than search for the proverbial needle in the haystack, we would examine the factors that led to the steady progress by black students in Northern Catholic School. The school was no different in size from two other Catholic schools (approximately 700 students and approximately 30 per cent black students) and only different in class composition from the one mentioned earlier, which had more African, dual ethnicity and middle-class black students. It was not by any means a 'highflying' school in terms of its position in the national league tables. It is at any rate commonly accepted that league tables do not and cannot measure accurately a school's actual achievement because of the complexities of schooling, of the environment and because of the diverse concerns of schools. As we state in Blair and Bourne (1998, p. 69),

> 'good systems' do not necessarily by themselves guarantee successful attainment for all groups of students, nor do league table measurements currently take into account value-added factors and the hard work put in by teachers who want to provide a curriculum that is relevant to a very diverse student intake.

League tables which tell us the percentage of students who obtained high grades in their examinations do not tell us *which* students received these grades and can therefore mask the failure of schools in relation to particular groups of students. A factor which stood out for Northern Catholic School was that there was a qualitatively different response from the black students at this school about their experience of schooling, and as mentioned, black students were making more progress academically than in any of the other schools with a comparable intake.

How a school can make a difference

On the whole, schools in Britain have not succeeded, despite attempts by the multicultural and antiracist movements, in creating environments in which black students as a whole feel the sense of belonging which comes with acceptance of who they are. But in order to accept and respect students' identities, it is necessary to know them and to understand them. This seems to be a particularly tall order in an environment which is ethnically, linguistically and religiously diverse. However, it is this overall student-centred culture and philosophy within the school that is at the root of 'effectiveness' for all students. To achieve such an environment requires a culture change which goes beyond well-meaning policy or statements of intent. Changing a school's culture cannot be done overnight but requires courage and patience, and most of all a deep sense of commitment and a genuine desire to provide equality of opportunity for all students.

Understanding the issues and concerns of black students

An examination of the literature which focuses on issues of 'race', ethnicity and education in British schools reveals an interesting and important fact – that black secondary school students, regardless of where they are in the country or what school they attend, seem to speak with one voice about the nature of their experience of schooling. Our own interviews with black students confirmed what many researchers have documented: that black students feel they are unfairly treated by teachers (i.e. 'picked on'); they believe that teachers often operate with racial stereotypes which are demeaning; that this outlook on the part of teachers affects their attitudes to black students; that teachers have low expectations of them; that teachers discriminate against them; that they do not treat them with respect; and (a complaint common to all students) that teachers do not listen to them, and also that teachers always 'stick up for and support each other'.

Listening to and respecting students

At Northern Catholic, the school decided that in order to deal with the serious problem of black student alienation it was important to listen to the grievances that were brought to them by students, and then find strategies for developing a culture which created a positive learning environment for black students. Listening to students meant actively attempting to understand things from their point of view. The headteacher listened to both the perspective of the students and that of the teachers about what they thought caused the poor behaviour and poor relations within the school. It was important for the students to know that the headteacher would not always 'stick up for teachers', especially when they were wrong. Complaints of racism were never dismissed as a symptom of the 'chip on the shoulder', but were properly investigated and, especially where a teacher had been unaware of the racial nature of their actions, this was explained so that the teacher could see the effects of their actions on the students. This non-judgemental approach was found to be necessary because of the complex nature of racism which can sometimes be unintended, unconscious and unacknowledged (Mac an Ghaill, 1988; Gillborn, 1997). In contrast, in another school, the black student who reported to the headteacher that he had been treated by his teacher in a racially discriminatory way was questioned about his own attitudes to school, told about his history of poor behaviour and then accused of 'reverse racism'. There was in this school a high level of disaffection amongst the black students, especially the boys, who were also disproportionately affected by exclusions.

An aspect of listening to students and respecting their point of view related, at Northern Catholic, to the manner in which information was gathered and used. It was important, as the deputy headteacher stated, that it was made clear to students that they would be believed unless, after investigation, the facts proved to be different. This approach was just as supportive to teachers, who realised that this was not a licence for students to make false accusations or try to gain an advantage, but was inherently about creating a fair and just system. If teachers respected students' rights to be heard, and in the process learnt about the issues that affected students and why, this was more likely to improve relationships within the school than an approach which was authoritarian and dismissive of students' concerns. Teachers were thus encouraged to reflect on their words and actions to understand how these were viewed by students. They were also encouraged to discuss with students rather than immediately resort to punishment when certain types of behaviour were unacceptable. In this way, a culture of mutual respect was developed and one in which black students felt assured that their concerns mattered to the school, would be investigated and appropriate action taken. The deputy head stated that

> The key to good relations in our school is that we take time to listen to students. We give them a fair hearing. If students feel that you will listen to them and investigate things properly, and sometimes you spend a lot of time listening to something you knew all the time, but the bottom line is, they know you will listen to them.

Respecting student cultures

One of the concerns that black students have is that their histories are excluded from what is considered to be valuable knowledge in the school curriculum. Not only is it excluded, moreover, but what exists is sometimes found to be eurocentric or racist. The restrictions placed on the school curriculum by the demands of the National Curriculum inhibit attempts by schools to place the histories and cultures of minority ethnic groups within the mainstream academic subject area. The feeling of marginalisation of black students was recognised at Northern Catholic, and attempts were made to meet this concern by the introduction within the Personal and Social Education (PSE) programme of a six week course in Afrikan Studies which was taken by all students in the school. This was later followed by a six week course of Irish Studies to reflect another major ethnic group in the school.

The initial introduction of Afrikan Studies was, as can be expected, controversial and greeted with less than enthusiasm from some members of staff and parents. It clearly required courage and perseverance, not only in ensuring that the course was introduced but in gradually persuading staff that it was important and useful.

Understanding and responding to adolescents

A factor that is often omitted in research, and certainly one that seems to be absent in teachers' dealings with black students, is that their identities go beyond the question of 'race' or ethnicity to embrace those factors which they share with all young people, namely, the fact of growing up. It is often assumed that when individual black boys misbehave, it is a factor of their 'race' rather than of their adolescence. It seems likely that this would lead teachers to treat black students differently from white students and explain the pervasive feeling amongst black young people that they are treated unfairly. It is also assumed that in order to create a positive learning environment for black young people, one need only address questions of racism and discrimination and ignore the need to understand black young people *as young people*.

A vital component of teacher education should be to help teachers understand the ways and the needs of adolescents. Many writers have pointed to this phase of development as being particularly difficult for the young people themselves. Adolescents, as Hargreaves *et al.* (1996) put it, 'are complex, diverse, and unpredictable'. These characteristics are part of young people's attempts to grow and become more independent. [. . .]

In many schools, this quest for independence is punished rather than harnessed for the benefit of the young people themselves and the school. In some schools in our study, however, staff showed sensitivity and an ability to engage constructively with the dilemmas of youth. They understood the pressures of the peer group and attempted to work with this rather than condemn it. In these schools, suspensions and expulsions were few or non-existent because staff took an approach which was empathetic rather than hostile towards young people.

Head of year (Southern International School):

> We very rarely permanently exclude. A student would have to have done something horrendous for it to get to the stage of a permanent exclusion. It's very rare, for example, in a case of violence, for students to go home not having made up. We talk through problems with students and help them find alternative ways of dealing with situations.

At Northern Catholic, the head of the school understood and responded to what one headteacher described as 'the fantastically strong stereotypes in the society of what people think black boys are like'. These stereotypes included the belief that where black boys were gathered in a group, there were likely to be drugs or they were preparing to do something antisocial like 'mugging'; that black males are violent and threatening; that they have no interest in education and therefore 'underachieve'; and generally that black males spelt 'trouble'. The headteacher of Northern Catholic School made it clear to the black students that she understood what they had to face, and assured them that such attitudes towards them by teachers would not be tolerated. But, whilst she offered her full support to the students, she also tried to ensure that they took responsibility for themselves and others around them. It was made clear, for example, that a change in the school culture could not occur without their full co-operation and contribution. Furthermore, not only were they encouraged to take responsibility for themselves, but also to play their part in the community, for example, helping to organise a youth conference.

There was thus an understanding that black students were not only adolescents with all the problems of adolescents, but that they were adolescents who were situated differently from their white peers both within the culture of the school and of the wider society. It was wrong therefore to compartmentalise their experiences into either 'race', or youth; it was necessary to see and appreciate the complexity of their experiences as young-black-males/females. [...] Often, it was the personal interest shown in an individual by a teacher that could make all the difference.

> *Student*: (Mrs B.) called me to the office the other day and she says, 'I've seen a spark and I don't want it to die. You've got the ability and you can do it. Do you mind me mentoring you? When you get your coursework, show me; when it's finished, show me.' She wants to monitor everything – my attendance, my punctuality, and I will gladly go along with that because I know that she is doing it because she really cares. She is a really good teacher.

Partnerships with parents

Discussions with black parents reveal very similar concerns to those of their children (Blair and Bourne, 1998). Parents have complained about teachers making assumptions about their personal characteristics on the basis of stereotypes about black people. Teachers sometimes assume that black parents are aggressive and this makes them feel intimidated, thus hindering their ability to relate to black parents. One parent stated

> Most (black) people were born in this country, went to school in this country, and half of these teachers, we used to play with them. So why are they finding us so aggressive?

Amongst the stereotypes held by teachers is an assumption that black parents are not interested in their children's education because they do not always attend 'Open Evenings' where parents meet with teachers to discuss the children's progress. Such arrangements, say parents, are often a waste of time because teachers do not give them quality information about academic progress but focus on behaviour, or else they report that the children are 'doing fine' when this is not reflected in the children's work.

> Usually when I go to Parents' Evenings, it's like, 'Well, she is doing fine'. It is such a generalisation. I want specifics, and they don't seem to be able to give me specifics. You know, I'll say, 'How is she doing in the particular subject?' and they say, 'Fine'. I mean that is why a lot of us are walking the streets because everything was 'fine' at the Parents' Evening.

Parents also report being 'fobbed off' by the school when they want to take up a concern, and that when they do go to the school, they are treated with disrespect not always by the teachers themselves, but sometimes by reception staff. Parents talk about being 'talked down to' by teachers and generally treated, on the basis of their colour and class, as second-class citizens.

How do schools that are 'successful' for black students avoid these mistakes? As with students, the most effective ways of gaining the parents' support and co-operation was to listen to their concerns, consult them about and give them a voice on important issues, both pastoral and academic, and perhaps most importantly, show them respect by acting on their concerns and not merely involving them in a tokenistic way. At Northern Catholic School, an Association of Black Parents and Parents of Black Children was formed. They met in the school and discussed the issues relating to the education of their children, issues which they wanted to take up with the school. These were then reported to the headteacher, or, through the governor representative, to the board of governors. Availing the parents of the school in this way, and then taking up their concerns, also helped to create an environment in which previously disempowered parents felt more confident to join the school's governing body and take an active part in decisions made about and for the school. The headteacher also made it her business to try to understand the issues for the black communities by involving herself in community affairs and getting to know the communities from which the students came. She forged strong relationships with people in the black community. Through this personal education, she understood that her role in the education of black students did not begin and end at the school gate. She understood that black people, young and old, were subject to police harassment and intimidation and she was sometimes called upon by black families to vouch for their children's character where these children came before the law. She also helped and advised parents to find legal support where students in the school were called before the criminal justice system. This intimate understanding of the political issues which beset the lives of the students and their parents gained this headteacher the respect and trust of the black parents. One parent said this of her:

> (Black) parents have the confidence to come to her as a friend. She is seen as a friend in arms, struggling together for the good of their children.

[...]

Strategies for involving teachers in school change

Attempting to change a school is a difficult and slow process because, as Hargreaves *et al.* state,

> educational change is not just a technical process of managerial efficiency, or a cultural one of understanding and involvement. It is a political and paradoxical process as well...educational change which promises to benefit all students...threatens many entrenched interests.
> (Hargreaves *et al.*, 1996, p. 163)

General change is difficult enough, but entrenched interests are particularly threatened when the type of change required involves an examination of and deep reflection on one's own beliefs and value systems. The half-hearted and sometimes failed attempts in the 1970s and 1980s to implement multicultural and antiracist education bear witness to this difficulty (Troyna, 1992). But change is difficult because it is also about

> transforming sophisticated relationships not simple behaviours, in complex classroom situations and organizational systems, whose purpose and direction are politically compounded and contested.
>
> (Hargreaves *et al.*, 1996, p. 168)

At Northern Catholic, the headteacher recognised the potential difficulty of convincing teachers that change was needed, and that this change had to embrace the whole philosophy and culture of the school and not just the disciplinary measures taken against misbehaving students. She was convinced that not only were there gross injustices being perpetrated against the black students with particular reference to the black boys, she was sure that no single strategy would be sufficient to change the climate of hostility and conflict in which the black students and teachers were engaged. She needed to be sensitive to the grievances brought to her by the black students as well as take account of the sensitivities of teachers whose very identity as professional was threatened.

The strategy adopted embraced both multicultural and antiracist methods. On the one hand, a course on Afrikan Studies was introduced, initially outside school hours and attended voluntarily by students, and then as part of the compulsory Personal and Social Education (PSE) programme in which all students took part. This strategy, which was interpreted by some teachers and parents as favouring black students, met with some opposition. To address this, meetings were organised in order to discuss the basic philosophy of the school and to gain a unified understanding of what equality of opportunity meant in practical terms. It was also explained that unless the issues which affected the black students could be effectively tackled, the relationships in the school would continue to negatively affect the whole of the school community, and black students would continue to 'underachieve' in relation to other students. The headteacher stated,

> I've been quite outright in saying that whatever strategies we use to help black students raises the achievement of the white students and of the whole school because if there is a social problem, it helps to change the atmosphere.

Teachers were encouraged to discuss their fears and misgivings and to ask questions in a climate of openness and honesty in a non-judgemental environment. Parents too were invited to express their feelings and to come to the school if they had questions or wanted to discuss the implications of the Afrikan Studies programme. Alongside the implementation of the Afrikan Studies programme, teachers received in-service education on issues of equality of opportunity.

Another strategy was to get teachers and students to define together what they wanted from their school. As a Catholic school, Year 9 Tutors and their students

(12–13 year olds) took 'retreats' together every year, and this was an occasion for all to learn about better communication, conflict resolution, the school's educational and moral mission, and for teachers to get to know their students and 'bond' together outside the normal routines and environment of the school. Out of these meetings and 'retreats' emerged a Code of Behaviour for the whole school and one which applied to the staff as much as it did the students. This Code of Behaviour defined what was acceptable and not acceptable behaviour and, importantly, provided guidelines for resolving difficulties in a respectful and conflict-free environment.

The process of gaining the co-operation of teachers was a long and, according to the headteacher, a hard one. It took six years before she began to feel that there was much more of a united front in the school. The black students were given assurances that racism and unfair treatment against them would not be tolerated and that they had the ear of senior management in the school if they had any grievance. All parents were given the assurance that if their children had a serious grievance, this would be heard by senior management, and together with the parents, the complaint would be investigated and something would be done about it.

The political rationale for addressing the concerns of groups and not only of individuals was explained to the teachers, who were informed that such action applied to all students regardless of ethnicity. These combined strategies, and the headteacher's perseverance in the face of sometimes very strong opposition, finally seemed to pay off so that it was the teachers themselves who were at last able to appreciate the benefits of the more peaceful environment in which they were working. Black students began to feel confident that the one issue which most affected them, that of being racially discriminated against, would at last be taken seriously. A further benefit, which the open discussions and the ability to engage with controversial and difficult subjects allowed the school to do, was to address the issues that affected adolescents as adolescents without the clutter of racial stereotypes. The level of mutual trust that developed enabled the school to introduce changes that were of benefit to the whole school community. Teachers were able to develop an understanding of not only black students' needs but the needs of all students, and to experience the benefits of this for their own teaching.

Conclusion

The case of Northern Catholic High School is an illustration and not a template for what can be done to change the schooling experiences of black students. Every school operates within its own context and with its own set of problems and issues. That the problems faced by black students in British schools are not confined to specific areas of the country, and that they are just as likely to apply in situations of low as well as high black student population, have been well demonstrated in research. The example of Northern Catholic should therefore offer some encouragement. Black students need to know that they are not only welcome and wanted in the school, but that they will be treated fairly, their cultures will be respected, the political issues that beset them as black people will be understood and form part of the school's sensitivities and responsibilities toward them. They need to know that their particular needs will be recognised as complex and comprising their ethnic and 'racial' identities as well as their needs as 'children' or young people, but also that their differences will be appreciated.

A major criterion in achieving this kind of positive environment for black and all students is teachers who are willing to learn and genuinely understand the issues that affect their students.

Hargreaves *et al.* (1996: 6) state that

> Change is most effective, not when it is seen as a problem to be fixed, an anomaly to be ironed out, or a fire to be extinguished. Particular changes are more likely to be implemented in schools where teachers are committed to norms of continuous improvement as part of their overall professional obligations.

Regretfully, changes relating to 'race' and ethnicity are usually regarded as 'a problem to be fixed' and 'an anomaly to be ironed out'. This was undoubtedly the case for many teachers at Northern Catholic. What was needed was not only strong and determined leadership and a clear vision of what was right for the school, but enough teachers who were committed 'to the norms of continuous improvement' to create the momentum for change and provide the support needed for this to be effective. The extent to which the united 'Catholic' philosophy helped the process is open to speculation. The most important 'mission' was that of ensuring that none of the students who attended this school, and none of their parents, should feel in any way marginalised or discriminated against. To achieve this requires from any senior management in a school the ability to throw off the 'baggage' of assumptions that we all carry and which play such an important part in influencing how we see others and how we relate to them.

What is needed, as one headteacher said, is the ability to create in a school a 'we' ethos and not an ethos of 'them' and 'us' which divides teachers from students and black from white. Unfortunately, black students in many schools are consciously or unconsciously experienced as 'Other' (Blair, 1994). Changing this situation is the real challenge facing teachers who not only care about their students but genuinely want to make a difference to their lives.

Notes

1 I use the term 'black' here to refer to people of African descent whether they be from Africa or the Caribbean. The term is also used to refer to people of dual heritage where one parent is of African descent.
2 Approximately 98 per cent of teachers in British schools are white. Most black children will therefore be taught by white teachers, and some might never have a black teacher throughout their schooling. In writing about 'teachers', therefore, it is assumed in this chapter that the teachers are white.

References

Blair, M. (1994) 'Black teachers, black students and education markets', *Cambridge Journal of Education*, 24, pp. 277–291.

Blair, M., Bourne, J. with Coffin, C., Creese, A. and Kenner, C. (1998) *Making the Difference: Teaching and Learning Strategies in Successful Multi-ethnic Schools*, London: DfEE.

Channer, Y. (1996) *I am a Promise: The Schooling Achievement of British African-Caribbeans*, Stoke-on-Trent: Trentham Books.

Connoly, P. (1995) 'Racism, masculine peer group relations and the schooling of African/Caribbean infant boys', *British Journal of Sociology of Education*, 16(2), pp. 75–92.

Cullingford, C. and Morrison, J. (1997) 'Peer group pressure within and outside school', *British Educational Research Journal*, 23(1), pp. 61–80.

Driver, G. (1979) 'Classroom stress and school achievement: West Indian adolescents and their Teachers', in Saifullah Khan, V. (ed.) *Minority Families in Britain: Support and Stress*, London: Macmillan.

Eysenck, H.J. (1971) *Race, Intelligence and Education*, London: Temple Smith.

Fordham, S. (1996) *Blacked Out: Dilemmas of Race, Identity and Success at Capitol High*, Chicago: University of Chicago Press.

Fordham, S. and Ogbu, J. (1986) 'Black students' school success: coping with the burden of "acting white"', *The Urban Review*, 18(3), pp. 1–31.

Foster, P. (1990) *Policy and Practice in Multicultural and Antiracist Education*, London: Routledge.

Gillborn, D. (1990) 'Race', *Ethnicity and Education*, London: Unwin and Hyman.

Gillborn, D. (1997) 'Young, black and failed by school: the market, education reform and black students', *International Journal of Inclusive Education*, 1(1), pp. 6587.

Gillborn, D. and Gipps, C. (1996) *Recent Research on the Achievement of Ethnic Minority Pupils*, London: HMSO.

Green, D. (1982) Teachers' influence on the self-concept of different ethnic groups, unpublished PhD thesis, cited in Troyna, B. (1993) *Racism and Education*, Buckingham: Open University Press.

Hargreaves, A., Earl, L. and Ryan, J. (1996) *Schooling for Change: Re-inventing Education for Early Adolescents*, London: Falmer.

Herrnstein, R.A. and Murray, C. (1994) *The Bell Curve: Intelligence and Class Structure in American Life*, New York: The Free Press.

Jensen, D. (1969) 'How much can we boost IQ and scholastic achievement?', *Harvard Educational Review*, 39(1), pp. 1–23.

Mac an Ghaill, M. (1988) *Young, Gifted and Black: Student–Teacher Relations in the Schooling of Black Youth*, Milton Keynes: Open University Press.

Measor, L. and Woods, P. (1984) *Changing Schools*, Milton Keynes: Open University Press.

Mortimore, P., Sammons, P., Stoll, P., Lewis, D. and Ecob, R. (1988) *School Matters: The Junior Years*, Wells: Open Books.

Nehaul, K. (1996) *The Schooling of Children of Caribbean Heritage*, Stoke-on-Trent: Trentham.

Noguera, P. (1997) 'Reconsidering the "Crisis" of the Black Male in America', *Journal of Social Justice*, 24(2), pp. 147–164.

Nuttall, D. and Goldstein, H. (1989) 'Differential school effectiveness', *International Journal of Educational Research*, 13, pp. 769–776.

Ogbu, J. (1988) 'Understanding cultural diversity and learning', *Educational Researcher*, 21(8), pp. 5–14.

Rattansi, A. (1992) 'Changing the subject? Racism, culture and education', in Donald, J. and Rattansi, A. (eds) *'Race', Culture and Difference*, London: Sage.

Reynolds, D. and Cuttance, P. (1992) *School Effectiveness: Research, Policy and Practice*, London: Cassell.

Scott-Jones, D. (1996) 'Motivation and Achievement: Implication of Minority Status', Discussion Paper presented at the annual meeting of the American Education Research Association, NY, April.

Smith, D. and Tomlinson, S. (1989) *The School Effect: A Study of Multiracial Comprehensiveness*, London: Policy Studies Institute.

Tizzard, B., Blatchford, P., Burke, J., Farquhar, C. and Plewis, I. (1988) *Young Children at School in the Inner City*, Hove: Lawrence Erlbaum Associates.

Troyna, B. (1992) 'Can you see the join? A historical analysis of multicultural and antiracist education policies', in Gill, D., Mayor, B. and Blair, M. (eds) *Racism in Education: Structures and Strategies*, London: Sage.

Wright, C. (1992) 'Early education: multiracial primary school classrooms', in Gill, D., Mayor, B. and Blair, M. (eds) *Racism in Education: Structures and Strategies*, London: Sage.

Part II

Curriculum and pedagogy

Where special needs
are constructed

Chapter 6

Exclusive tendencies

Concepts, consciousness and curriculum in the project of inclusion

Peter Clough

Introduction

This chapter outlines and examines an argument which is, at once, very much of the age and (perhaps, therefore, also) morally and politically suspect. The argument has a prima-facie simplicity: we have exclusive structures in our institutions because those same structures organize consciousness, little wonder that our schools and our curricula *include* some at the same defining moment as they *exclude* others, when the very process by which individual identity is formed is just such a selective and ultimately discriminatory affair. Now such a constructionist point of view could be seen as a journalist – if not omnibus – truism were it not for the fact that a majority of calls for inclusive educational systems take for granted their moral necessity without proper regard for the very political conditions that mediate their *emotional* cceptability. So we might wonder whether an inclusive philosophy is not only naïve, but also dishonest because it assumes what it seeks to establish; that is, that inclusion is morally necessitated and *structurally* indicated: get the structures right one might say, and humanity will follow. However, it cannot be assumed that inclusion is a simple 'given' of natural life, a necessary property of consciousness or culture (or, therefore, of the curricula which mediate them). Indeed, exclusion may be necessarily as much at the centre of consciousness and social structure as inclusion, so that the argument for inclusive education is a much more complex matter than is contained in the belief that a naturally inclusive mind is hindered from, its true moral expression in socially inclusive structures.

[. . .]

Recent developments in UK special education

The changes which have affected education in the UK in recent years have been the more remarkable in special education. These include

- the increasingly explicit politicization of educational structures and processes;
- the wide- and deep-ranging development of legislation which increases the regulation and control of education through central policies;

- at the same time as this, the development of certain areas of responsibility (most importantly, funding) to schools;
- the consequent 'marketization' of schooling, and the increasing separation, both within schools and in the broader institutions which maintain them, of managers from professionals;
- the development of an accountability ethos which effectively promotes instrumentalism within the curriculum.

[...]

An even more noticeable change, however, is in the area of the curriculum. In the old dispensation, the greater part of what went on in special schooling was a matter for schools – and frequently individual teachers – to decide; curriculum could be as arbitrary as were many of the decisions which had led to a child's particular placement. Now, of course, a statutory National Curriculum in the UK affects – if only by technical default – the education of all learners, and the degrees of freedom open to teachers in their selection of curricula are considerably more limited.

Perhaps the greatest change, however, is in the culture of special schooling. Effectively as cultures unto themselves, special schools and 'special' departments in mainstream schools were distinctive by nature of a broadly deficit-centred ideology which – relatively unhindered by regulation – could issue in practices accountable to a notion of individual pathology (Golby and Gulliver, 1979). [...] Teaching intentions were regulated – and mediated – more by implicit traditions of professional practice and personal preference than by any explicit, mandatory and essentially externally imposed requirement. The introduction of statutory funding, curricular and assessment frameworks brings this culture of child-centred education to a crisis, since the organizing principle of management becomes one of accountability to structures hierarchically far removed from the immediate and daily needs of any child (though they are surely *intended* to guarantee the meeting of such needs).

Old wine in new bottles?

How radical are these changes beyond the phenomena, of structure? How do they affect, for example, the degrees to which teachers will embrace instances of learning difficulty and inclusive processes? Can these changes ever seriously erode an arguably fundamental principle and purpose of special provision, as claimed, for example, by Dessent (as long ago as 1983, but enduringly characteristic):

> Whatever else special education [in mainstream or segregated provision] involves, it is first and foremost an administrative and organisational system whereby one group of professionals are invested with responsibility for handicapped and 'difficult-to-teach' children. At the same time, other groups are absolved from such responsibility... [Special education's] *historical roots lie in*

the need to remove responsibility for teaching children with SEN from teachers in normal schools.

(Dessent, 1983; emphasis added)

I should suggest that these roots are still vigorous, however much academic re-conceptualizations of special education (as integrative or inclusive) may have rearranged the furniture of provision (Corbett, 1998). For unless teachers in the UK *opt* during their initial training to teach children with learning difficulties, they do not expect to do so. Thus is created a culture of teachers with a tendency to exclude.

Let me briefly rehearse the spirit of the changes which the Warnock Report and subsequent Education Acts' (DES, 1981, 1988) pursued. At the centre of the Act was a view of learning difficulties as relative phenomena – specific events tied to particular learning environments, rather than enduring conditions reflecting stable abilities and disabilities. The perceived source of difficulty is moved outside of the learner's head, as it were, to his or her learning environment, while action on those difficulties moves correspondingly from the child to the curriculum again which those difficulties are noticeable. As Wedell (1985) put this: 'The concept of special educational need is a relative one and need is seen as the outcome of the interaction between the resources and deficiencies of the child, and the resources and deficiencies of his [*sic*] environment.'

This leads to what might be called a curricular conception of learning difficulties. In this account,

> special educational needs are not noticed in a vacuum, as it were; they appear against a background of 'normal' ability and performance which gives them relief; they are noticed because the students fail to meet the requirements of a given curriculum. They are ways of locating and describing the points of mismatch between individual understanding and performance on the one hand, and the notional demands of a given curriculum on the other. They are inevitably norm-referenced, and the norms which give them their distinctness are in the first instance those of the given curriculum. However, we have not in the past typically admitted and considered this background; to be sure, the child's engagement with the curriculum tells us something about him or her, but it also tells us a great deal about the curriculum. Thus we have tended to reify a notional disability rather than attend to the broader and much more elusive curricular data of which any given 'failing' is an abstraction. Let us say finally, then, that learning difficulties only occur in specific and describable contexts, though too often we generalise the difficulty and fail adequately to describe its context.

(Clough, 1998)

The date of this reference tells its own story but it has a logic and a rhetoric which have struggled to survive the raft of political upheaval which has effectively changed the very language of education (Corbett, 1996). Such definitions – of curriculum and learning difficulty – belong now to the privileged language of the academy, and would be laughed out of most school staffrooms. Such a conceptualization was not, of course, 'wrong', but it depended for its life on very different political (and hence resource) fuels from those which drive education in the late 1990s. There is an increasing return to popular (and, indeed, governmental), views of 'failure' (of individual students, teachers and, indeed, schools), low attainment disaffection and non-attendance as defects without meaning outside of the individuals concerned. In this way, the signals of institutional failure can be muted, the experiences of the individuals marginalized and their 'difficulties' picked off with minimum tearing of the fabric of the *status quo*.

Teachers making policy/policy-making teachers?

It is in the nature of traditions that they evolve slowly, and that their features remain in professional consciousness and practice long after their original bestowal of meaning may have disappeared. (Cyril Burt, for example, may be academically discredited, but the legacy of his work is ineradicable.) It is in the nature of traditions that they may go along for the most part unreflectively and uncritically, but that it takes vigorous, wide-scale and well-explicated revolution to overturn them. Is it likely, then, that a new dispensation of inclusivity can seriously erode the *status quo* of tradition which has its roots in much deeper structures of society than the simply educational?

In the end, it is teachers who mediate policy through their activities in and out of the classroom, through their participation in the realization of curriculum. But in the case of students with learning difficulties, this curriculum is still unavoidably infected, with notions of child-deficit. Through teacher education (as a function of a broader academic tradition) psychology has imposed frameworks of interpretation which have fundamentally conditioned teachers' understandings of what happens in their classrooms and schools; psychology has elaborated categorical conceptions of personal, educational and social life which directly affect the decisions taken daily about every child whose performance in the classroom is in any way remarkable.

The point is an important one if we are to understand how the present system (of broadly exclusive provision) is supported not merely in the structures of society (such as its institutions), but necessarily *in the structures of experience of the individuals who participate in that culture.*

An illustration

What follows is an illustration of some of the ways in which recent SEN policy in the UK has directly affected school practices and teacher attitudes. In 1991, I carried out a survey of nearly 1000 mainstream teachers' perspectives on SEN, in 16 secondary schools divided equally among four English LEAs. Several items in a lengthy questionnaire sought to explore the teachers' willingness to integrate children with various learning difficulties into their classrooms and schools; and, in particular, three separate though clearly conceptually related questions pursued their

- commitment to broad inclusivity;
- views on banding by 'ability';
- professional commitment to teaching pupils with SEN.

Table 6.1 shows a collapse of these three items to indicate those teachers who answered unequivocally positively to three 'key' integrative/inclusive statements.

Even before statistical sophistication, it is clear that something special is happening here, as revealed by the LEA3 scores. I would emphasize that each of the LEAs had explicitly articulated integration policies: that each had – variously within five years previous to my survey – undertaken some extra SEN-focused initiative; that each had an elected, advisory and administrative staff wholly committed to integrative principles; and that, by and large, the pattern of institutional distribution of students with SEN was common throughout the four LEAs. How, then, do we explain the LEA3 responses (which, in their tenor, were consistent throughout the whole of the questionnaire's 45 central items)?

Crudely it can be said that what chiefly distinguished LEA3 from the other LEAs was that it puts its money (and considerably more of it) where its mouth was, and while all LEAs demonstrated vigorously written and stated policies, those of LEA3 were more transparently enacted. Resources were visibly and considerably attached to the development of supportive structures, *for both students and staff*; importantly, these included not only relatively generous staffing of in-school and out-school support teams, but the promotion – through financial inducement – of a broader bedrock of structures, continuous with an integrative principle (such as mixed-ability teaching across the curriculum).

[...]

Table 6.1 Percentage of teachers in agreement with all three 'key' statements (*n* = 986)

	LEA1	LEA2	LEA3	LEA4
Teacher who said: 'All or most students with special educational needs should be educated in mainstream' *and* 'I would NOT like banding by ability' *and* 'I am happy that my job involves teaching ALL pupils'	18	23	47	30

Discussion

It appears to be true – if a truism – that resources can buy attitudes; the corollary, of course, is that positive attitudes can atrophy in keeping with the shrinking of resources. But what is it in human experience which not only permits but effectively structures that relationship? Quite how in experience do resources correlate with teacher attitudes, conceptualizations and practices?

Three concepts of inclusiveness

At the beginning of this chapter, I characterized some of the features of both the psychometric and sociological approaches to learning difficulties. The arguments against the former are well-rehearsed (see e.g. Barton, 1996) but critique of the other perspective less so. In particular, and in this context of argument about inclusion, sociological approaches appear to operate through the kind of critique and research, which identifies difficulties in path of inclusion, as though these were just obstacles to something that is natural and inarguably good. This is often accompanied by a rhetoric (of 'the struggle': Barton, 1996) to support the political implementation of inclusion. Both this research and rhetoric derive from a perspective which assumes that social and mental structures are isomorphic, in the sense that a presumed naturally inclusive mind is hindered from its true, moral expression in socially inclusive structures by various imposed and immoral exclusive practices. This is in contrast, of course, to the opposing psychometric view that mind and society are intrinsically exclusive and competitive.

How might an analysis of the concepts of inclusion and exclusion allow us to advance beyond these positions, and define the research agenda, in a new way? More 'specifically, we can ask what can we *mean* when we use these concepts? For there is a number of possible ways of forming and using concepts of inclusion and exclusion, and these depend upon particular understandings of concept formation and use. By way of conclusion, I shall outline three possible concepts of inclusiveness.

- The first is the traditional theory of abstraction, which states that concepts are formed through our identifying resemblances between things (Bolton, 1972), and then generalizing from these to form classes. On this basis, the task of forming judgements about inclusion and exclusion is that of attending to real resemblances and differences between people, and placing them inside or outside classes. These judgements are based upon inspection of data and, consequently, are of a universal nature (e.g. 'All children with such-and-such a Learning Difficulty should be . . .').
- The second view arises, from a critique of the first. As Husserl (1901) pointed out, we would not generalize from one item to the next if we did not already possess some idea enabling us to see how items resemble one another. So, what is important in forming a concept is the application of a particular perspective or principle. In this case, the argument over inclusion/exclusion is about

which principles are to be applied in order to group or separate individuals. This second perspective is commonly seen as supporting a pluralist and contextualist view (although there is no logical necessity in elevating pluralism to a universalist principle of inclusiveness).

• A third view is a synthesis of the first two. We can borrow from Hegel (1894) here, for there is a parallel between his doctrine of three mental functions, and the foregoing description of the nature of concepts. The first function, which Hegel calls 'Understanding', is a conceptual activity which isolates and fixes boundaries. It places events in categories which are seen as independent, not requiring other ideas either for development or contrast. Then we have a second function called 'Dialectic proper', which opposes the separatist system of Understanding as absurd, as presupposing the things it excludes, for things cannot meaningfully be credited with the character given to them except in the setting provided by other seemingly external, seemingly irrelevant factors. Finally, the Hegelian dialectic posits a third function, which is called 'Reason' or 'Speculation', fixation and whose purpose is to undo the neat isolation and fixation of the first thought function while, at the same time, preserving the distinctions which it has introduced. From this perspective, contextualization and categorization require each other as necessary parts of the same process. The sort of thinking required here is a long way from the dogmas of (psychometrically oriented) exclusion and the too-easy rhetoric of inclusiveness.

This is difficult work which does not issue in an obvious programme of research enquiry. I would suggest that what is broadly needed is much more close-order analysis of professional judgements in practice in various contexts; in this way, I suspect, we should see that there is really no prior definition and theory of inclusion/ exclusion, since it is made and remade again and again − or not − in practice. As Wilson and Cowell (1984) have it,

> We have to find out what principles and assumptions control the thinking (and hence the decisions) of those concerned [with SEN] ... For ... the assumptions are often hidden, not only from the interviewer but from the person interviewed. Much time and effort is required grasp the shape and style of a person's deepest thoughts. [And] in the case of handicap [*sic*] ... it would be unwise to start from any particular view about identification and 'treatment; We need rather ... to map out the views and concepts of people in the business without any implication that they measure up, or fail to measure up to a pre-established picture ...

Conclusion

Primarily and by definition, institutions exclude, cultures exclude and curricula exclude. Curricula have always been a means of exclusion; they have always been the means by which, ultimately, this group of students is separated from that.

Decisions about 'ability' based on psychometric or other forms of assessment lead ultimately to decisions about what can and should be studied. Such decisions themselves reach deep into ideologies, for the curriculum is and always has been a selection from culture for particular ends. Of course, this seems to be more glaringly the case with the introduction of the National Curriculum, but it is so in any culture in any time; what and whom we choose to teach are vital determinants of the part which those students are able to play in shaping a society's development.

In order to bring about a more truly inclusive schooling and society, we need to start from a recognition that exclusive principles are no less at the co-structured heart of 'organism and organization' (Williams, 1965) than are inclusive intentions. We have to understand more about the ways in which inevitably limited resources may be correlated – sometimes quite subtly – with attitudes, and we have to find a way of understanding teachers' resistance to inclusive practice without pathologizing, or even demonizing it. For the dynamics, of such resistance are complex, and their occurrence is growing. Actually, the bulk of the empirical work which gave this project its character derived from extensive life-historical exploration, and these are the data which ultimately give some plausible life to a rational resistance. There may be in the margins of the profession a very small minority of teachers whose attitudes to exceptionality are vile, but they are not to be confused with that larger portion who struggle uncomfortably to articulate a growing resistance. The motif of resistance and of a tendency to exclude is more imaginatively captured by the words of Andrew, a 44-year-old Head of History in a 1200 student 11–18 school:

> 'I don't have any difficulty with the kids like this [with SEN] . . . I mean I have no practical or . . . whatever, political difficulty with them in my classes. . . Well, I do have practical difficulties and that's the point that *is* the point. I teach a subject [History] which is . . . finally non-negotiable in content, I mean in examinable content, and . . . I suppose in the way it has to be learned. And taught. So if I'm going to succeed . . . personally, that is, and professionally and if the school's going to succeed in the [local press], I've got to go for the academics, haven't I? And that means just not having the kids who can't make it in the class . . .

References

Barton, L. (ed.) (1996) *Disability and Society: Emerging Issues and Insights* (London: Longman).
Bolton, N. (1972) *The Psychology of Thinking* (London: Cassell).
Clough P. (1998) Bridging 'mainstream' and 'special' education: a curriculum problem. *Curriculum Studies*, 20 (4), 327–338.
Corbett, J (1996) *'Badmouthing': The Language of Special Needs* (London: Falmer).
Corbett J. (1998) *Special Educational Needs in the Twentieth Century: A Cultural Analysis* (London: Cassell).
Department of Education and Science (DES) (1981) *Education Act 1981* (London: HMSO).

Department of Education and Science (DES) (1988) *Education Reform Act* (London: HMSO).

Dessent, T. (1983) *Making the Ordinary School Special* (Lewes: Falmer Press).

Golby, M and Gulliver, R.J. (1979) Whose remedies, whose ills? A critical review of Remedial Education. *Journal of Curriculum Studies,* 11, 137–47.

Hegel, G.W.F. (1894) *Hegel's Philosophy of Mind* (trans. W. Wallace) (Oxford: Clarendon Press).

Husserl, E (1901) *Logical Investigations*, Vols I and II (Halle: Nicmeyer).

Wedell, K. (1985) Future directions for research on children's special educational needs. *British Journal of Special Education*, 12(1), 22–26

Williams, R. (1965) *The Long Revolution* (Harmondsworth: Penguin).

Wilson, J. and Cowell, B. (1984) How should we define 'handicap'? *Special Education: Forward Trends*, 11(2), 33–35.

Chapter 7

Pedagogy, observation and the construction of learning disabilities

Carol A. Christensen and Carolyn D. Baker

The challenge of critical social research

Traditionally, children who experience school failure requiring the support of a resource teacher have been identified as having a learning disability. The term was introduced by Kirk, who defined it as 'retardation, disorder or delayed development in one or more of the processes of speech, language, reading, writing, arithmetic, or other school subjects resulting from a psychological handicap caused by possibly cerebral dysfunction. It is not the result of mental retardation, sensory deprivation, or cultural or instructional factors' (Kirk, 1968, p. 398). The definition established that learning disability exists as a within-child disorder arising from neurological or psychological-process impairments.

The internal-deficit orientation of learning disabilities continues to be reflected in current definitions so that the field of learning disabilities has been dominated by psychological perspectives and current practices are grounded in the assumption that failure is due to a real, physical entity, which exists inside the heads of children, and requires accurate identification and treatment for remediation. Thus, systemic procedures are designed to seek out and classify the learning disability, and to respond to it appropriately. These processes include assessment, individualised planning and the provision of 'special' education. Critical social research on learning disabilities demonstrates that the identification of students with learning disabilities does not necessarily function in the way that was intended. Carrier (1990, p. 21) suggests that the assessment process is fundamentally social in nature, involving a 'panoply of unspoken assumptions, covert cues and responses'. Individualised educational planning meetings frequently do not function to ensure appropriate educational provision for the child. Rather, they are intensely political. Reynolds (1984) refers to the educational team decision meeting as a 'capitulation conference', where parents and often teachers capitulate to the authority of the psychologist.

A central issue that has emerged from social critiques of the field is the question of whose interests are served by categories such as learning disability. Traditional perspectives assume that these categories work in the interests of the child. However, social analysis suggests that they may often serve the interests of professionals (Tomlinson, 1982). Thus, a small number of researchers have argued that in practice, the apparent neutrality of the processes of identification, assessment, educational planning and provision is an illusion. In other words, the procedural safeguards designed to ameliorate the condition, in fact, provide a formal mechanism for the creation of learning disability through social processes (McDermott, 1993).

Despite these critiques, the actual practices of identifying, assessing and treating learning disabilities have held fast to psychological perspectives based on the rhetoric of 'in the best interests of the child', and the professional field has been extremely resistant to social analysis. Thus, Dudley-Marling and Dippo (1995) argue that, while the field of learning disabilities has enriched itself by drawing on diverse traditions in medicine and psychology, it has remained isolated from developments in social and critical theory.

Purely psychological approaches have been unable to explain the educational practices related to learning disabilities largely because the creation, and treatment of learning disabilities are forms of social practice (Christensen *et al.*, 1986). McDermott (1993, p. 272) has argued that 'there is no such thing as LD, only a social practice of displaying, noticing, documenting, remediating and explaining it'. In other words, the processes by which a child is transformed from 'normal' to 'learning disabled' are fundamentally social, rather than psychological in nature. The social processes by which this transformation occurs are situated in the day-to-day lives and interactions of teachers and students, specialists and administrators. They are 'submerged in the routine of teachers' work and thoughts (so that) frequently there is no call for teachers to articulate them' (Carrier, 1990, p. 211).

This is not to suggest that school failure does not exist or to deny that some children find learning much more difficult than others. However, it is argued that the institutional production of school failure is shaped by social, as well as psychological factors and that a coherent understanding of school failure cannot be obtained without an analysis of how these social processes work.

Relatively few researchers have systematically investigated the continuum of the social processes underpinning learning disability. Little is known about how these categories emerge from the day-to-day lives of teachers and students in classrooms. However, those researchers who have examined this issue have provided some interesting insights into how classroom interaction and discourse functions to designate some students as having a 'disability', while others are seen as performing satisfactorily.

Hargreaves *et al.* (1975) argued that identification and referral of pupils can only be understood within the context of ongoing classroom interaction. For example, they found that being identified as a disruptive student was not an issue of the level of noise a student creates. Rather, it depended on how skilled the student was in negotiating the classroom social organisation - not being caught making noise at times prohibited by the teacher.

Similarly, Hull *et al.* (1991) demonstrated the way in which a 'remedial' student could be identified because of her frequent violations of classroom discourse rules. Classroom discourse was dominated by initiation, reply, and evaluation (IRE) sequences. The teacher would initiate a student comment, the student would reply and the teacher would evaluate the comment. For example:

> *Teacher:*   How about some of the rest of you? (initiation)
> *Student:*   I, I just seen *Like a Prayer.* (reply)
> *Teacher:*   Okay, *Like a Prayer,* all right, good.

(p. 302)

Hull *et al.* (1991) argued that the rules for IRE sequences were quite clear and that it was inappropriate for any student to interrupt the sequence, unless invited to speak by the teacher. However, Maria, the remedial student, did not abide by this structure. She persistently interrupted the sequence. While Maria's interruptions were not necessarily disruptive of the flow of the lesson, they were intrusive and inappropriate. In addition, Maria seemed to pursue topics after the teacher had signalled her intention to move on. Hull *et al.* found that the teacher often ignored relevant and insightful comments that Maria made. Even though the teacher indicated that Maria's written work was good, at times showing logical thought and organisation, she continued to evaluate Maria's academic skills based on her inappropriate verbal behaviour. In an interview the teacher commented:

> Maria is becoming to me the Queen of the Non Sequiturs. You know, she really is just not quite... That's, that's why I'm sort of amazed at times at, at her writing level, which is really not really not too bad... Because her thinking level seems to be so scattered that I would expect that her writing be a lot more disorganised and disjointed.

(Hull *et al.*, 1991, p. 310)

Hull *et al.* argued (p. 311) that 'Maria's interactional patterns in class were not just an annoying conversational style. Her bothersome conversational habits became evidence of a thinking problem – evidence so salient that it goes unqualified even in the face of counter evidence'.

In his case study of 'Adam', McDermott (1993) found that learning disability was less an inadequacy inside Adam's head and more a consequence of 'the arbitrariness of the tasks Adam is asked to work on... and the interactional dilemmas thrown in Adam's way as he moves through school' (p. 279). According to traditional psychometric criteria Adam qualified as learning disabled, however, McDermott found that in everyday life situations, Adam's 'disability' disappeared. 'He proved in every way competent, and, more than most of the children he could be wonderfully charming, particularly if there was a good story to tell' (p. 278). In classroom tasks with low cognitive demand Adam performed capably, provided that he had a supportive social environment. For example, when working with a supportive peer, he could complete tasks successfully, sometimes reading instructions independently. However, if the interpersonal environment became more hostile, Adam's performance deteriorated dramatically. Rather than completing the task, Adam concentrated on avoiding the appearance of incompetence.

Unfortunately, use of an incompetence-avoidance strategy merely compounded the problem. [...] Central to this cycle of avoidance and failure was public humiliation based on exposure of the learning disability. Adam consistently acted in ways to avoid such exposure. However, McDermott argues that once Adam's learning disability had been identified and named it became a visible element of the classroom discourse. 'Adam's LD generally played to a packed house. Everyone knew how to look for, recognise, stimulate, make visible and depending upon the circumstances, keep quiet about or expose Adam's problem' (p. 287). Thus, 'looking for Adam's LD has become something of a sport in Adam's class' (p. 291). His difficulties lay not so much in the inherent difficulty of material he was required to learn or his own inherent inability to deal with that material, but in the social organisation and patterns of interaction within the classroom. Adam's difficulty arose because he 'cannot address the material without worrying whether he can get it straight or whether anyone will notice if he does not' (p. 291).

Pedagogy as an observational filter

Thus, existing evidence indicates that the social processes in the classroom exert a powerful influence on who is perceived to demonstrate imperfect learning and is labelled as having learning disabilities. In the studies reviewed earlier, the teacher's pedagogical practices provided the conditions, the possibilities, for identifying children as experiencing learning disabilities. The organisation of classroom activities acts as a filter through which the teacher can or cannot see what children can do. We suggest that the social construction of learning disabilities, while substantially the work of the teacher and possibly the other students, is not work that is disconnected from how the classroom is organised in the first place. That organisation, it seems, is not entirely the invention of the teacher. The curriculum and school work plans have a place in shaping what the classroom pedagogy entails, and how and where the children's activities become visible or not, to the teacher.

The classroom

The data used in this chapter were collected in a Grade 2 classroom in Queensland (Australia). In many contexts, the term learning disabilities is used to refer to children who are experiencing problems in acquiring basic academic competencies to the extent that they require support beyond that provided by the classroom teacher. In Australia, the term 'learning difficulties' is generally used, rather than the term learning disabilities. However, the more universally recognised term – learning disabilities – is used here.

Initially, the teacher (SH) was interviewed to obtain information on the curriculum and teaching strategies she used in the classroom. She was also asked to describe the students in the class. Literacy lessons were videotaped approximately every 4 weeks over a period of 6 months. Following the penultimate videotaped lesson, the teacher was interviewed after viewing segments of the videoed lesson. She was asked to explain her purposes in teaching the particular content and utilising particular pedagogy. She was also asked to discuss her understanding of student behaviour during the lesson.

A conceptual framework

Following examination of all the videoed lessons, we developed a theoretical framework to indicate the relationships between the multiplicity of factors which seemed to shape classroom pedagogy and the identification of children as having learning disabilities. These factors are portrayed in Figure 7.1.

Although the factors are represented in boxes we do not see them as discrete phenomena. Rather, they should be thought of as overlapping elements each of which plays a role in the construction of classroom experiences for teachers and students. While we have used arrows to indicate directions, we mean to describe flows of discourses and practices. While we have retained the elements identified in the social constructionist literature, we have looked also outside the classroom to include some 'prior' influences that bear on what happens in the classroom. This does not dislocate the teacher and classroom interaction from the centre of the action, but it does situate them inside various requirements or demands coming from outside, suggesting that the identification of learning difficulties is perhaps more systemic than has been recognised.

Impact of curriculum development process

Fundamental to the classroom practices in the school appeared to be the curriculum development process. School-based curriculum development is strongly

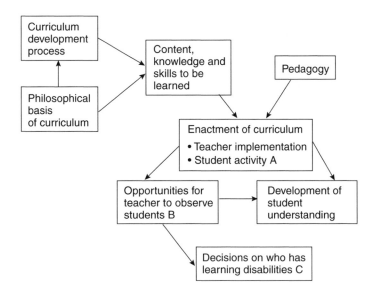

Figure 7.1 Factors influencing teacher's decisions on who has learning disabilities.

encouraged by government policy. In the school we studied, the literacy curriculum was set by a school committee that consisted of 'upper-school' teachers. The upper-school refers to Grades 5–7. In developing the curriculum, the committee appeared to be more familiar with and more sensitive to the literacy needs of upper-elementary students than very young students. The committee strongly endorsed an interdisciplinary or integrated-curriculum approach and required that the entire school work as a cohesive whole by teaching the same underlying concept or theme at the same time across all the grades in the school. Thus, the whole school studied the same genre (e.g. fiction) or theme (e.g. dinosaurs) simultaneously. [...]

Conceptual confusion and enactment of curriculum

In addition to constraining classroom practice, the policy appeared to have a number of unintended consequences for students. For example, it appeared that the very young children we observed were often confronted with literacy tasks that were conceptually very difficult for them to manage. At times, even the teacher seemed to be unequal to the demands of the task and appeared conceptually confused:

SH: Echidna...and it's one of our special animals, because this echidna lays eggs and also looks after its babies. A lot of animals that lay eggs don't look after their babies, they just leave them. Birds do, snakes and turtles don't often, OK? Frogs hardly ever. Alright? So we're going to have a look at this book . . . (Teacher opens book and holds it up for students to see). Here we have a picture of the echidna. We've got them around... (Teacher read text) It's a slow moving, and usually harmless (Teacher closes book). What does it do when it gets into trouble? Simi?

The lesson continued indicating that echidnas rolled up into balls when threatened, had spines, ate ants, dug fast, laid eggs, were mammals, fed their young milk and were warm blooded. SH explained what was meant by warm-blooded. The lesson then abruptly shifted direction to focus on the main literacy-related content of the lesson, the genre of the text:

SH: OK we'll read a little bit about the echidna. Is this book, do you think, will this be a narrative book or a fiction book?
Shaun: Fiction.
SH: Non-fiction, sorry I'll get you all confused. OK why do we know this might be something that's going to tell us facts?
Shaun: That it's not true?
SH: Do you think it's a not true book, a narrative? Or a true book – tells the facts and non-fiction.
Matty and Trevor: True.

SH:	OK Hands up those who think it's a true book, it's a non-fiction book. (Trevor, Matty, Simi, Wesley, Heidi, Paige, Martin raise hands) Hands down. Hands up those who think it's a narrative, and it's going to tell us a story, (Joshua raises his hand). OK so why do you think, the people who think it's a true book. Why do you think it's going to be a true book? It's going to tell us the … facts. (Simi puts up his hand and the teacher nods to him.)
Simi:	Because it might come true.
	(SH looks at Matty).
Matty:	ummm, because they made it ummmm real, made it real.
SH:	Well what about the cover. What makes you think that this is going to be a true story? Trevor?
Trevor:	()
SH:	True. We'll have a look. Well the animal looks real, it's not wearing any clothes, it's not wearing glasses. OK now what happens in our narrative stories, like Possum Magic.
Trevor:	If they did wear glasses they would be funny.
SH:	Very funny.
Matty:	Yeah. If we saw a real one with glasses, that would be real …
SH:	We've got a table of contents which shows us …
	Who thinks it's a non-fiction book? It's a real book. Who thinks it's going to tell us the truth now? (most students raise their hands). Tell us what we know about these animals at that time? Wesley you still think it's a narrative book – it's going to tell us a story? Why?
Wesley:	()
SH:	Who else thinks it's a narrative? Shaun do you think it's a narrative, it's going to tell us a story?
Shaun:	Umm, yes.
SH:	Well let's read a little bit of it. We'll go over to our page. Look, see how it's set out. Tells us where abouts in Australia these are found, the map of Australia and the dark bits. It tells us the length, where it lives, it's habitat, OK? And then it tells us something about it, it gives us a description and tells us it's scientific name. Is that a story?
Student (chorus):	No.
SH:	No! That's a report. It tells us about something … You've got a short beaked echidna. Echidnas live everywhere – look at it, all blue. It lives almost everywhere from forest to desert. And it's going to tell us about it. It's going to tell us the truth, which is a non-fiction book. If it says 'one' day an echidna went to visit America and on the way they had some Pavlova, would that be true or false?

Matty: False.

SH: Would it be a story, a narrative or a fiction – non-fiction – you
                are getting me confused.

In teaching genre theory, the concepts of truth, non-fiction, facts, real, report, false, story, fiction, and narrative, seem to be intertwined and appeared at times to become confused. It seemed that SH was suggesting that there were two fundamental types of text, and that each could have multiple labels. One was true, non-fiction, real, a report and contained facts. The other was a narrative, fiction, a story and false. The confusion was compounded when terms, such as 'true story' and 'real book' were introduced into the discussion. The point that the teacher is struggling with a multidimensional lesson could mean that the observations that she can make about children's abilities through such an activity might not be fully free of turbulence.

Structure of lessons and the invisibility of reading

This dialogue was typical of the lessons we observed. Further, lessons were usually divided into two segments. They began with the children seated together on the floor. Initially, the teacher conducted a dialogue, similar to that reported previously. Then the children moved to their desks to complete an activity. The activity usually involved cutting and pasting a worksheet and usually occupied the majority of the time allocated to literacy.

During the initial phase of the lesson, the teacher appeared to try to develop concepts and ideas through questioning the children. She only rarely provided specific direct instruction. These sessions also seemed to be characterised by talking about the activity of reading rather than engagement in reading. In the six lessons we videotaped, we never observed children reading individually for an extended period. Occasionally, there was whole-class choral reading of words or phrases, or a single child would be asked to read a word or a sentence displayed to the class at the front of the room. Thus, from the lessons we observed we were unable to make informed judgements about the children's competence in reading and writing. However, the teacher could be expected to be making some such judgements, and we proceed to investigate how this might be done.

In interview, SH explained that individual reading was undertaken at home. In other words, opportunities for the children to read extended text were confined to books that the children took home to read to parents. This practice was in part the result of the resources available in the classroom. There was only a single copy of any title available, so that whole class or small group shared reading of extended written text was not feasible [. . .]:

Interviewer: So what's your reading program like?

SH: We have readers that go home every night. We've got 25 different books. So every kid gets a different book. We can't read them in class. They go home sight unseen... And the range of books is amazing – they go from five words to a chapter book, and there are some with no words at all.

Interviewer: How often will they take a book home?

SH: Most will take it home every night. (I've) Got a couple that haven't bothered bringing them (their book) back or have one all semester, and because I've said 'You bring it back or you'll pay for it'. They've brought it back. And that's it. That's all they've had.

Interviewer: So they've read one book all semester?

SH: One book.

Interviewer: Whereas other kids might read a book every day.

SH: Twenty four.
And it's part of their homework... the spelling is not the be all and end all just because they're writing. They need to read as well. And they (some children) don't see that as important.

Interviewer: So is it the kids who are already good who tend to do all the extra reinforcement, and the ones who are behind tend to do nothing?

SH: Yes.

Thus, it seems that the teacher herself does not hear the children reading extended text. She reads books to them, but there are no books that the children read to her in class. Books are designated to home reading, which, of course, she cannot see. The inherent problems in this approach were highlighted later in the interview when SH discussed children's home backgrounds:

SH: ... these exceptional (good) kids have always had it. They've been read to as kids, that metacognitive stuff. They know how a book goes.

Interviewer: Before they even start school?

SH: Yes... They automatically know (about correct formatting of books) because they've been read to so often.
Whereas there are some kids don't even have that basic literacy knowledge. And don't see any sense in reading... (for good kids) it's (reading) a real life experience. Whereas some of them probably would only know cigarette packets and stuff. It's sad, isn't it? I got a note on the silver part of a cigarette packet. They (a parent) pulled the silver part out, flattened it and wrote a note on it.
Even their parents' writing is shocking. It's always little 'i'. 'i want' (little i not capital I for I). Their spelling is shocking.

Interviewer: How do they check their kid's homework if they can't write themselves?

SH: It's funny that they want them (their children) to spell, but they can't spell themselves. Anyway it's not really that important. Now days with computers...

The use of home reading as a core element in the literacy programme limited opportunities for SH to facilitate the children's emerging reading skills and her opportunities to observe their development in reading. Again, we call attention to the classroom pedagogy as a site for observation, and wonder how and where the observation occurs.

[...]

Pedagogy and opportunities to observe student learning

The classroom demonstrated a context in which the opportunities available to observe those children who were experiencing literacy problems were constrained by the intersection of a number of factors. School curriculum policy dictated the content to be covered, the complexity of some concepts being taught and the nature of the pedagogy focusing on dialogue resulted in a series of teacher/ question–student/answer sequences. These sequences provided the primary opportunity for the teacher to observe student competence. As we have pointed out, the teacher's attention to individual children reading actual texts was limited. Yet, the teacher was able to identify children's reading competences. How was she able to do this? It appeared that children who were judged competent were those who could decipher teacher cues to answer questions in the way that the teacher wanted.

How the teacher was able to see

Now, we turn from our description of classroom activities to interviews with the teacher. Our questions here are what does the teacher seem to have noticed? Where and how did she notice these things? In an extract of the lesson on decoding strategies and dinosaurs, Wesley, Aaron, Casey, Amanda, Heidi, Joshua and Casey were asked to respond to the teacher's request for ways that unfamiliar text could be decoded. Wesley, Heidi, Trevor and Joshua gave answers that the teacher regarded as correct. In the lesson, SH endorsed each of their answers. When discussing the students in her class SH indicated that Wesley and Heidi were exceptionally good students. She described Wesley as 'One of the top group, (who is) very academic...'. She admitted that Wesley was not perfect. 'He's getting a bit cheeky, he likes to push his luck. He doesn't mean to be cheeky, he means to be funny. Once he knows the difference he's fine. They're so cute at that age.' Along with Wesley, Heidi was described as 'exceptional at everything. She finishes all her work, no matter what. Always one of the top finishing people'.

Joshua and Trevor were seen as achieving satisfactorily, but not quite as outstanding as Wesley and Heidi. It is interesting to note that although Joshua's answer that you could 'read on' was not judged completely wrong, it did not receive the same level of endorsement that Wesley or Heidi's answers received. SH indicated that Joshua had merely restated a previously confirmed correct strategy ('That means the same as read ahead'). While Trevor's answer was accepted unconditionally, he offered it tentatively, as a question. He did not present his contribution with the unequivocal confidence evidenced by the 'exceptional' students, Wesley and Heidi.

Wesley, Heidi, Joshua and Trevor contrast with Aaron, Casey and Amanda whose answers were all unacceptable. Amanda failed to answer the question and both Aaron and Casey suggested that the words could be 'sounded out'. However, this was not an acceptable answer to SH. This is ironic because in analysing the cutting and pasting activity that formed part of the lesson, it is clear that the use of letter–sound cues to decode unknown words was the only strategy that could successfully lead to completion of the activity.

While Wesley and Heidi were regarded as excellent students and Joshua and Trevor were seen as making satisfactory progress, Aaron, Casey and Amanda were all described as experiencing learning disabilities and receiving support for their reading. Although two of their answers could be considered technically correct, the teacher judged them as inaccurate as they were inconsistent with her own philosophy of reading. Because of the nature of the pedagogy in the classroom, answers to teacher's questions are one of the few mechanisms that students have to demonstrate competence (or incompetence). It seems that these 'wrong' answers are part of the basis for SH's decision about who has a learning difficulty.

Getting the answer right

At times, the particular answer that the teacher was seeking during these question–answer sequences was obscure, so that as observers we were unclear as to what would constitute a legitimate answer. However, some students seemed to be able to intuit the 'right' answer, while others were consistently 'wrong'. As with the discussion of reading strategies we sometimes found the teacher's judgement of answers perplexing. However, it appeared that students who gave 'correct' answers were seen as capable and those who gave 'incorrect' answers were seen as having learning disabilities. It needs to be remembered that for teachers enacting this kind of classroom discourse structure, at least some right or correct answers are necessary to maintain a sense that the teacher is competent (Baker, 1991). Thus, the students who get right answers even where the questioning is game-like or obscure are crucial in allowing the pedagogy to proceed. Those children who produce a capable teacher are therefore capable themselves.

Another example extends this point further. Following a lesson on dinosaurs, SH gave a lesson on dragons. The lesson began by looking at the cover of the book and deciding that the book was about dragons. They then talked about the characteristics of dragons and SH asked:

SH: Does it look similar to a dinosaur?
Students: Yes. No.
(chorus)
SH: How does it look like a dinosaur? What are the similarities between that
            and a dinosaur?

Trevor: Scales.
SH: Hands up please. Yes, Matthew.
Matthew: Big feet.

The lesson continued discussing the similarities between dinosaurs and dragons, which included, long tails, claws, sharp teeth, tails, sails, ears and eyes. This was followed by a discussion of differences between dragons and dinosaurs:

SH: What's the main difference between a dragon and a dinosaur?
Casey: They have tails.
SH: How do we know dinosaurs are real?
Wesley: They've got fossils. Cause they, they got fossils.
SH: We have fossils of dinosaurs. Do we know that dragons are real?
Students: No.
(chorus)
SH: So what do we call those animals, starts with mmmm.
Aaron: Marsupials.
Heidi: Make believe.
SH: Make believe, that's a good one, I like that. So they're make believe. Make believe or fantasy.

The question 'what do we call those animals?' marked a critical point in the dialogue. When initially observing the lesson, we were unable to deduce the 'correct' answer when the question was asked and saw Heidi's answer 'make believe' as quite inspired. However, after viewing the video several times, reading the transcripts and reading her interviews it became clear to us that SH wished to contrast non-fiction text about dinosaurs with fiction about dragons. It appeared that students who were judged as exceptionally good were able to follow SH's line of reasoning across a sequence of lessons and come up with answers to questions that to the naïve observer were completely opaque. Aaron, who was seen as having a learning disability was unable to do this. He appears to have cued his answer from the prompt 'starts with mmmm', recalling an earlier lesson about marsupials. Heidi, in contrast, was able to leap across lessons and retrieve the magic word.

As observers it often appeared to us that SH's lessons lacked a logical structure. However, it seems that students who excelled in this classroom were able to impose a coherence to the lessons by showing their thinking processes to coincide with the teacher's. They were able to make sense out of scattered references and unannounced shifts of topic in ways that the other children, and we the researchers, could not. When teachers hear this being done, they hear their own competence as a questioner being validated. Whether this is literate competence or competence in reading the teacher's mind is a question that researchers have posed before. It is the obverse that we are concerned with here: that a student's inability to restore the teacher to competence becomes a sign that the child is deficient.

Seatwork as demonstration of competence

The second opportunity for SH to observe students occurred when students were engaged in a seatwork activity. These activities consisted of completing a prepared worksheet and often involved cutting and pasting pictures or copying small pieces of text. SH's interview comments indicate that these activities provided her with information she used to make judgements about which students were experiencing learning disabilities. Those students who were efficient at completing their work and showed manual dexterity in completing the task were regarded as competent. Those who were slow to finish, did not attend to the task or were very clumsy in the execution of the activity were seen as demonstrating learning disabilities. At no time did she mention children's competence in understanding or producing written text as mechanisms for recognition of learning disabilities. In fact, she indicated that she suspected that some of the children identified as having learning disabilities probably do understand the material ('Do you understand what you need to do?' 'No'. 'But the probably do'), but they choose to perform poorly by being inattentive or using up time until the lesson is completed:

Interviewer: How do you come to notice that students are having learning disabilities?

SH: They won't be finishing their work. Their writing will be really messy. 'Can you see these lines? There are lines on this page, you've avoided all of them'. Sometimes they have trouble even articulating what they want or something like that and you notice that. They often always the last to finish. They will have to go to the toilet. 'I have to go to the toilet'. 'Can I go to the toilet?' Very good avoidance tactics.

Interviewer: Yes.

SH: Yes. 'I can't find something'. I'm swinging off my chair. I'm talking to someone. Anything to avoid that task, and that's when I'll bring them over and say to them 'OK what is your problem? Can't you do this? Do you understand what you need to do?' 'No'. But they probably do, but they know that there are certain time limits here and they just might go over the time here and it'll have to stop. They forget they'll have to do it some other time. Last few weeks of school it's been in their lunchtime... they are given a paper and pencil and they lose their place and they have to get it done. That works for some of them but then they are so good at avoidance they don't even do it then. 'I did some'. And they might have written two things and you are thinking half an hour, And then you think 'Yeah, that's right. That's about what you do in my class'.
...There is a whole lot of things you look for and you think 'That's a sign'. Pencil grip is a sign. Brain gym is really good. If they can't cross over, you know how you've got to touch your left leg with your right hand, if they're having troubles with that, you know. You know someone's got a problem. It's always the ones with learning disabilities that

can't do it. I do it every day for 10–15 minutes, and as soon as they get it, they start understanding a few things as well.

Interviewer: … They can't touch their right foot with their left hand?

SH: Yes, they can't cross over. In Year 1 they're funny. Because they'll write some of their sentences and their pencil will stop somewhere and they'll grab it with the other hand. They won't cross over that line … And that's when you think 'oh, they've got big problems here, they haven't decided what hand they're going to use' …

They are still having problems with fine motor skills. A major one. Gross motor can be part of it. They are usually not very good at Phys Ed. either.

Although the views articulated by SH on the relationship between motor skills and learning disabilities indicates a traditionally popular perspective on the causes of learning problems, it is not supported by empirical research (Shepard *et al.*, 1983; Ysseldyke *et al.*, 1983). Yet it provides a comfortable theoretical basis to account for her decisions about students.

Another pertinent point about SH's activities of noticing is that she very rarely makes eye contact with students, in either part of the lesson and she seems to have little sustained interaction with any of the students. In viewing the videotapes we have tried to work out what student activities are in her line of vision such that she could have any idea about how children are doing academically. We have located right and wrong answers that are in her line of hearing, and 'pencil grip' and other physical signs in reported in the interview data. These lines of hearing and vision correspond exactly to the activities that make up her lessons. In this respect, we see enactment of pedagogy as the filter through which observing and noticing can be done.

The sociology of observing children learning literacy

SH seems to locate signs of understanding or lack of understanding in the body, through a glance being able to find children who do not look or move or act as if they know what they are doing. These complement, on occasion, the various motivational ascriptions that the teacher expresses concerning individual people. Effectively, what the teacher has proposed as domains of signs of competence are not unique to her. Such domains have been identified before, although the specific details within the domains will vary by case. At least some of the signs this teacher is reading as clues to children's reading competence have been captured before in the phrase 'looking like a reader', found initially in Cochrane-Smith (1985). Baker and Luke discussed this 'image of the child as an active reader' (Cochrane-Smith, 1985, pp. 25–26) as follows:

> This concept, 'looking like a reader', is in effect a description of the pedagogic gaze turned onto the student's body–mind relation … To 'look like a reader' – by accident, fortune or design – is effectively a cultural and political resource

in the classroom. To not have acquired the look of a reader is a liability. Within this semiotic, [the] teacher's theory of signs, the body is turned into a surface of the mind, and the teacher becomes a reader of that surface.

(Baker and Luke, 1991, pp. 261–262)

The operative term applied to the argument in this chapter might be the notion of 'surface'. This surface becomes a substitute for deeper investigation of what children can do conceptually, particularly when the pedagogic circumstances are as demanding as they are in most classrooms. Teachers rely on such surface readings as a kind of default sign system. The signs relate specifically to how children inhabit the classroom – a concept extended by Luke (1992) through Bourdieu's notion of 'habitus' to describe how the 'body literate' is inscribed in early literacy training. We consider that our interview question, 'How do you come to notice that students are having learning disabilities?' is a crucial one in our investigations. In this teacher's answers we see a listing of physical signs and imputed motivational dispositions that are taken to stand for 'learning disabilities'. At one level, these signs make sense given the curriculum and pedagogy in this classroom. They are identified in relation to the specific activities that are used to organise and to teach the students. These signs are not independent of the pedagogy, but instead, their listing by the teacher is a compelling account of what she takes her pedagogy to be.

Conclusions

It is conceded that this classroom represents a single example of an approach to teaching literacy. It is one demonstration of the relations between enactment of curriculum, conditions or opportunities for teacher observation, and decisions on who has learning disabilities (domains A, B and C on our map). Both school policy and the teacher's classroom practices were underpinned by a whole language approach to literacy with attention to genre theory. This philosophical approach intersected with a set of pedagogical practices that defined the space in which the teacher could make observations about the competence or incompetence of students. As naïve observers we found that the classroom did not reveal information about children's competence to read and comprehend text. Rather, it distinguished between those students who were capable of using a range of covert cues to follow the teacher's reasoning in order to answer questions to her satisfaction and those who could not. It also distinguished between children who were conscientious and diligent, and who were neat and tidy in their execution of motor tasks, and those who were not. In this way, it appeared to us that the pedagogy played a central role in defining who was clever and who was learning disabled in the class. We conclude that studies in the social construction of learning difficulties should take into account how the teacher's observational practices and conclusions about children need to be situated firmly within an investigation of how teaching and learning are locally organised, and furthermore, within an investigation of how the curriculum is handed down for local enactment.

References

Baker, C.D. (1991) Literacy practices and social relations in classroom reading events, in C.D. Baker and A. Luke (Eds) *Towards a Critical Sociology of Reading Pedagogy*. Philadelphia: John Benjamins.

Baker, C.D. and Luke, A (1991) Discourse practice: a postscript, in C.D. Baker and A. Luke (Eds) *Towards a Critical Sociology of Reading Pedagogy*. Philadelphia: John Benjamins.

Carrier, J. (1990) Special education and the explanation of pupil performance, *Disability, Handicap and Society*, 5, pp. 211–227.

Christensen, C.A., Gerber, M.M. and Everhart, R.B. (1986) Toward a sociological perspective on learning disabilities, *Educational Theory*, 36, pp. 317–332.

Cochrane-Smith, M. (1985) Looking like readers, talking like readers, *Theory into Practice*, 14, pp. 22–31.

Dudley-Marling, C. and Dippo, D. (1995) What learning disability does: sustaining the ideology of schooling, *Journal of Learning Disabilities*, 28, pp. 408–414.

Hargreaves, D., Hester, S. and Mellor, F. (1975) *Deviance in Classrooms*. London: Routledge and Kegan Paul.

Hull, G., Rose, M., Fraser, K.L. and Castellano, M. (1991) Remediation as a social construct: perspectives from an analysis of classroom discourse, *College Composition and Communication*, 42, pp. 299–329.

Kirk, S.A. (1968) The Illinois Test of psycholinguistic abilities: its origins and implications, in I. Hellmuth (Ed.) *Learning Disorders,* Vol. 3. Sattle WA: Special Child Publications.

Luke, A. (1992) The body literate: discourse and inscription in early literacy training, *Linguistics and Education*, 4, pp. 107–129.

McDermott, R.P. (1993) The acquisition of a child by a learning disability, in S. Chaiklin and J. Lave (Eds) *Understanding Practice: Perspectives on Activity and Context*. Cambridge: Cambridge University Press.

Reynolds, M.C. (1984) Classification of students with handicaps, in E.W. Gordon (Ed.) *Review of Research in Education,* Vol. II. Washington, DC: American Educational Research Association.

Shepard, L.A., Smith, M.L. and Vojir, C.P. (1983) Characteristics of pupils identified as learning disabled, *American Educational Research Journal*, 20, pp. 309–311.

Tomlinson, S. (1982) *A Sociology of Special Education*. London: Routledge and Kegan Paul.

Ysseldyke, J., Algozzine, B. and Epps, S. (1983) A logical and empirical analysis of current practice in classifying students as handicapped, *Exceptional Children*, 50, pp. 160–166.

Chapter 8

Research case studies in teaching, learning and inclusion

Adrienne Alton-Lee, Christine Rietveld, Lena Klenner, Ngaio Dalton, Cathy Diggins and Shane Town

Introduction

The research case studies presented here have been designed to assist educators to reflect upon ways in which education can be inclusive in classrooms and school communities. Evidence from interviews with new entrant students in the ERU-DITE[1] Roadrunner study revealed the effectiveness of strategies used to educate the younger peers of a student with spina bifida at Roadrunner School. The teacher, Ms Nikora, devised her strategies in response to research Christine Rietveld carried out as part of her doctoral thesis (1994) on the participation of children with Down's syndrome (DS) in new entrant classes. Ms Nikora encountered this research in a teacher education course that included training in action research. Our account highlights the potential of interplay between research, teacher education and educational practice to inform teacher professional development.

Here we enable the reader to consider Rietveld's case study excerpts that were influential in Ms Nikora's approach. We describe Ms Nikora's strategies and then trace the responses of new entrant students to the strategies using a case study approach. In particular, we focus on the theoretical tools that Rietveld offers educators and the potential role of these tools to assist teachers in developing inclusive educational practice.

In presenting two of the research case studies we use a technique that has been entitled the 'interrupted narrative'. We present the reader with a critical decision faced by a teacher and ask the reader to reflect upon what they might have done in that situation or what they think would have been an effective response and why, before we go on to present, what the teachers actually did. Our purpose is three-fold. First, we use prediction to engage the reader more directly in reflection upon the interplay between theory and practice. Second, the interpolation of an interrupted narrative highlights the use of theoretical tools in equipping teachers to draw upon a range of creative strategies appropriate to particular contexts. Third, the interrupted narrative technique encourages and focuses debate about the nature of effective teacher intervention.

[. . .]

We use research case studies to illustrate the ways in which two alternative theoretical models of disability influence practice: the 'social constructionist' and the 'personal tragedy' models. Ms Nikora's experience illustrates the potential of these models to assist educators.

'Social constructionist' and 'personal tragedy' models

While there have been many influences historically on the ways in which educators and communities think of disability, and a range of terminologies used to represent the views held, we have found the terms 'social constructionist' and 'personal tragedy' to be useful for teachers. 'Personal tragedy' is a term applied to the model that posits disability as a problem or deficit located within the individual that requires 'fixing'.

[. . .]

The 'social constructionist' model rejects a focus on remediating the individual through a focus on the individual. The social constructionist model sees disability not so much the result of a person's impairment, but as a product of social factors in the contexts in which s/he participates that create barriers and limit opportunities for equal participation. In terms of this model's application to the chalk face or whiteboard of the classroom, the emphasis is on the teacher in managing the context and environment to provide appropriate educational experiences for all students including those with identified disabilities. The social constructionist model fits in with ecological theory that is based on the transactional relationship between a person and her/his contexts including the relationships between contexts and wider systems impacting on more immediate contexts. From our perspective the social constructionist model rejects a distinction between the 'mainstream' and the 'included disabled'. Rather the model requires a shift to a universalizing discourse of difference within which a programme is designed to meet the diverse and fluid educational needs of all students (Town, 1996, 1998).

Using the 'social constructionist' and 'personal tragedy' models to understand educational practice

Ms Nikora encountered these two models when Rietveld's research used as the focus of a lecture and tutorial in a university programme for teachers seeking to upgrade their Diploma qualifications. Observational data from Rietveld's doctoral study in progress provided vivid illustrations of educational practice underpinned by the two models. Rietveld undertook continuous narrative observations of three children with DS from pre-entry visits to each child's school through five consecutive days from the time the child arrived at school. A further 18 hours of observation of each child was carried out subsequently, spread at different times of the day over the next month and at the end of the school term.

Rietveld recorded the following account of 6-year-old Mark's experience in the playground during an interval break:

[Mark is in the playground standing and looking around. James comes up to Mark.]

James: Hello, hello, hello. [James gets very close to Mark's face.]

[Mark backs off a little.]

Mark: No.

[James goes off to a nearby friend in the adventure playground.]

James: Look at that boy there. He said 'No'. Come and have a look. He goes like this with his tongue.

[James imitates putting his tongue in and out of his mouth. James pokes his tongue out at Mark. Mark walks off a little and watches children playing on the adventure playground. James returns with another two boys as well as the first boy.]

Boys: Hello, hello, hello.

[The boys say hello to him over and over and laugh at him. One of the boys throws his lunch paper at Mark after screwing it up first. Mark looks at the ground and shakes his head. Peter squeals at him and pats his cheeks. The others make growling noises at him then laugh.

The boys leave for a minute and then return and continue saying 'Hello' to Mark over and over. Mark pokes his tongue out at the boys.

[A teacher-aide walks by.]

TA: I hope you boys are being nice

James: We're just saving 'Hello' to him . . .

[The teacher-aide introduces Mark to the boys and suggests that they play with Mark. They ask Mark if he wants a swing. Mark does not respond. The boys leave and Mark stands on the path looking around.]

TA: Come on. [The teacher-aide is holding out her hand to Mark.]
We'll find William. [William is another child with a disability the teacher-aide is there to support.]
Let's go to the adventure playground.

[Mark follows the teacher-aide.]

In this case Mark's isolation, within the school playground was evident at the outset of the observation. Mark's difference became the focus of James's attention. Mark's actions at the outset of the incident were not socially inappropriate towards James. Rather, James's actions towards Mark such as the overly close proximity were socially inappropriate. It is clear from the observation that Mark did not welcome James's attention and found it to be disconcerting and undesirable. The incident escalated when James brought other boys over to join in taunting Mark. Mark was then subject to inappropriate physical contact and the mocking behaviour of the other boys who growled as if he were an animal, object or not fully human. If such interactions form the basis of a child's peer relationships they will inevitably affect his development of self-worth (Hatch, 1988). He is likely to internalize the view that he is of inferior status and an undesirable playmate, without knowing why. Developmental processes such as self-agency, advancement of language and other skill development will be negatively affected.

The teacher-aide's response to the situation she encountered was to challenge the boys. They readily justified their behaviour as friendly greeting behaviour. The teacher-aide directed the other boys to behave in a friendly way. They apparently complied but Mark understandably did not want to play with the boys and rejected their prompted invitation. The teacher-aide resolved the problem by providing physical comfort or compensation to Mark, when she held out her hand, and suggested that he play with another disabled student.

When we have used this observational excerpt in teacher education, it has had a powerful impact on teachers. The case highlights the cruel isolation and suffering students can experience within the peer culture in a school playground. Hahn (1997) put forward an argument for rejecting a paternalistic policy of protecting disabled children from the negative responses of peers: 'The insults of the playground can be cruel, but learning to cope with offensive comments there probably represents indispensable preparation in acquiring the social skills they may need in later years' (p. 321). Repeated experiences of peer abuse may, however, undermine rather than support the developmental processes that would enable such learning of social skills.

The compensatory behaviour that marks a personal tragedy approach was exemplified in the teacher-aide's hand holding behaviour that typically in our culture would have been socially appropriate only for a much younger child. The personal tragedy perspective is apparent also in her complicity in the social marginalization of Mark within a peer group of difference and disability. We have found that for teachers, this case vividly conveys a sense of the enormity of the challenges confronting educators seeking to support effective inclusive practices.

We have used a second case from Christine Rietveld's doctoral research to show a teacher's approach to inclusion that exemplifies the social constructionist model. The context was a junior school class where a small group of children were engaged in block play during 'Choosing Time'. Ian added some more cars to the block building in progress and broke the structure the group of children were building together.

> *Alan:*   Ian! No, Ian.
> *Brent:*   [To Alan] Tell the teacher.
> [Alan tells the teacher]
> The teacher arrives at the scene and . . .
> [Interrupted narrative]

We interrupt the narrative at this point as we did in the teacher education programme Ms Nikora experienced. We use the interruption of the narrative to invite the reader/audience to generate and reflect upon possible effective actions that the teacher might take.

Here, we take up the case study again.

[The teacher arrives at the scene and looks.]

Teacher: [To Alan]. If there's a problem, tell Ian what it is. Tell Ian if there's too many cars, it'll [the structure they have built] break. Tell him where he can put the cars and blocks.

[Alan and Ian sit down on the mat. Ian picks up a car.]

Alan: [To Ian]. In there. In there. [Alan shows Ian where to put the car.]

Ian: No. [Ian says 'No' but does put the car where Alan showed him and drives it around. Brent, Alan and Kate also drive their cars around each on their own part of the block structure.

[The children continue to drive their cars around for 2 minutes.]

In our discussion of this case study with teachers we emphasize the teacher's careful assessment of the situation and her decision to focus on Ian's peers. The teacher rejected Brent and Alan's framing that Ian was the problem because of his less developed block building skills. The teacher intervened to assist Ian's peers in problem solving and using a communication strategy to help Ian learn why his action caused a problem in the building task. She explained to them how they should interact with Ian appropriately to give him feedback and help him to learn and use appropriate building skills. In our experience, teachers consider the strategy to have been remarkably successful. For educators who have worked with junior children, 2 minutes of ongoing, amicable and productive cooperative play is compelling evidence of a successful teacher intervention! As a consequence of the teacher's intervention all the children in the block play group have had an opportunity to learn a problem-solving skill from the teacher that can he transferable across contexts.

Ms Nikora and the collaborative research endeavour

The two case studies vividly illustrate the contrast between a personal tragedy and social constructionist model in action in educational practice. Ms Nikora was a new entrant teacher who had encountered these two cases from Rietveld's research in an in-service teacher education course. She was one of a group of teachers who stated that they were deeply challenged and affected by the research. Ms Nikora later specifically identified Rietveld's theoretical framework as influential in her planning and decision-making about her class programme. We have been fortunate to be able to carry out a collaborative classroom research study to explore the interplay between research, theory and practice in Ms Nikora's class programme.

[. . .]

The Roadrunner context

Roadrunner School (a pseudonym) is a small state primary school located on the rural/suburban margin of one of the satellite cities in the greater Wellington region. At the time of the study there were 125 students in the school. The school was assessed according to the Ministry of Education's socio-economic indicator for schools as in the low socio-economic band. The ethnic mix of the school comprised 26 per cent Maori, 64 per cent Pakeha/European, 6 per cent Samoan, 2 per cent Tokolauan and 2 per cent Rarotongan students.

The case study was set in the reception or Years 0 and 1 class that took in new entrants to the school and comprised 18 children at the time of the study.

Data gathering

Five cameras, four with zoom lenses and one with a wide-angle lens, were mounted in the classroom to provide an ongoing video record encompassing the classroom space used. A mobile movie camera was also used to maintain a sequential visual and audio record of the teacher's activity. [. . .]

A portable tape recorder was used after teaching sessions to maintain an ongoing debriefing record with the teacher and to capture each observer's perspectives upon what was happening. The teacher's reflections were also recorded from time to time when she wished to make a comment upon the progress of the unit.

Both the visual and audio data were used to construct a continuous record of the audio transcript and a detailed descriptive record of the student involvement. Copies of student drawings and writing have been scanned into the record. These records have been supplemented with the transcripts of individual interviews with students, before and after the unit, about the unit content. Pre- and post-unit interviews that focused on the teacher's intended learning outcomes were carried out with 15 students in the class and 13 of these students remaining, at Roadrunner School were interviewed again a year later.

Interviews have been and continue to be carried out from time to time with the teacher around the case study development process supplemented on occasion by her written reflections on her intentions and perspectives.

Ethics

After negotiating entry to the school and receiving the support of the teacher, principal and Board of Trustees for the study we sought written permission from the parents for their children to participate in the study. [. . .] The first author informed them about the reasons for the study and nature of the data-gathering procedures.

As is evident in the availability to children of an 'off' switch on the wireless microphones, we have balanced our methodological concern with obtaining data that will give us insight into the lived culture of the classroom with our ethical commitment to the children's rights to maintain privacy. Throughout the study the principle guiding data-gathering procedures with the children was that the children should have as much agency as possible in the process and our access to data was subject to their choice. For example, although the children had agreed to wear microphones and participate, they could choose to turn off their wireless microphones and/or decline an interview. We taught the children to use the portable tape recorders and they controlled the 'on', 'off' and 'pause' buttons during the interviews deciding when the interview would or would not proceed. The children actively took up these opportunities.

A contract was drawn up with the teacher explaining her rights to be involved at each stage of the research process. Permission was sought from other adults or students working in the class from time to time if their interaction with the students occurred during the unit.

Retrospective data analysis

Our observational and interview data revealed that Ms Nikora had been effective in her approach to supporting inclusion and challenging personal tragedy perspectives for the new entrants at Roadrunner School. The detailed reconstruction allowed us to trace retrospectively the strategies that she used. The purpose in the analysis has been to identify and make explicit the theoretical principles underlying the specific strategies used by Ms Nikora so that those principles can be adapted by other teachers to other contexts to support effective and inclusive educational practice. [. . .]

Zack and the playground incident

Zack, a student in a Year 5 class at Roadrunner School had spina bifida. Some weeks before Ms Nikora's unit planning Zack had had a seizure in the playground and collapsed. Some of the new entrant children had witnessed the incident and the arrival of an ambulance to take Zack to hospital. Ms Nikora was concerned that children thought that Zack had died when he went into a deep sleep after his seizure.

> I think it was Ellis; it was either Ellis or Campbell. I just can't remember off hand. Um, there was Caitlin . . . just a group of them . . . I can't remember who was the one who said he had died. It happened at lunchtime and they came back and [they] had questions. Huhana, she was out standing up yelling, 'The ambulance is here!' They were all concerned . . . once one person had brought up the word 'dead'.

At the time of the incident Ms Nikora attempted to reassure the students: 'We had to do some reassurances that Zack was actually OK. We . . . made cards for him and talked about [him being] at hospital but . . .'. Ms Nikora remained concerned about the incident and the children's fear; their lack of understanding and their misunderstandings. She explained that she was concerned both for them and for their attitudes towards Zack in the future. Ms Nikora reflected also that Rietveld's research and the personal tragedy model had raised questions for her about the absence of an explicit whole school approach to supporting inclusion at Roadrunner School.

She reflected upon her previous implicit assumption that effective inclusion in Zack's case had been primarily an issue for Zack's own teacher.

In response to her reflections on this incident and its consequences Ms Nikora decided to educate her new entrants about Zack and about spina bifida. In addressing this issue directly, Ms Nikora aimed to assist the effective inclusion of Zack in the school.

Interrupted narrative

Before we proceed in reporting what Ms Nikora did, we invite readers to identify strategies that they might use in such a situation. From Ms Nikora's perspective the new entrants' witnessing of Zack's collapse has created attitudes of fear and misinformation. The event has contributed to a situation where the personal tragedy perspective has been evident in the attitudes of younger children in the school.

Before proceeding with our account of Ms Nikora's approach we wish to take the reader into the new entrant class 25 minutes after Zack had been invited to join the class for an afternoon session to explain about spina bifida. The students were asked to record (through drawing and writing) what they had learned about spina bifida in their 'Thinking books'. New entrant Caitlin who was sitting alongside Zack at a table had not recorded anything in her book, ostensibly because there were no pencils in the container at the table. When Caitlin announced earlier that there were not enough pencils at the table Holly gave hers to Zack and retrieved an extra one from a container at another table. Caitlin made no perceptible effort to find a pencil. Zack had turned away from Caitlin, demonstrating parts of his wheelchair for another new entrant student, Fa'afetai, at Ms Nikora's instigation. Ms Nikora has focused Fa'afetai's attention on the wheelchair and Caitlin who had overheard the conversation called out.

Day 1, Task 19, 13. 58'00"
Caitlin: Zack gets around in a wheelchair! [giggles]
[Caitlin takes the handle of the wheelchair and starts pushing. Zack puts the brake on and re-orients the wheelchair away from Caitlin as he returns to a conversation he is engaged in with Fa'afetai and Ms Nikora.]

Day 1, Task 20, 14.01'45"
[Caitlin has not worked on Task 19 so has not yet begun her task. Other students have finished and are now moving to play with blocks or read books.]
Caitlin to Zack: I said 'Where's the pencil?' I'm getting angry.
Caitlin to Zack: Hurry up! I'm getting angry [laughs].

Day 1, Task 20, 14.03'00"
Caitlin to Zack: I know why you're a bit smaller
Zack to Caitlin: 'Cause I'm in a chair.
Caitlin to Zack: No, because you're in a wheelchair.
Zack to Caitlin: That's what I meant.

Day 1, Task 20, 14.03'45"
Caitlin to Zack: [whispers in Zack's ear with her hand across her mouth]
            Spina bifida boy. Hee hee.
Day, 1, Task 20, 14. 03'45"
Caitlin to Zack: [calls out softly]
            Hey, spina bifida boy.

At this point Ms Nikora overhears Caitlin and . . .

Again we invite readers to consider how Ms Nikora might respond to Caitlin's comment and why?

Ms Nikora's approach

Ms Nikora chose to use a curriculum-focused approach to inform the students about spina bifida and to enable them to interact appropriately, with Zack within the school community. We have identified the four major strategies Ms Nikora used in her overall approach:

• Social studies curriculum integration
• 'Personal tragedy' critique
• Multiple positionings
• Curriculum application in the school community.

[. . .]

Social studies curriculum integration

Ms Nikora used the ongoing social studies programme to educate her students about spina bifida in order to inform the students, to enable them to act appropriately and supportively to Zack, and to support effective inclusive practice within the wider school community. Spina bifida was not the focus of the unit but rather a context used to help the students better understand the diversity of experiences of Christmas and the concept of people in the community who help us.

Ms Nikora integrated her objectives for the students' learning about spina bifida and Zack into the ongoing programme rather than making it a special mention or isolated topic. This approach is similar to that identified by Banks (1994) as a key dimension in the construction of effective multicultural curriculum: content integration. In the content integration approach to transforming mainstream curriculum, content reflecting diversity is integrated into key instructional points.

The vehicle for Ms Nikora's approach was a social studies unit 'Christmas in Hospital', that she taught to the class of new entrant students over a three-day period. Ms Nikora decided to combine a focus on spina bifida with a focus on the celebration of Christmas. Because the unit was timed to occur in late November, Ms Nikora decided to use the children's growing excitement about Christmas as an impetus for her social studies programme. However, she planned her unit to avoid stereotyped portrayals of Christmas. Rather, Ms Nikora intended that the social studies curriculum should provide a consideration of the Christmas festival that reflected the diversity of experiences the new entrant students might have at Christmas. To achieve her purpose, Ms Nikora selected as a key resource a New Zealand social studies resource kit. The kit prepared by Kelvin Smythe (1996) contained a story and a set of 22 large pictures about Tyler, a 4-year-old boy with spina bifida. Tyler had spent Christmas in hospital having an operation. Her planning focused on the key objective for the unit: Achievement Objective 2 in the second draft of the New Zealand social studies curriculum statement Culture and Heritage Strand: 'Children will describe how they celebrate Christmas and compare it with (the way Tyler spent his Christmas when he was four years old)'. Ms Nikora used this story about a boy's experience of having an operation in hospital at Christmas both to exemplify a different kind of Christmas experience and to inform the children about spina bifida.

Ms Nikora's intention to inform the students about spina bifida was evident throughout the unit as she provided a range of tasks and contexts for the class to learn specific facts about spina bifida:

Day 3, 13.47'30"
Ms Nikora: What can you remember, Kim?
Kim: The bones don't join up together.

Day 3, 13.39'30
Ms Nikora: Can anyone tell me what spina bifida is?
Holly: Your, it's the thing that makes, 'cause some of the bones at the back of your spine are gone so something has to squeeze out the other side.
Ms Nikora: You're so right.
Holly: And you're born with it and you can't walk.
Ms Nikora: Just like Holly said a cyst grows through a split in their spine.

Day 3, 14.26'00"
Ms Nikora: And this word, 'drip'? Does anyone know what a drip is?
Huhana: It's a drip that you put in your hand, and like an injection . . .

The information that you are born with spina bifida appeared to alleviate fears that Caitlin harboured for her own susceptibility to the condition.

Day 1, Task 19, 13.57'00"
[The new entrants are talking while recording their individual Thinking Book entries.]
Caitlin: Eight year olds don't have spina bifida maybe
Holly: Because you're borned [sic.] with it.
Caitlin: I wasn't borned [sic.] . . .
Holly to Huhana: [spelling spina bifida]-I – N – A

Day 1, Task 19, 13.57'15"
Caitlin to Zack: I wasn't born with spina bifida (inaudible) never!

Ms Nikora was constantly reflecting throughout the unit on the extent to which her focus on specific content information was successful with the students. She struggled with moderating a balance between introducing new information and consolidating what the students, had learned. On reflection she would not have attempted to teach the concept of hydrocephalus which she initially included because both Zack and Tyler had the condition.

Because the context of hospital was central to Tyler's story, Ms Nikora planned also to develop the children's understandings of the nature of 'hospital' from a social studies perspective. Accordingly, Ms Nikora selected Achievement Objective 1 in the Social Organisation and Processes strand: 'Children will collect and present information about people in the community that help us when we go to the hospital.' One of the students in Ms Nikora's class, Huhana, had recently had an accident on the slide in the school playground, broken her arm and been admitted to hospital to have her arm set.

Ms Nikora used the Social Studies curriculum as a vehicle to address an issue of diversity within the Roadrunner school community. This approach met Brophy and Alleman's (1992) assumptions that ideal social studies curricula should be relevant to long-term goals and life applications outside of school. The approach also drew upon the social studies curriculum to help the students participate in informed and responsible ways within there own school community contemporaneously. What they were learning about in social studies was directly linked to their own experiences and community. Ms Nikora emphasized, as central to her planning, the role of the national Social Studies Curriculum aim to enable children's 'participation in a changing society as confident, informed and responsible citizens'. She perceived the valuing of community and interdependence as integral not only to social studies curriculum but also to the cultural values of Maori: 'Social studies should promote the community sense. The idea of working together rather than in isolation has implications for a lot of children in my class because from the Maori cultural side of it, you do work in together. It's not the individual that's emphasized . . . the whole community thing is important'.

'Personal tragedy' critique: reflective and responsive management of personal tragedy positionings in enacted curriculum

Throughout the interviews and debriefings about her planning and day-to-day progress during the unit, Ms Nikora mentioned the influence of her critique of the personal tragedy model on her approach. She described that influence as affecting decisions she made to exclude resources and to adapt resources. She also used the personal tragedy model as a tool to aid her reflections on the children's responses to Zack. While the 'personal tragedy' model was a useful tool for classroom practice, the model is a blunt instrument when trying to interpret how children do perceive people with disabilities and why they respond in the ways they do. A useful area of further research would be to identify the kinds of, and the origins of, perspectives and views that students do hold that influence their 'othering' of peers.

Ms Nikora explained that she wished to distinguish in the new entrants' thinking the person, Zack, from the disability, spina bifida: 'The person needs to be seen before the disability . . . I was wanting to get across to them that, you know, Zack does have this condition, but that 95 per cent of the time he's all right. It's just something he has to live with, just like Barry has asthma and he has to go off to hospital like that'.

Throughout her planning for the unit, Ms Nikora used the personal tragedy model as a tool to assist her resource selection and usage.

> The major change that I've made today . . . Zack's video – when I viewed it I could see it from an adult's perspective . . . it was great that Zack was so independent and he could use his parapodium. However, the other day when Caitlin . . . said 'Spina bifida boy!' I thought that she was going into the personal tragedy . . . you know, 'Poor little thing – you've got it and I haven't. And so then I viewed the video again last night I asked my husband to sit in on it and see what he thought. He thought it was definitely, 'Look at this poor kid. He's down there rolling on the ground trying to get into his parapodium. . . . It does make him look as if he's totally different'. So, I thought 'Well, he doesn't know, Zack . . . and if that's his sort of view, then I could see from there that my five year olds may not be mature enough to see that it's the independence you know, that's being highlighted; not the poor little kid rolling around on the ground trying to get into it'. So I've decided to cut that out because I don't want that to come across.

[. . .]

Ms Nikora attempted to influence the personal tragedy approach played out by Caitlin on Day 1, and exemplified in the Interrupted narrative we presented earlier. We return to that incident to explore Ms Nikora's response to Caitlin's taunts.

Ms Nikora chose not directly to challenge the nature of Caitlin's comments. This choice reflects her commitment to using an educational rather than a disciplinary process. Her approach is congruent with the views of many students interviewed in the Understanding Learning and Teaching Studies whom, when asked about teacher interventions in peer abuse, commented that direct teacher interventions generally make the consequences in the peer culture much worse for them, not better. However, we have selected this issue for our interrupted narrative focus because we consider it a complex and crucial issue for teachers and students. Research approaches that address the complexity of the contextual processes involved are needed to help inform educational practice that can facilitate student safety and well-being in our schools and communities.

When Ms Nikora heard Caitlin's comment to Zack she moved over to Caitlin apparently using physical proximity and a very firm intonation to halt Caitlin's comments. Ms Nikora refocused Caitlin on the task at hand through a series of questions after eliciting an admission from Caitlin that she had done nothing for the set task:

Day 1, 14.04'00"

Ms Nikora to Caitlin:	Right. What have you drawn your picture about? What did you learn about spina bifida?
Ms Nikora:	What did you learn about spina bifida?
Caitlin:	Oh. [Looking at her blank Thinking Book page] Nothing there.
Ms Nikora:	No.
Ms Nikora:	Well, what are you going to draw your picture about? What did you learn about it? What did you learn? What part of your body does it affect?
Caitlin:	Your spine.
Ms Nikora:	Right. You could draw your − a spine.

Ms Nikora left Caitlin to continue with a specific task and turned her attention to Zack:

Ms Nikora to Zack:	What have you learnt about spina bifida since you've had it? What has been the most important thing for you?
Zack:	That it's sore.
Ms Nikora:	That it's sore, is it? What's the most painful part? In your head?
Zack:	Mmm.
Ms Nikora:	Your head aches and that.
Zack:	Yes.

Ms Nikora did not acknowledge directly Caitlin's hurtful comments to Zack either to Caitlin or to Zack. However, our reading of Ms Nikora's interaction with Zack suggests that she used the opportunity to acknowledge the pain he experienced and to provide reassurance for him that may have been intended to address more than just his physical pain.

Because we did not have an active microphone continuously recording Caitlin's interactions during the unit we cannot be sure of what else happened. Our other microphones recorded no more gleeful taunts from Caitlin to Zack by Day 2. However, the attitude of diminution was apparent in Caitlin's interactions with Zack when she used a diminutive name in addressing him during the morning of Day 2.

Day 2, 11.15'30"

Caitlin/Zack:	Hello, Zack, Zackie.

Questions of intersections between gender arid disability arise out of these data. The data provide evidence of a 5-year-old girl using diminutives and taunting towards a boy who was four years older than her.

It is likely that Zack would not have been subject to Caitlin's taunts had he not been part of Ms Nikora's programme. Our presumption is that the evidence from the study indicates that the overall effect of the programme would have been to generate a more knowledgeable and respectful peer community for Zack within the school. There was evidence to support this view. [. . .] Also there is some evidence in the research literature that the helper role can be beneficial to the learning of the helper (Webb, 1982). However, Hahn's (1997) assumption that exposure to the cruel insults of the playground will help students to develop social skills is problematic. Critical questions about the well-being of Zack and other students within abusive peer subcultures should remain at the forefront of research and practice.

Ms Nikora's used her critique of the 'personal tragedy' model when interacting with the new entrants as she elaborated upon their ideas in their Thinking Books:

> Day 2, 11.12'30"
> [Huhana is drawing a wheelchair and Ms Nikora stops to talk to her]
> *Ms Nikora/Huhana:* Because people with disabilities . . . we need to treat them?
> *Huhana/Ms Nikora:* Kindly.
> *Ms Nikora/Huhana:* Yes, with respect.

Ms Nikora's reframing of personal tragedy portrayals of people with disabilities was reflected in Barry's self-correction as he reported back to the class what he had learnt on the second day of the unit:

> Day 2, 11.21'15"
> *Ms Nikora/Class:* What did you learn?
> *Barry to class:* Someone helps Zack in a – just ask Zack if I could push him and I could.
> *Ms Nikora:* Right, then. You ask, and that's the most important thing. Well done Thank you.

In summary, while Ms Nikora was proactive in excluding personal tragedy portrayals from curricular resources or in adapting and transforming such portrayals, she rejected the approach of being directly critical or challenging when she encountered evidence of such an attitude in the new entrants. Ms Nikora's primary approach to the presentation of Zack in enacted curriculum was to make apparent to the children *evidence* of the range of Zack's competencies and to model informed, respectful and appropriate way's of behaving with Zack.

Multiple positionings

> the problem of curriculum becomes one of proliferating identifications, not closing them down. . . . But . . . more is required than simply a plea to add marginalized voices to an already, overpopulated site.'
>
> (Britzman, 1995: 158)

The multiple positionings approach provides an implicit counteraction to the narrow personal tragedy positioning. Ms Nikora used multiple positionings to re/present, in this case, people with a disability through varied positionings. We have identified here four distinct multiple positionings strategies she used.

The older peer helper positioning

Some weeks before the social studies unit began, Zack joined several other 9-year-old students who came into the class regularly as cross-age tutors to provide help to the new entrant students.

Ms Nikora's strategy of using Zack as older peer helper was descried to generate a context wherein Zack's abilities and strengths were self-evident to the new entrant children and directly helpful to them. Zack's provision of help for the younger children ensured that in the first direct contact they had with Zack, Zack's capabilities were featured. Zack was initially, directly introduced to the new entrants in the roles of older student and helper rather than being positioned as different and/or disabled. His positioning as helper, mentor and older student was integrated into an ongoing cross-age tutor programme rather than established as an isolated or one-off intervention.

The timing of this strategy was also critical to Ms Nikora's approach. She intended to influence the new entrant students' initial perceptions of Zack so that they would think of him as a person with a range of abilities and strengths *before* they learnt about or focused upon his specific disability. Through establishing in the children a substantial personal experience of Zack as someone with abilities, Ms Nikora aimed to pre-empt or overcome a deficit perspective about or personal tragedy perspective on Zack in the new entrants.

To evaluate Ms Nikora's strategy we included in our pre-unit interviews with the new entrants an open question about Zack. Each student was asked: 'Who is Zack?' Of 15 students interviewed before the unit, 13 identified Zack in some way. We were particularly interested in their initial comment or association. Six students mentioned Zack's wheelchair as their first association. One child identified Zack by his classroom number, Room 2. Five new entrants surprised three different interviewers by giving in their initial comment the explanation that Zack was the, person who helped them to skip. For example, they replied that Zack 'helps us to skip'; 'came in for skipping to hold the rope'; 'helps me to skip'. Huhana, noticed the interviewer's eyes widening in surprise at her description of Zack and explained further: 'You don't just teach people by showing you know. You can teach them by telling!'

[. . .] A year later 8 of the 11 students who had been in Ms Nikora's class and were still at the school mentioned Zack's role as an older peer helper when asked about him. In effect, almost three-quarters of the children we interviewed remembered Zack for his helping role. Only one child, Caitlin when interviewed a year later remembered only that Zack was in a wheelchair.

The 'one of many' positioning: multiple stories of children with spina bifida and/or hospital experience

[...]

Through including Zack's story as one of several stories of spina bifida, Ms Nikora achieved several pedagogical purposes. The use of multiple stories provided an effective way to scaffold the children's learning. Ms Nikora provided the children with access to similar information using a variety of contexts, thereby achieving both novelty and repetition. The repetition is likely to have helped the children to construct new knowledge through repeated opportunities to encounter new curriculum content (Nuthall and Alton-Lee, 1993). The use of pictures, written vocabulary and real-life demonstration was interwoven, within the unit to provide rich learning opportunities for the children.

Over and above the effectiveness of the strategy for supporting children's knowledge development, we wish to highlight the importance of the strategy in the positioning of Zack. Zack was *not* singled out as the only example of a child with spina bifida. Rather he was one of at least five different children that were presented to the class as examples of children managing their lives with spina bifida. While the stories addressed the disability they also provided information about a range of capabilities of the children with spina bifida. The use of multiple stories may be critical in the design of curriculum. If Ms Nikora had focused only on Zack, then not only would the wealth of rich educational resources apparent in her programme have been lost to the students, but also Zack would have been presented as a special, different and individual case. From our perspective the use of multiple stories mitigates against the 'freak' positioning that can occur inadvertently when a curriculum intervention focuses just on the disability or difference in one individual.

The sequencing of Zack's story within the multiple stories was also a critical dimension of the strategy. An analysis of the way Ms Nikora structured the curriculum sequence revealed that although Zack was the major focus of the curriculum content he was not the first encounter the children had with curriculum content about spina bifida.

Ms Nikora did not use Zack's actual experience to introduce spina bifida. Rather, she used the teaching resource developed by Smythe depicting the story of 4-year-old Tyler, a Christchurch boy with spina bifida. The story focuses on Tyler's experiences in hospital at Christmas, when he had an urgent operation to drain the fluid that had build up around his brainstem. .

Through focusing initially on Tyler's story, Ms Nikora used the experiences of a real New Zealand child without that child being present when the new entrant students grappled with the nature of the disability.

[...]

Ms Nikora's strategy of using Tyler to introduce the topic of spina bifida enabled the children to explore their ideas, fears and misunderstandings freely. This strategy may have enabled the children to be more sensitive to Zack because they already had some knowledge and understanding to bring to their encounter with Zack in his role as a curriculum resource.

By using hospital as another focus context in the unit and including the hospital stories of children within the class and of children in stories read to the class, Ms Nikora structured a wider focus on shared experiences in community.

Although the children learnt that people are born with spina bifida and that they would not develop spina bifida they also learnt that children go to hospital for many different conditions. The multiple stories depicting a range of shared and overlapping contexts illustrated similarities as well as differences in the experiences of children the new entrants learned about, including, children in their own class community.

Zack as authoritative informant

Ms Nikora's avoidance of a personal tragedy positioning for Zack was evident also in the way in which she introduced him as a direct curriculum resource. While Ms Nikora used Zack as a key curriculum resource, he was not positioned by Ms Nikora as a passive object of study or example. Rather, Zack was presented to the class by Ms Nikora as an expert authority on spina bifida who could take the teacher's role in some part:

> Day 1, Task 17/18 Transition, 1.42'15"
> *Ms N:*   Thanks for sharing that with us, Zack. That was really good to have someone who knows all about because Ms Nikora didn't.

> Day 1, Task 18, 1.43'15"
> *Ms N:*   This boy's name is David [looks at the book and points to the picture] and he's twelve years old. And he was born with spina bifida. [Looks at the class and then at Zack and smiles] Just like Zack told us.

> Day 1, Task 19, 13. 51'30"
> *Ms N:*   I want you to write down what you've learnt – maybe from the book or something Zack has taught you.

Zack explained and demonstrated spina bifida to the new entrant class. He told the children that a person is born with spina bifida and showed them the curve in his spine. He explained about the need for an operation and the headaches he had because of his hydrocephalus. Then Zack discussed the implications for his mobility of having spina bifida.

The outcome of Ms Nikora's strategy of positioning Zack as in authoritative expert about spina bifida and teacher was evident in post-unit interviews with many of the children. For example, Huhana explained that 'Zack told the children why he ended up in a wheelchair' and Brian said that 'Zack showed us how his wheelchair worked'. Both students' responses positioned Zack as an active and knowledgeable informant.

[. . .]

The 'one of us' positioning: Zack the cricketer

Ms Nikora, in reflecting upon Zack's collapse in the playground, was concerned 'that they would see him [Zack] as out there'. Ms Nikora designed her programme to counter the emphasis on the differences of spina bifida and the position of Zack as 'other'.

Ms Nikora's view that students with disabilities are part of us and not 'other' influenced her pedagogy and her use of language in the classroom. For example, after Ms Nikora had brought Zack into the classroom as a peer helper and expert on spina bifida for the afternoon session on the first day of the unit, she introduced a new task apparently unrelated to the unit. She asked each child including the cross-age tutors to draw a picture showing what they were good at.

> You may have wondered why, after Zack had . . . came up in the first day, why I got them to do the picture of the things they were good at. It was to include Zack, you know, so that they could see that Zack was just like one of them. He was good at things as well. I don't know why I thought about that last night, but I just had a feeling that nobody had questioned why I put that in my planning because it didn't seem to relate to the 'Christmas in hospital' [topic]. But it was just that inclusion sort of thing.

In subsequent class discussion of individual responses, Ms Nikora focused on Zack's strength as a cricketer. Cricket is not only a sport that many of the children would have experienced directly, but also a highly valued activity in New Zealand culture and a highly valued traditionally masculine cultural practice. Among the frequent opportunities Ms Nikora took to emphasize Zack's cricketing prowess to the class, the following teacher comment reflects her inclusion of two boys, Zack and William, in a sporting strengths category.

> Day 1, 14.28'15"
> *Ms Nikora/class:*   I have learnt today that Zack [is] good at playing cricket and William [is] good at playing soccer.

Ms Nikora also used the 'people who help us' aspect of the social studies curriculum achievement objective to position children with spina bifida as like all of us in needing help at some time or other.

[. . .]

Social studies curriculum application: new entrant students as knowledgeable and skilled participants within a community of mutual support

Ms Nikora designed her unit not only to make the students more knowledgeable but also to provide them with appropriate applied strategies and skills. The students were taught wheelchair protocol so that they would have the knowledge and skills to assist people in wheelchairs in appropriate ways. The skills were introduced by Rachel, the expert from the Crippled Children's Society and demonstrated by Zack using his wheelchair as a key resource.

> Day 2, 11.02'45"
> *Rachel:*   . . . This might give you some hints about assisting someone who uses a wheelchair. . . . Things to say and things to do.
>
> Day 2, 11.05'15"
> *Rachel:*   Do ask me if I want to be pushed. That's really important.

Both Rachel and Ms Nikora emphasized the importance of asking someone in a wheelchair whether they want to be pushed before providing any assistance. This message had a profound impact on the students. Brian and Simon engaged in an extended discussion about the appropriate way to negotiate pushing a wheelchair.

> Day 2, 11.08'00"
> [Private conversation between Brian and Simon]
> *Brian/Simon:*   If you push them too fast they might fall out and the seat might . . . if you push them too fast the seat belt will come away and they'll fall out.
> *Simon/Brian:*   If you don't put the seat belt on and then. . . .
>
> Day 2, 11.10'15"
> *Simon/Brian:*   Don't push. You have to ask if they push . . . ask push.

Huhana rehearsed the message about asking and then decided to focus on that issue in her Thinking Book entry.

> Day 2, 11.18'00"
> Huhana talking to self as she works in her Thinking book: Do ask me if you want to push me.

Ms Nikora made provision for two children to actually go out into the school grounds and practise wheelchair protocol under the supervision of a student teacher: Fa'afetai and Ellis. It appeared that she made this decision because she considered the in-class opportunity insufficient for Fa'afetai who had little English language and Ellis who had difficulties with hearing and sight and did not have either his glasses or his hearing aid at school that day

> Day 2, 11.09'00"
> *Ms N:*   Would you mind, Zack? I know Fa'afetai would like to help you out in the playground but he's not quite sure how to push you safely. Would it be all right if Mr Kitson went out with Fa'afetai and

you and Ellis and had a practice at making sure they ask you first then . . .

Day 2, 11.10'30"

Mr Kitson:	OK. Fa'afetai and Ellis, you come here. Zack is going to show us, right? What's the first thing we have to do when, if we want to push, Zack ? We have to say, to ask?

[Mr Kitson models asking]

Mr Kitson/Fa'afetai:	You ask. You say: 'Can I push you Zack?'
Fa'afetai/Zack:	[Zack puts his hand up] Ahhhh I pussh [*sic.*] you, Zack?
Mr Kitson:	Does Zack mind if he pushes? Is that all right, Zack?
Zack:	Yeah.

Day 2, 11.13'00"

[Observer notes that Fa'afetai pushes Zack very carefully.]

Ms Nikora's combined strategies described hitherto had a striking impact on Zack's physical positioning within the class. Whereas Zack had previously sat on the edge of the class grouping to talk to the children, by the second morning of the unit programme his wheelchair was noticeably situated within the midst of a group of new entrant children. Zack literally moved from the margins of the class to the centre as the 'Christmas in Hospital' unit progressed.

[. . .]

Summary and reflection

We have identified the links between Ms Nikora's encounter with Rietveld's research and its power to illuminate a theoretical framework that had a profound impact on Ms Nikora's own practice. We have considered in-depth, strategies Ms Nikora used in her social constructionist approach to supporting inclusive educational practice at Roadrunner School: Social studies curriculum integration, 'Personal tragedy' critique, multiple positionings and curriculum application in the school community. We have made transparent four of the multiple positionings Ms Nikora used to position Zack: as an older peer helper, as one of many people (including us) who have shared experiences, as authoritative informant and as one of a community of us that is inclusive of diversity. By making transparent such strategies, we intend that they provide tools for other teachers to use, critique, develop and adapt to support effective inclusive programmes and practices in their own contexts.

Note

1 Educational Research Underpinning Development in Teacher Education Programme funded by Pub Charity, Inc.

References

Alton-Lee, A., Diggins, C., Klenner, L., Vine, E. and Dalton, N. (2001) Teacher management of the learning environment during a social studies discussion in a new-entrant classroom in New Zealand. *Elementary School Journal*, 101 (5), 549–566.

Banks, J. (1994) Transforming the mainstream curriculum. *Educational Leadership*, May, 4–8.

Brophy, J. and Alleman, J. (1992) Planning and managing learning activities: basic principles. In J. Brophy (ed.), *Advances in Research on Teaching*, Vol. 3 (Greenwich: Jai Press).

Britzman, D. (1995) Is there a queer pedagogy? Or, stop reading straight. *Educational Theory*, 45, 151–165.

Hahn, H. (1997) New trends in disability studies: implications for educational policy. In D.K. Lipsky and A. Gartner (eds), *Inclusion and School Reform* (Baltimore: H. Brookes), 315–328.

Hatch, J.A. (1988) Learning to be an outsider: peer stigmatization in kindergarten. *Urban Review*, 20, 59–72.

Nuthall, G.A. and Alton-Lee, A.G. (1993) Predicting learning from student experience of teaching: a theory of student knowledge construction in classrooms. *American Educational Research Journal*, 30, 799–840.

Rietveld, C.M. (1994) From inclusion to exclusion: educational placements of children with Down Syndrome. *Australian Journal of Special Education*, 18, 28–35.

Smythe, K. (1996) *Christmas in Hospital: A Social Studies Unit For Junior and Middle Levels* (Hamilton: Developmental Publications).

Town, S.J.H. (1996) Is it safe to come out, yet?: the impact of secondary schooling on the positive identity of ten young gay men, or that's a queer way to behave. In *Resources in Education*. ERIC Documentation Reproduction Service No. ED 395 262.

Town, S.J.H. (1998) Is it safe to come out, yet?: the impact of secondary schooling on the positive identity of ten young gay men, or that's a queer way to behave. Unpublished doctoral dissertation (Victoria University, Wellington).

Webb, N. (1982) Student interaction and learning in small groups. *Review of Educational Research*, 52, 421–445.

Part III

Striving for inclusive pedagogy and curricula

Chapter 9

Learning 'how' and learning 'why'

Watching teachers in Asia move towards more inclusive styles of work

Janet C. Holdsworth

[...]

The issue

I feel very strongly that successful integration/inclusion cannot happen merely because a person accepts an intellectual, philosophic or moral argument. The problem is that, in many instances, 'the western perspectives' on disability and special educational needs assume that once the argument is accepted, the practice will automatically follow. Thus there is an emphasis on the 'why' and a great distrust of the 'how'.

I would like to suggest that a consideration of the relationship between theory and practice leads one to a different viewpoint, and that this can help in the urgent task of creating 'Schools for All'.

Once an issue is seen as a 'moral imperative' it becomes nearly impossible to discuss the difficulties of implementation. This is graphically shown by Bricker (1995) in writing about the problems of implementation in American schools. Following assurances that she does not support segregation, Bricker writes,

> ... Rather, my difficulty comes in the simplistic and naive declarations about how to achieve this goal [of full inclusion]. The content of many written documents and verbal presentations suggest that we, like the Nike commercial, 'Just do it.' On the contrary, I believe considerable thought and planning are required...
>
> (p. 180)

The very fact that Bricker felt that she had to devote nearly two pages of her paper establishing her right to criticise current practice by showing that she is not 'anti-inclusion' and has a 'history of long-term involvement in developing integrated programs for young children with disabilities...' is indicative of the way the issue has been seen as a moral and legal and value-laden question. She feels that even to suggest that current practice is not good enough will leave her 'lined up with those on the wrong side' [of the fence]. This she finds 'at the very least disconcerting'.

After giving very pertinent observed examples (see Box 9.1) and detailing what she considers to be necessary for success, Bricker concludes, in a colleague's words:

> Like many things in education we tend to bulldoze ahead based on 'principle' with little thought given to how to make that principle truly supportive of the development of all children. Of particular concern is the fact that little empirical effort is invested in describing what is happening in the integrated environment and how to support efforts so that better things happen.
>
> (p. 192)

Where educationalists talk of 'accepting principles', development agencies and non-government organisations (NGOs) tend to use the term 'awareness raising' to describe the process of changing people's concepts and ideologies. In the 'development business' in poorer countries, agencies sometimes assume that once teachers are 'aware' then they can 'Just do it' in the same way that Bricker describes the US teachers are expected to have no problems once a principle has been accepted.

However, my experiences in Asia would suggest that 'awareness raising' provides no solid basis for change. This is partly because the ideas presented cannot be openly argued against. Anyone who disagrees or has doubts has clearly 'failed to have their awareness raised'. They must therefore be stupid, or cruel, or unfeeling, or just plain wrong. As none of us like to be labelled in this way we stifle our doubts and concerns about 'how' and agree on the surface. What happens then depends on the power of the individual and the options open to them; some may simply refuse by leaving the job; some may say, 'Well I agree in principle, but it won't work here because . . .'; most doubters will lose motivation and resort to passive resistance so that when it fails (which it will under these circumstances) they can mentally adopt an 'I told you so!' attitude.

The second problem with 'awareness raising' is that the issues cannot be fully understood without personal experience. The relationship between theory and practice is not linear – first you learn the theory and then you 'do' the practice. No, the relationship is dialectical with practice both being informed by theory and building theoretical understanding. Each are returned to over and over again enriching each other.

Similar ideas also inform modern management theory. Klien (1998) uses arguments on organisational learning capability as it relates to NGOs. Using a division of learning into how and why Edmonson and Moingeon (1998) argue that competitive business advantage is gained only when management knows when to use each resource. They also say that it is wrong to assume that learning why is a superior activity. In applying this idea to development Klien gives the following example:

> NGOs sometimes fail to find the proper balance. After 'discovering' the importance of learning WHY, an NGO lagged behind preparing their new managers in the 'arts of the business', the HOW. Thus there were managers in the field offices who were aware of the strategic challenges to the ethos of the organisation, but did not know the 'commonalties' in terms of procedures for

monitoring and evaluating, financial control, Human Resources etc. They were clearly 'limping' and their capacity as managers was certainly limited.

(Klien, 1998, p. 11)

I would like to argue that the same is true in teacher development, and that whilst there are cultural (and very great resource) differences, help with how speeds the learning process in most situations.

The American chair and the Lao needle

Becky was 5 years old when she enrolled in a summer preschool programme in Oregon, USA. She showed developmental delay and had problems with speech. She was closely observed by Eileen Hughes as part of a doctoral thesis called 'Narratives from the Sandbox'. The observations were used by Bricker to support her discussion and shown here in the chair story (Box 9.1).

Nikonh was 3 years old on entering a kindergarten in a small provincial town 400 km from the capital of Laos, Vientiane. The school had just joined the Lao Integrated Education programme initiated by the Lao Ministry of Education and supported by SCF (UK) and UNESCO. He has very low vision, is undersized and has additional skin problems. The observations in the needle story (Box 9.2) are mine.

The most significant point of difference between these two stories is that, in their day to day work, these two teachers behaved quite differently towards the child with special needs. In the first case, the actions of the American teacher led to increased isolation and 'specialness' for the child, while the actions of the Lao teacher led to

Box 9.1 The Chair

> In the first week of school, Becky fell out of the small chairs in the class... Because Becky lost her balance on the small chairs in the classroom, she used a slightly larger chair positioned against the wall at the table. While this was a solution to the tipping chairs, it created a place away from the children and hence a special place for Becky.... The children came to learn that this was her place and never used it themselves. If she was bothering them they directed her back to this place. (When Becky comes back, Ashley is standing in front of her [own] chair as she paints. Becky goes to move Ashley's chair; Ashley tells her, "This is mine. Yours is the one over there," pointing to Becky's table and chair against the wall. The teacher tells Becky, "Here is one... Now go to your table"). There were a few occasions by the end of the summer school session in which Becky initiated finding a chair at another table (and did not fall out). However by this time, the children had learned that Becky's place was against the wall.
>
> (Hughes (1993) quoted in Bricker (1995))

Box 9.2 The Needle

When I first saw the classroom and Nikonh, it was clear that the teacher was trying to work in new ways that had been introduced to her in a workshop during the school holiday a few weeks before. Despite the overcrowding and the pitifully few bits of equipment, she had decorated the wooden walls with some pictures and was trying to ensure all children got a chance to play with the two wooden puzzles by splitting them into two groups. Unfortunately this had led to a 'competition' between the groups, and although sitting in one of the groups Nikonh was unable to take part. After the puzzles were completed the teacher worked with Nikonh by himself while the assistant organised a game. This meant that he was also excluded from the game. Later the support team talked with the teacher about her lesson and related it to some of the training she had received. Support was continued by the local team and through further contact with other teachers in the programme.

One year later, I again visited this classroom. This time it was a bright and welcoming place full of pictures by children and games and toys made from junk and natural materials. There was a hum as children chatted and worked in different groups. And Nikonh had 'disappeared'. No, he was not in the small group with the building blocks (made from off-cuts); he was not in the group listening to a story being read by the assistant; neither was he in the group making patterns with pebbles on the dark wooden floor. Then I saw him bent over his work threading patterns with some others and chatting to a neighbour. I was amazed because I did not know how he could take part in this activity. The children were threading short pieces of transparent drinking straws and small squares and circles of scrap fabric onto plastic string. This required the careful placement of the end of the soft string into the hole at the end of the straw pieces and gently pushing the string through being careful not to let it bunch up inside. I knew that there was no way Nikonh had sufficient vision to do this by sight like the other children.

As I bent over his shoulder to watch, I noticed the needle. He was using a home-made needle made from a sliver of wood with a hole punched in the end. I smiled and looked across to the teacher. 'Is that all right?' she said. 'Oh Yes!' I said, 'It is excellent!' 'I was only trying to put in practice the need for "small changes in activities" so that all children could take part', she replied.

increased inclusion, greater access to the curriculum and a normalisation of the child's social life. As can be seen, inclusion is accomplished in the fine detail of the interaction between teachers and children.

Like the Chinese teachers, the Lao teachers had also had some quite clear instructions which related to the particular issues and decision making faced by them in the classroom. In the example in Box 9.2, the teacher refers to the need to find 'small changes'. This comes directly from the directions that had been given in the training workshop:

> The education offered to children with special educational needs is based on the standard kindergarten and primary school curricula. The children are expected to take part in all normal school activities with the least amount of change or extra help that is possible.
>   This is accomplished firstly by:
>
> • finding ways that children may take part by using a variety of methods and activities;
> • making small changes in activities that will enable a child to take part in an activity that would otherwise not be possible – such as providing large clear writing for a child with poor vision, or a similar (but easier) puzzle or question for a child with learning problems.
>
> If this is insufficient, then by:
>
> • providing the child with the least amount and the least intrusive form of help that is needed.
>
> And if this is still insufficient, by:
>
> • planning and carrying out additional activities in school aimed at reducing the particular difficulties the child is facing;
> • planning activities with the family so that additional training and help can be given by them.
>
> (Management of the Lao Integrated Education
> Programme: Guidelines, 1997)

It is tempting to speculate whether Becky's teacher could have provided a more inclusive setting if she had also had some simple direct instructions as a guide to action, and whether such guidance would have been welcome. Directions do not necessarily reduce freedom of action. In this instance, following a simple direction to find the minimal changes needed, increases teacher autonomy by putting in her hands the need to use her own professional skill and judgement to the full.

If Becky's teacher had been directed to try and find minimal solutions, it is possible that the following less isolating solutions could have been tried. With a special chair, the teacher could have tried any of the following:

• making every child's chair 'special' by gluing names and/or symbols on them and encouraging all children (including Becky) to move their own chairs to the places they wished to work;
• only using the chair when absolutely necessary and encouraging Becky and all other children to use all the chairs including the 'big' one;

- breaking the barrier in children's minds by placing very popular games and activities on 'Becky's table' so that there is competition to use the table, including sitting in the big chair;
- choosing the big chair herself when reading a story, but not making it more Becky's by asking permission. 'I like this chair – it's a bit bigger.';
- moving the big chair to a different table each day;
- helping Becky to sit on the small chairs in easy circumstances – for example, if children are sitting round the teacher for story time, chairs could be put closely together so that Becky's neighbours would prevent her failing off;
- noticing that everyone sent Becky to 'her chair' and stopping it happening.... 'No Ashley. Becky can sit at this table if she wants to.';
- getting rid of the chair as soon as Becky showed that she was beginning to manage small chairs;
- as soon as Becky had demonstrated the ability to sit on a small chair, encouraging this by placing Becky's chosen activities on a different table next to a small chair.

Without the chair, the teacher could have tried these:

- watching Becky closely to see under what circumstances she fell off and minimising the difficulties in those circumstances – this could mean, for example, placing another small chair with its back to the side of the chair Becky was sitting on so as to produce a corner seat or teaching her to put her feet more squarely on the floor so that she was more stable, or using her arm to steady herself against the table;
- using other children as above;
- praising Becky for sitting carefully and encouraging her in her struggle to use small chairs, thus making 'using school chairs' a personal goal for her to achieve;
- lending a school chair to the family for a few weeks so that they too can help Becky learn to sit without falling off by using it while doing easy and enjoyable things like watching the television.

All these are creative solutions which rely on teachers increasing their problem-solving skills. I would like to suggest that, had Becky's teacher been given straight-forward instructions, and some support as she began to incorporate the new ways of working, she would have found these (or other) more inclusive answers for Becky. Furthermore, the skills she developed would have informed all her teaching and thus would benefit all children in her class. It is this aspect that makes me confident that inclusive types of teaching bring benefits for all Children and not just those with designated 'special needs'. As it is, Becky's teacher was not only unable to consider these other solutions, she was unaware of the additional problems she was creating by further isolation of Becky in the classroom.

It is possible that the access American teachers have to resources and special education expertise works against inclusion. In both Laos and China, teachers must make their own equipment from available materials. This is quite a burden but it does mean that there is every incentive to provide minimum rather than maximum changes. The provision of a special chair may have been seen as necessary long-term need (rather than a temporary solution to be discarded as soon as possible) but as soon as it was installed, the isolation of Becky from other children and the restriction of both the activities available to her (to those set out on her table) and choice of friendships (to those children at her table) increased. Furthermore, if the chair was bought with special funds allocated to Becky, it is natural that staff and children would see the chair as exclusively 'belonging' to Becky. And if the funds for the chair have been applied for, argued for, and 'won', there may be enormous pressure on all to ensure that Becky actually uses the chair so as to justify the purchase.

Another significant difference is that in Laos and other developing countries, the class teacher is the person responsible for the education of all children in her class – including those with special needs. In western countries, access to expertise can both help the teacher and also hinder inclusion as the 'expert' may see their responsibility as directed only to the one or two children 'designated' as having special needs. It is quite possible that the advice given is aimed at 'individualised' solutions which mimic standard special school practice. As the class teacher's decision making is handed over to another who is seen as more knowledgeable, she may back away from bringing her creative (minute by minute) problem-solving skills to the situation.

However, having acknowledged these additional problems (which, curiously enough, relate to the problems of wealth not poverty) for many western teachers, I would still maintain that the main difficulty is a product of a misunderstanding of the relationship between theory and practice; the, relationship between the 'why' and the 'how'.

Taking off

There is always the danger that when directions are given or people are specifically taught how to do something they will apply this in an unthinking non-creative way. Is it possible for teachers to begin by following instructions on how to do it, and yet gradually upgrade their understanding of why and thus become highly creative and innovative practitioners – taking off on a solo flight?

Experience in Asia suggests that, given the right circumstances, this learning process is entirely possible. At a certain point in the learning spiral, teachers can and do 'take off' by themselves; producing an inclusive style of teaching which can be a joy to watch.

During his visit to China and after watching many teachers in different schools, Ainscow was able to 'tentatively' suggest three levels of implementation. In order to facilitate discussion, his notes are reproduced in full here, before I go on to provide an illustration.

> *Level 1* – Pre-implementation.   Here teachers may not have been exposed to the ideas of the innovation or, if they have, have not yet introduced them into their classroom. Typically lessons are well planned, lively and stimulating, with content usually at an interest level that is appropriate for the children. Activities are mainly directed by adults to the class as a whole, with limited use of play, group activities and individual teaching. Additional adults may observe the lesson, or carry out preparation and clearing-up tasks. Since the emphasis is on achieving conformity of response it is difficult to integrate children with special needs.
>
> *Level 2* – Standard Implementation.   Here teachers who have been exposed to the innovation use its recommended approaches in their day-to-day work. This means that the day has been restructured in order to include group and individual teaching sessions, alongside whole class activities. Teaching is still mainly directed by adults. However, there are also play sessions which are intended to encourage independence and provide children with a certain amount of choice. Additional adults may observe the lesson, carry out preparation and clearing up tasks, and encourage children with special needs to participate. Integration of children with special needs is possible but is difficult with those who do not conform to requirements.
>
> *Level 3* – Creative Implementation.   Here teachers who have been exposed to the innovation adapt and develop its recommended approaches in order to facilitate the participation of all children in lesson activities. The elements of restructuring referred to at level 2 are all present but are used flexibly. Teachers are sensitive to the feedback of individual children and use varied methods to encourage participation. Additional adults share a variety of roles that are intended to support learning. Since the emphasis is on participation the classroom is becoming more 'inclusive'.
>
> (Ainscow, 1996, personal communication)

Level 1 should be familiar to most readers and is the situation in standard traditional classrooms. Level 2 and 3 are more interesting. In this context, level 2 is the result of following initial 5 day training workshops. Making use of the fact that the large classes (up to 45 children were taught by a team of two teachers, the instructions included using small group discussion (not more than 12 children) so as to increase interaction and increase involvement of children; more use of open questioning; play (including imaginative play); individual work with children when needed; observation and planning; child to child help; and a variety of activities. At stage 2 these are demonstrated but strictly adhered to. By stage three, teachers confidently and flexibly use all their experience and stop holding rigidly to the formula. Box 9.3 gives an example of this situation.

Box 9.3 Mirrors and emotions

Class of the oldest kindergarten children (5–6 years): 36 children present: two teachers (T1 and T2); 'Morning exercise' was held outside on this cold but sunny day. This is a standard feature of Chinese schools but here it had evolved into complex 'circle dancing' with simple equipment such as bottle top shakers or chopsticks to bang together like drum sticks. The children then entered the classroom in which tables were placed in 6 groups, and chose where they wished to sit. There are three small mirrors on each table.

Activity 1 – led by T1.   Following a time to play with the sunlight on the mirrors, the teacher asked the children to use the mirrors and their neighbours to consider the way emotions showed in facial expressions. This led a full class discussion on smiling, then crying and then angry faces. There was a very lively discussion in which children's contributions were accepted and built on. For example crying might happen 'when Mum or Dad tells me off . . .'; 'when you fight with a friend . . .' Similarly, 'I get angry when someone tries to scare me', etc. T2 was with the children listening to shy children and encouraging them to contribute – 'Lei lei has a good idea – go on tell everyone'. This was followed by an activity in which children used paper shapes placed on paper circles to create expressions. Choice and creativity were encouraged and half way through 4 children who had finished were invited to create new ones on the blackboard. At the end of this activity children were encouraged to walk round and look at everyone's work, after which the mirrors were taken outside for more play with sunbeams and some free outdoor play. [. . .]

Activity 2 – led by T2.   After gently calming the children by doing some hand exercise and talking about hands so that the children gradually quietened as they joined in, she introduced seven craft activities. One was entirely new and this she carefully demonstrated and gave brief instruction for the others. Children could choose which table to join (knowing that they would eventually get the chance to do everything). The six tables offered a range of difficulty thus enabling more T1 and T2 help with the difficult ones and independent working at others. Work took place with children chatting, helping each other and teachers helping and talking with children. Of particular note, was the group working on the tiled wall outside. The mural was entirely in children's hands with changes being made by erasing parts or by adding or altering the picture; 'I don't think the rainbow has enough colours yet. I think I'll add some more . . .' 'This bus has been here a long time. Shall we change it to something else?'

My observation notes only gives a pale reflection of this enormously busy, warm-hearted classroom, so it is perhaps worthwhile detailing some of the aspects which contributed to the inclusive nature:

- the classroom was no longer wholly teacher-centred, although an observer could see how carefully this was planned...the teachers' roles have changed to one in which they 'direct' and 'facilitate' the activities rather than dominate them;
- children were active all the morning and very involved in all the various different parts of the session;
- interaction was high and children's contributions were encouraged and used by the teacher;
- there was sensitivity towards the desires and needs of children. For example T1 allowed a short play with the mirrors before and after the activities and also supported children making 'angry' faces and did not ask them to describe the more difficult angry looks;
- when making the faces with coloured shapes T1 allowed 4 children who had worked quickly to create bigger ones on the board thus providing examples for those finding it more difficult as well as stretching the more able children by asking them to repeat the activity in a new way;
- Children's work was valued and all children were encouraged to look at classmates' pictures;
- teachers studied children's responses as part of their ongoing monitoring and understanding of individual children;
- choice and creativity was encouraged – this is very unusual in traditional settings;
- a mixture of autonomy (on easier craft tasks) and help (with more difficult ones) was available.
- cooperation between children was encouraged and this includes whole class cooperation on the painted wall – something which I believe would be very useful in the very individualised classrooms of some western cultures.
- team teaching seems effortless when practised in this way and the benefits are obvious. This team approach even went as far as T2 assessing the results on the activity led by T1. Discussion will take place later.

At the same time the elements of the curriculum are all there. For non-Chinese readers, it is worth pointing out that kindergartens need to include many pre-reading activities. These include a good knowledge and understanding of shape, good hand–eye coordination, and the ability to memorise sequences of movement. 'Delicate' craft activities, description of shapes, and dance sequences all prepare children for the complexity of reading, and then writing, Chinese characters.

[...]

Conclusion

[...]

It is not simply a matter of telling teachers what to do but of enabling refection on those experiences brought about by working in new ways. It was the experiences of holding small group discussion that enabled these Chinese teachers to feel what could be gained through higher levels of interaction with children. The encouragement to experiment led them to try to see whether this could be transposed back into whole class teaching and then opt for a mixture of small group discussion and whole class discussion with the new higher levels of interaction.

Moving beyond the directions and applying the lessons gained in earlier more directed ways of working brings about new professional skills and the confidence to experiment. It is experimentation and the ability to reflect about the needs of children, about their varied strengths and weaknesses, about the choices in methodology and how to maximise the potential of all children that make for inclusive styles. At the beginning of the change process, help with how to do this is needed if each teacher and each school is to travel that road. Leaving teachers (like Becky's teacher) without such help means that learning opportunities for both teachers and children are lost. This seems such a pity – the investment in training and support are so very small and the gains can be so large.

References

Ainscow M. (1996) The Integrated Education Project in Anhui – Towards a Theory of Implementation: personal communication.

Bricker D. (1995) The Challenge of Inclusion, *Journal of Early Intervention*. Vol. 19, No. 3 pp. 179–194.

Edmonson and Moingeon (1998) The How and Why of Organisational Learning in Mastering Global Business: Financial Times.

Klien R.E. (1998) Management and Change in the Profit and Non-Profit World: unpublished paper.

Lao Ministry of Education (1997) Management of the Integrated Education Programme – Guidelines: Lao MoE/SCF(UK).

Chapter 10

Creating and using inclusive materials, collaboratively and reflectively

Jonathan Rix

An introduction to the obvious

In the mid 1990s, I was involved in adapting some Year 10 (age 14–15) geography materials that explored the development of the Norfolk Broads and issues surrounding their sustainability. The materials took the form of a booklet with pictures, text and a wide variety of activities. The text and activities were intended to be easily accessible, making minimal assumptions about both prior geographic and linguistic knowledge. The activities reinforced both academic and language development and encouraged students to explore issues in many different ways. Students could work their way through the booklet at their own speed, though there were plenty of opportunities for them to work together or to bring in personal experience and previous knowledge. The booklet was primarily produced for students who had English as an additional language, but was also used by a wide variety of students in the class alongside a more linguistically complex booklet. These two booklets represented a six-week course of work. There was always an overlap in the conceptual content of the booklets and often an overlap in activities, particularly those which were open-ended. Students with all sorts of differing characteristics successfully worked through these topic booklets, carrying out the activities with enthusiasm. This form of working was one which the students had experienced before, and reflected the close team-teaching approach that the class teacher used with myself and others. We felt that it was a successful working relationship. We were also pleased that students who had only recently arrived in the UK often managed to achieve E, D or C at GCSE.

So why was it that half way through our second term of using these materials one student, Ceylan, just did not seem to understand the work when everyone else did? Even when it was explained to her in first language, Turkish, Ceylan would become confused. She was not a student who found school work easy, but her incomprehension was not what we expected. To start with we just repeated ourselves, explaining the concepts in different ways. She seemed to understand the explanations but then became confused again shortly after. So we asked her questions and got her to ask questions, hoping to reveal the core of her misunderstanding. In week 3, with the help of some bilingual support, we identified that our problem was the notion of erosion. We went back through the booklet, discussing the activities and the text. Ceylan understood both of these aspects. We still could not understand what the problem was. Then in week 4, I was again talking through this with her (she was very patient with us!) discussing the use of reeds as barriers to bank erosion, pointing at the diagram in the booklet to underline my point and Ceylan was nodding. Suddenly the nodding stopped. 'What reeds?' asked Ceylan. I explained in English what reeds were and then flicking through the glossary we had prepared pointed to the Turkish translation for the word. For the first time in four weeks Ceylan looked annoyed. 'No!', she stabbed her finger at the picture, 'What reeds?'. It was one of those moments. All became clear. She could not see the reeds in the picture. She could just see a load of straight lines that she took to be our visual representation of the bank eroding. Our simple explanatory image was the problem. To Ceylan our reeds did not look like reeds at all, and so our visual point of reference was not supporting what we were saying but working against it. For four weeks we had been searching for a way to get her to understand. It transpired that it was the clearest part of our explanation that was the barrier. It was the bit we hadn't thought to question.

Good practice?

In many ways this story acts as a very neat exemplar of failure and success from the viewpoint of inclusive pedagogy. It involves a number of sound pedagogical and curricular techniques that would fit well within any class where there is an attempt to be inclusive. There is team teaching, joint planning and preparation, differentiation, a wide variety of examples from which to learn and transfer concepts, multiple representations of information, opportunities to practice skills, open-ended learning techniques, group work, inclusion of student experience, bilingual support, a concern with formative assessment and performance-based assessment of learning. For 3–4 weeks, however, all of this was failing to generate the expected learning outcomes. It is quite possible to say that it was the use of all of these inclusive measures that managed to stop Ceylan slipping through the net, but I felt at the time that it was only because Ceylan kept on trying that we achieved a breakthrough. Other students may well have given up a lot earlier and we would have failed entirely.

In hindsight, I can also see that at the core of our success was our determination to make sure that Ceylan was included in this part of the teaching and learning. There were four of us involved across the period of time, each bringing different areas of expertise. We talked about our dilemma in the classroom, corridors, staffroom, support-team rooms, smoking room and on the bus. We shared a mindset that meant Ceylan's learning was our challenge and our problem as much as it was hers. As it turned out, we probably learned more from the experience than she did.

Thinking with others

If we wish to maximise participation in learning situations it makes sense to encourage the widest possible participation in the creation and use of learning materials, beginning with the teaching teams working with the students and the learning materials and involving all the relevant support teams. We can in this way seek out contradictions within our work and ask the awkward questions that may reveal possible barriers to learning. This collaborative approach can range from the level of comments passed to each other in the classroom to widely attended planning sessions. It can occur within or across departments or schools or teaching teams.

It is not uncommon for teaching staff to complain that they do not have appropriate time and resources made available to them to effectively carry forward such collaboration. In many schools and Local Education Authorities (LEAs) there will be some truth in this, but blaming lack of resources can be an avoidance tactic as much as a genuine barrier. LEAs will occasionally provide funding for in-school or inter-school projects to develop materials and all schools have the option to use INSET days for teams to plan and develop resources. Regular departmental meetings can be organised in such a way that time is made available for collaboration, as can the timetables of teaching staff. I am fortunate enough to have been party to all of these whole school approaches in a typical inner city comprehensive school, not particularly renowned for its inclusive achievements. I have also been fortunate to see small initiatives having a considerable impact on both teaching and learning.

One of the great advantages of collaborating with a wide variety of teaching staff is that we increase the chance of cross-curricular working. This increases the possibility of giving students multiple opportunities to interact with information and for that information to come to them in a variety of ways. This in turn increases the chances of learning for all (Blamires, 1999; Lewis and Norwich, 2001).

Teaching teams are more likely to find ways of linking together the various parts of the curriculum for themselves and for pupils. Askew *et al.* (1997) demonstrated, in relation to mathematics, how this 'connectionist' approach most effectively enables pupils to learn. The breadth of experience available within teaching teams facilitates expanding this connectionist approach across a variety of curriculum areas. In the example at the start of this chapter, this meant that the team could immediately draw on the knowledge and experience of the geography class teacher, two language support teachers – one of whom spoke Turkish and a special education support teacher. The support teachers in particular had a good understanding of what was going on in other subject areas. There were a number of occasions when support staff were able to build upon the ideas explored in the Norfolk Broads project within other curricular areas, most particularly science. But we were also able to bring our experiences and ideas gleaned from supporting in other contexts. Following on from our experiences with the booklet, for example, the class teacher drew upon my experience in teaching drama to create an erosion exercise. This was used on two separate occasions, once in the main hall to demonstrate river erosion and once on a beach to demonstrate coastal erosion. On both occasions the pupils had to act out the roles of the water and the soil.

This connectionist approach can be both informal and formal, of course. As well as looking out for momentary opportunities to create subject links, there are numerous possibilities for planning those links more completely. For instance, by examining historical scientific figures through drama (Pantidos *et al.*, 2001) or history (Galili and Hazan, 2001), we can make learning about scientific knowledge more effective since the context for that knowledge is better understood. We can also raise issues that would typically be seen as non-academic and in so doing not only explore those issues but underline the relevance of the subject area. We can for example link sex education and personal and social education with primary science lessons (Tunnicliffe and Reiss, 1999), or by examining current events within science make connections between physics and citizenship (Campbell, 2002). Highlighting links between typically disconnected humanities and sciences may break down those curricular barriers for many students, often in a very surprising way. Richards and Gibbons (1998) describe a possible series of lessons that would explore pentangles in conjunction with a medieval poem, Sir Gawain and the Green Knight. Exploring such a link between English and Maths, and notions of change across the ages, opens up all our thinking. We need not limit these links to one or two subjects either. Why not have a wide variety of lessons in a second language? Tucker (2001) describes an inspirational programme that has integrated Spanish into an ongoing art, music, library, PE and ICT curriculum in elementary schools in a suburban district of Pittsburgh, Pennsylvania.

Drawing from others

Collaboration is not only a connectionist tool for designing the curriculum; it also offers ways of working. It is a fundamental process within the constructivist classroom. Cormack (1999), for example, reports that when teachers who typically did not use collaborative talk activities did so, all students benefited and particularly those who often did not succeed in class. Similarly, involving students in group activities, encouraging thinking aloud and reciprocal peer tutoring can have a positive impact on reading (Idol, 1987) and writing (Baker *et al.*, 2002) and is popular with pupils. Mastropieri *et al.* (2001), for instance, report that pupils wished to use peer tutoring across the curriculum.

It is important that inclusive principles underpin the collaborative process too. Boaler *et al.* (in Chapter 4, this volume) for example point out that only one-sixth of students they interviewed were comfortable with working within groups setted by ability. Collaboration that draws upon inclusive principles allows us to draw on the strengths, interests and learning styles of different members of a teaching and learning group. The recommended use of Total Communication procedures for people with Down syndrome, for example, along with the use of simplified language and clear behaviour policies means that in trying to best meet their needs, we can enhance the learning opportunities and environment for all pupils (Rix, in press). Similarly a number of teachers have expressed to me that the physical rearrangement of a classroom to enhance access for a pupil who uses a wheelchair can have huge benefits on the interaction and collaboration of everyone in the class.

A process of creating

Meaning is something that we create. As we carry through any process of learning we create our own meaning to describe and explain that process. If we can create a meaning which coincides with the majority we are more likely to feel included within the whole. If we cannot operate effectively within the systems created by others we attach a meaning that sees us as excluded (a pupil who struggles to carry out mathematics tasks can soon see themselves as bad at maths or the pupil who struggles to understand a number of poems can soon sees themselves as non-poetic). A very effective way of counterbalancing this exclusionary pressure is for the individual to become involved effectively in the creation of that which might otherwise exclude them.

I have enjoyed working as a facilitator on many creative collaborative processes. For many of us (not all!) understanding the process has been revelatory and empowering. I describe here one activity that I have initiated with all kinds of people from ages of 5 to 85, mixed together in a wide variety of ways in informal community and formal educational settings. The end results of this activity have been various, including creative writing, performances, academic essays and scientific experiments. The process has been used flexibly, being adapted to meet the demands of space, numbers and individual learning and working styles.

The process is initiated by introducing a schema (Idol, 1987). This could be a list of 15 questions which take you through classical story structure, or the main questions you'd want to ask about why Macbeth murders people, or how to carry out a specific scientific investigation. The schema can be created by the group or provided for them. Typically the group of people would then sit in a circle with a piece of paper each (and a scribe if necessary). They write down a line to answer one of the questions, then pass the paper on. This carries on until all the questions are answered. At the end there are as many different versions of the piece as there are people, and everyone has written all of them. This in turn becomes the basis for the next stage of activity.

In many ways the success of this approach is that it involves everyone within the discourse of that area of work. By opening up the process it becomes easier to understand its development, its purpose and its impact. This involves people with a creative, collaborative and reflective process out of which they construct their own meaning in the light of the shared, guided, experience.

There have been two contexts in which this way of working has been particularly satisfying. One involved a group of over twenty prisoners serving life sentences, writing a play across a period of a year. The other involved a group of pupils with English as an additional language producing detailed essay plans for writing assessed GCSEs English essays. In the first instance, we were able to complete a play that belonged to a group of prisoners despite fluctuating group membership. At one level the craft of play construction was stripped bare through discussion, analysis and the act of writing; at another more fundamental level, we created a broad sense of ownership of a piece of theatre. In the second instance, we enabled pupils to more clearly understand the process and construction of an academic essay as well as assisting them to complete a course requirement and gain a satisfying sense of achievement. In both these instances, we were able to overcome systemic constraints by opening up processes. We reduced any sense of threat by making the focus one simple question, which still had some significance in the whole.

Pulling and pushing in different directions

Collaboration is not a magic pedagogic wand, of course. The act of collaborating brings with it a wide variety of potential pitfalls. These pitfalls should not act as a disincentive however. Part of being reflexive is the consideration of the impact of your ways of working. Part of the reflection must be about processes, methods and other systemic behaviours.

During recent years, I have been working with students from the United States and each year as a classroom activity, I ask them to brainstorm the problems they have faced through collaboration and teamwork. The lists of reasons they give for barriers to effective teamwork are chastening. Typically they include the following:

- there is a lack of leadership;
- there are too many people trying to be leaders;
- teams are made up of people who agree or think about things in the same way;
- teams don't have a balance in skills;
- teams don't understand their own strengths, abilities and preferences;
- work isn't allocated in the most appropriate ways
- too much energy goes into one area;
- members feel their talents and abilities are not being used to full potential;
- someone doesn't pull their weight;
- there is a general lack of motivation
- team members are not communicating and work in opposite/overlapping directions;
- people have an unavoidable incentive to agree with the boss;
- people can go along with someone who is stubborn or a bully;
- people tend to agree with those we most admire or like;
- people want to be accepted by the group and so say and do what is wanted;
- people don't want to share undesirable information;
- people share and receive information more openly if there is mutual liking and respect;
- rivalry with another group can get in the way;
- group cohesion means they dismiss valid external criticism;
- individuals come up with more original ideas than teams.

The problems we face during collaboration are not a reason to abandon it, of course. They can be counterbalanced if there is a healthy element of self-awareness and reflection. An example of this came when I was a support teacher on an

Intermediate Level GNVQ Health and Social Care course. The majority of the group had English as an Additional Language, with five other languages being spoken. The course required a considerable amount of collaborative work by the students. Whatever groupings the students were put into, or they put themselves into, they kept on demonstrating problems of the sort listed here. A course tutor, the course leader, the students and I had discussions about this but they did not seem to change matters. This was a particular problem because as part of the course they had to research, budget, invite guests, prepare and carry through a successful party for a group of local Primary school children. We decided that we needed to arrange some team building exercises. There was not a lot of spare time and so we decided to give over three tutor periods to the project. We created a number of light-hearted exercises that had to be carried out around the school. In each group, we included some known adversaries.

One exercise involved making up a jigsaw in turn; another involved some people having to leave the room to gather information which then had to be transcribed or drawn by another person in the room; another involved decoding a message. We then talked (and laughed) about problems we had encountered. At the end of this brief process, there was a change in the behaviour of the students. They did begin to try to confront internal group issues. Barriers about who people would work with (and on what they would work) were also broken down. I would not suggest that the problem was solved entirely. But it was the beginning of a process, which allowed all of us to deal with the pitfalls of collaborative practice and so build on the strengths. The party for the Primary school pupils was a success and all of the GNVQ students played an effective part within it.

Collaborative processes can be used to prepare and assess in all areas of the curriculum and can be used to break down the intellectual, physical, behavioural, social, cultural and systemic barriers that we all face when working or studying in schools. For collaboration to be at its most effective, however, we need to be aware of the processes involved. Collaboration without reflection means that the focus becomes the end product. Without reflection the significance of the learning that can occur within the cooperative process is diminished.

Conclusion

Inclusive practice requires that moments of learning are not just confined to students or the classroom. It is about all of us examining how we create our context. Cormack (1999) explores this notion in relation to teachers discussing the discourse surrounding students. He describes how staff were able to redefine their students following discussions about the impact of ability, gender, home life and social group on their teaching. By examining their underlying assumptions they were able to change their perceptions of what was possible within their classrooms.

Inclusive practice offers us this opportunity to explore our assumptions, open up our processes and ways of working so as to build bridges between experiences. The content of our lessons, and the methods and materials we use, must reflect both the opening of the process and the breadth of experiences of those involved. To create and best use materials and practices we need to work together, drawing upon and reflecting upon on each others skills, knowledge and experience.

References

Askew, M., William, D., Rhodes, V., Brown, M. and Johnson, D. (1997) Effective Teachers of Numeracy, Report: Report of a Study Carried Out for the Teacher Training Agency 1995–96, London, King's College.

Baker, S., Gersten, R. and Scanlon, D. (2002) Procedural facilitators and cognitive strategies: tools for unraveling the mysteries of comprehension and the writing process, and for providing meaningful access to the general curriculum, *Learning Disabilities Research and Practice*, 17(1), pp. 65–77.

Blamires, M. (1999) Universal design for learning: re-establishing differentiation as part of the inclusion agenda? *Support for Learning*, 14(4), pp. 158–163.

Campbell, P. (2002) A citizenship dimension to physics education, *Physics Education*, 37(3), pp. 191–196.

Cormack, P. (1999) What influences teachers' decisions about talk in middle years classrooms? AARE-NZRE Conference, Melbourne.

Galili, I. and Hazan, A. (2001) The effect of a history-based course in optics on students' views about science, *Science and Education*, 10, pp. 7–32.

Idol, L. (1987) Group story mapping: a comprehension strategy for both skilled and unskilled readers, *Journal of Learning Disabilities*, 20(4), pp. 196–205.

Lewis, A. and Norwich, B. (2001) A critical review of systematic evidence concerning distinctive pedagogies for pupils with difficulties in learning, *Journal of Research in Special Education*, 1(1). www.nasen.uk.com/ejournal

Mastropieri, M., Scruggs, T., Mohler, L., Beranek, M., Spencer, V., Boon, R. and Talbott, E. (2001) Can middle school students with serious reading difficulties help each other and learn anything? *Learning Disabilities and Practice*, 16(1), pp. 18–27.

Pantidos, P., Spathi, K. and Vitoratos, E. (2001) The use of drama in science education: the case of 'Blegdamsvej Faust', *Science and Education*, 10, pp. 107–117.

Richards, C. and Gibbons, R. (1998) Sir Gawain's Pentangle: interdisciplinarity in English and mathematics, *Changing English: Studies in Reading and Culture*, 5(2), pp. 135.

Rix, J. (in press) Building on similarity – a whole class use for simplified language materials, Westminster Studies in Education.

Tucker, G. (2001) Implementing a district-wide foreign language program, *Eric Digest*, EDO-FL-01-03 http://www.cal.org/ericcll/digest/0103implement.html – accessed on 30/9/03.

Tunnicliffe, S. and Reiss, M. (1999) Opportunities for sex education and personal and social education (PSE) through science lessons: the comments of primary pupils when observing meal worms and brine shrimps, *International Journal of Science Education*, 21(9), pp. 1007–1020.

Chapter 11

Towards an inclusive school culture

The 'affective curriculum'

Gerda Hanko

Towards inclusive education – a saga of insights and missed opportunities?

Recent spectacular incidents of revoked exclusions for misbehavior have added to distorting the inclusion issue as one of 'requiring teachers to teach disruptive pupils' by merely placing them in mainstream schools where they then damage the educational chances of other children. Research, however, suggests the need to understand inclusive education not as merely placing children in mainstream schools but as a 'connective pedagogy' (Corbett, 2001) which embraces emotional and behavioural difficulties (EBD) in the concept of diversity. Studies continue to point out that emotional and social factors affect all learning; show the connections between our feelings, our reasoning and our motivation; and emphasise that direct support strategies geared to meeting the needs of specific children should be developed as whole-school policies in relation to all children and understood by the staff as a whole.

This raises the question of what opportunities there are for teachers and non-teaching staff to help them to achieve such understanding. Recent studies of direct support strategies focusing on behaviour issues have shown these to be effective to the extent to which they

- address behaviour as well as curricular issues (e.g. Riley and Rustique-Forrester, 2002; Head *et al.*, 2003);
- raise awareness of the relevance of 'EBD skills' for most children in the mainstream (Visser *et al.*, 2002);
- promote in the staff an understanding of the kind of support needed for a school ethos of 'responsive pedagogy' (Daniels, 1996) which enables them to respond to the needs of all their pupils as well as to those of colleagues (Hanko, 2002a,b,c), and thereby ensure 'that no teacher or support staff feel isolated and alone in their teaching tasks' as it is realised that good practice can be widely shared (Corbett, 2001, p. 116).

All this re-emphasises what now appears to be buried in the Elton Report's analysis of 'the nature of the problem' (DES, 1989) as the virtues of an 'affective curriculum'. Teachers' own findings in earlier in-service courses about their own need for professional and emotional support had already confirmed 'that to the extent to which one becomes effective with one's most difficult children, to that extent one is also a better teacher with the whole class' (Teacher's comment, Hanko, 1985, p. 54).

Teachers' confidence in their own competence:

Mittler highlights that teachers need to be prepared to teach all children, and that this should be understood as both a personal and an institutional commitment. Apparently provocatively, he suggests that 'this task is nothing like as difficult as it may seem because most teachers already have much of the knowledge and skills they need to teach inclusively. What they lack is confidence in their own competence' (Mittler, 2000, p. 133).

It is revealing how readily groups of teachers can confirm the validity of both aspects expressed in this statement. When confronted with it at the beginning of a staff development session on working with 'difficult children', beliefs likely to impede their professional effectiveness surface in immediate reactions like: *'Kids shouldn't get away with bad behaviour'; 'my job is to teach mathematics; if they don't want to learn they shouldn't be in this school'; 'teachers are forced to do too much social work'; 'we are teachers, not therapists – we are not trained that way.'*

These beliefs highlight both a myth and current difficulties experienced by many teachers: the myth that only a specially trained expert can deal with special emotional and social difficulties; and the reality of thousands of stressed and despondent teachers calling a teacher support line for help about increasing work-place demands, conflict with colleagues and lack of support with difficult-to-teach children. However, when one asks these same seemingly negative teachers about any experiences where 'difficult' pupils changed their behaviour as the result of teachers changing their own, they easily cite examples: for instance, how hearing about a disruptive or otherwise 'disaffected' pupil's unhappy home circumstances had reduced a teacher's previous negative feelings about him, and how that pupil then, 'strangely enough', also began to respond differently in class.

Clearly, it is not difficult to raise teachers' awareness of what they already 'know': to argue that there are interactional aspects of learning, that social and emotional factors play a part in cognitive development, and that these factors should not be seen as additional to an academic curriculum but as an integral part of their professional task. So, what gets in the way of promoting practising teachers' insight along such lines?

Revisiting Elton

How to promote teachers' insight into such factors influencing learning, and at the same time develop their confidence to apply their insight, has been occupying educators in previous centuries and not only since the Elton Committee's report (DES, 1989). Asked to enquire into problems of discipline in schools, the committee recognised that difficult behaviour is not an individual problem but an interactional one linked to the quality of the day-to-day educational experience of pupils and their teachers. It thus set out to find ways to improve both the quality of the pupils' education in general and the job satisfaction of those who teach them. The committee suggested a solution in 'an all embracing affective curriculum' within which to teach values as well as knowledge and skills. If the importance of addressing the affective dimension of learning in this way were understood and pursued by all staff, this would clearly be to the benefit of all children's learning, rather than merely to that of a limited group, as it would also help to forestall the educationally disruptive consequences of disaffection about school reported by teachers and by so many children when challenged about their behaviour.

The Elton Report was published before the exclusion tide that followed the introduction of the National Curriculum with its contentious league tables and routine testing. The excessively competitive academic results-centred teaching climate to which it led resulted in academic failure and disaffection for some. It also reduced teachers' opportunities to attend to the affective dimension. [...]

Exclusion as an effect of an exclusive focus on negatively perceived overt misbehaviour

But there were warnings about centring inclusion concerns mainly on overtly displayed behaviour difficulties. Seeing this, for instance, as a potential shortcoming of the behaviour support plans of the late 1990s, Marshall (1998) warned teachers and behaviour support teams about the hazard of focusing merely 'on children who misbehave rather than on the wider range of children who have a range of difficulties... which would contribute to (atypical) behaviour which the support plan might not touch on because the [DfEE] circular doesn't require it to' (p. 19).

The consequences of the, by then alarmingly, rising exclusion rate from mainstream schools without sufficient support for the excluded were systematically analysed (e.g. Stirling, 1992; Parsons and Howlett, 1996; Fletcher-Campbell, 2001). Inflexible forms of assessment of pupils' progress and schools' academic results had become threats rather than an indication of need for support or a commitment to addressing pastoral needs through the curriculum. As a school's reputation and financial viability became dependent on surface success, headteachers previously sympathetic to offering extra support to difficult and underachieving pupils were now seeing them as a liability. Schools experiencing the tension between the business ethic and the professional ethic now saw such pupils' manifest problems as 'justifying' their removal.

Moving towards a more 'nurturing' connective school culture: developing 'therapeutic' intervention projects

Educators, alarmed by such educationally dysfunctional developments which affected even the teacher training institutions, now found allies in professional organisations to re-emphasise how much had been learnt from educational pioneers like Bowlby (1969), Bruner (1968), Erikson (1964) and Vygotsky (1978) about the importance of children's emotional and social experiences for their effect on the development of thinking, learning and failure to learn. Findings from attachment theory, now further strengthened by recent developments in neuropsychology and neuroscience (e.g. Schore, 1994; Siegel, 1999), could inform teachers about how children's responses to new learning are influenced by their early secure or insecure attachment experiences as they transfer these to new settings, and how 'good enough' teachers, as a crucial part of a 'facilitating environment' (Winnicott, 1965), can help children to supersede earlier insecurities if the connections between the affective/emotional and the cognitive/social dimensions of new learning are understood. Daniels (1993, 1996) reminded teachers of the complementary Vygotskian/social–cultural angle and how the basics of a 'responsive pedagogy' lie in the 'socially negotiated responsiveness to the learning potential of every child'.

The time was now ripe for the inspired revival of the nurture group experience (Bennathan and Boxall, 2000; Cooper et al., 2001; O'Connor and Colwell, 2002). [...]

Nurture groups were influenced by Bowlby's and Winnicott's findings on the link between early attachment experiences, new learning and the development of a sense of self. They were designed to bridge the divide between emotional, social and cognitive development for children who had missed out on such crucial pre-school experiences of care and trust. School-based strategies of developing teachers' skills to provide for such connectiveness also enabled them jointly to draw maximally on their own 'therapeutic' resources as they became more aware across the school that what is offered specially to the neediest was of relevance to all others.

The concept of 'therapeutic teaching skills' for mainstream teachers began to be seen as relevant for all teachers but not to be confused with therapy as such, for which teachers do, of course, have no mandate. Introducing the concept, the late Professor Ben Morris recalled how he was once taken aback by an invitation to give a talk to a conference on 'the caring element in the educational system'. Noting that this implied a 'non-caring element' in teaching, he feared that this would refer to most of the system according to the extent to which it aimed to make children 'fit in'. Discarding the reductive 'caring element' idea of the proposed topic, he developed instead the concept of 'therapeutic teaching skills' as essential for all teachers whose insightful commitment to each child's learning needs might then 'at the same time seek to ... change the system as well, however little' (Morris, 1991, p. 7) – clearly encouraging the exploration of the relationship between inclusion and institutional improvement which is now in the foreground of professional endeavour.

Therapeutic intervention projects at first endeavoured to meet the needs of those failing to thrive emotionally by offering them a 'healing environment' (e.g. 'The Place to Be' (Baxter, 1999); projects developed by the Pyramid Trust (Watson, 1999); and the 'A Quiet Place' project (Spalding, 2000; King and Chantler, 2002; Renwick and Spalding, 2002)). These were welcomed by schools as additional but separate short-term support programmes for individually selected children. The 'A Quiet Place' project, however, offered therapeutic support to their teachers as well, to understand how the child's participation in the project would impact on them. The use of insight into social and emotional factors in children's learning was thus noted as an as yet insufficiently supported aspect of teaching, thereby hinting at a crucial gap in teachers' professional development (Hanko, 2002a).

Growing recognition of the awareness-raising potential of working within a whole social classroom context led to programmes on how to foster all children's awareness and not only that of the neediest. Learning to understand their feelings as they were relating to others was to help all children to deal with both existing relationship problems and those that might yet arise. In approaches like 'Circle Time' (Mosley, 1993) children were encouraged to share solutions to situations that all of them would have experienced at some time, and would experience again such as feeling sad, lost, angry or disappointed. Ground rules had to be adhered to so as not to characterise such education in solely affective terms, merely boosting self-esteem while ignoring the cognitive angle. In 'Circles of Friends' (Newton and Wilson, 1999) the approach was structured so as to ensure the inclusion of individuals who face the greatest risk of rejection or isolation from the community in which they live. Anti-bullying approaches (Robinson and Maines, 1994) similarly focused on relationship building, problem solving and conflict resolution.

Working with specific packages of behaviour management programmes or working with 'multiple concepts'?

An education system that continued to divide children against each other meant the issue of 'managing the behaviour' of those who protested, through disruptive behaviour, against this 'non-caring element in the system' was at the fore. Teachers were soon offered a range of behaviour strategies, but were uncertain which to choose. However, as researchers like Kolvin et al. (1982) and experienced practitioners like Laslett (1982) had already shown, no one model can offer the practitioner in the classroom the full perspective. Their evidence pointed to the beneficial results of a flexible combination of methods as was shown by the teachers applying the insights they were deriving from reflecting jointly on their pupils' difficulties (Hanko, 1999): these teachers were clearly drawing 'systematically' (Dowling and Osborne, 1994) on all approaches they felt could assist them in the creation of a genuinely 'therapeutic learning culture' (Osborne, 1998), working flexibly rather than with 'any specific packages of programmes to promote good discipline in an assertive manner' (Corbett, 2001, p. 77). Working with 'multiple concepts' (Norwich, 1996), they were responding within the rationale of an integrative framework needed to understand the range and complexity of the interactive influence on behaviour (Frederickson and Cline, 2002).

Understanding the long-lasting benefits of affective and cognitive/social dimensions in curricular interaction

A recently developed 'resilience package' for vulnerable children (Place *et al.*, 2002) bases its rationale on Rutter's (1991) and Quinton's (1987) findings on the long-lasting effects which young adults who grew up in care institutions ascribed to their positive school experiences. They attributed those experiences to what their teachers had offered them in both academic and non-academic curriculum areas rather than through mere success in examinations. The 'resilience package' emphasises, as the most significant protective experiences that schools can provide for all children, an interactive curriculum which can help them to make sense of their experiences; to think and act independently; to acknowledge vulnerability but also to feel part of the world around them as they are helped to interact positively with it – in short, addressing the key factors of an inclusively 'affective curriculum'.

Knowing how to provide children with meaningful personal experiences: learning through addressing problems jointly

Observing inclusive school cultures, Cooper *et al.* (2000, p. 193) list key factors for providing vulnerable children with meaningful personal experiences. These entail gaining a sense of

- being valued as a person;
- belonging and involvement;
- personal satisfaction and achievement;
- being accepted and listened to;
- congruence between personal and institutional values;
- personal meaningfulness of the tasks of teaching and learning;
- efficacy, power to influence things for the better;

and achieving these key factors jointly. As was being realised, such factors, of course, matter for all children. But is there a single factor in this list that does not also matter for their teachers?

Focusing on this commonality, 'joint systems approaches' (Dowling and Osborne, 1994) were showing teachers how their understanding of children's educational problems could be enhanced by sharpening their recognition of the nature of their interactions with them and augmenting their abilities to create a meaningful curriculum for all. School-based joint problem-solving staff support approaches (Hanko, 1985, 1999; Barrow, 2002) were now advanced in which teachers were creating for each other the dynamic that enabled them to further develop their own thinking and learning, and their attitudes about children's difficulties in relation to teachers' own experience. For many it was, for instance, a revelation how the negative feelings that children can cause adults to have about them, can unintentionally influence the disaffecting messages teachers often send out to children. But it was also a relief when teachers could realise how their negative feelings not only need not get in the way of good teaching but, 'pedagogically' contained, could actually help to address those key factors and thereby enhance their therapeutic teaching skills.

Addressing the two-dimensional nature of pedagogical responsiveness, these staff development approaches were thus designed to foster an understanding of why children behave as they do, what more teachers can do to help them learn and how teachers may support each other in their professional task.

Conveying understanding unobtrusively at critical moments

It has been said that what school-age children hate most, above not being understood, is 'being understood'. The essence of an authoritatively affective teaching relationship will lie in conveying personal awareness unobtrusively, especially at critical moments of conflict. As mutually supportive staff development structures have shown, promoting insight 'interactionally', through shared conceptualising reflection, can facilitate the skill of responding appropriately at just such moments – what Claxton (1997) referred to as 'implicit know how' validated by the ongoing reflection.

It enabled for instance, one primary school teacher to transform a ten-year-old's violent anger into more 'manageable' feelings when she told him how sorry she was at his 'feeling so bad', wondering 'whether something was making him sad'. She did not press for an answer, yet was inviting him to 'think jointly' with her about his violent feelings. Unobtrusively she made him 'feel thought about' (Winnicott, 1965), while also stimulating an awareness of the complexity of feelings, such as a link between anger and anxiety, and suggesting that she had not taken his anger as a personal attack on her.

[. . .]

As to their choice of 'management' strategy, teachers learnt to accommodate in their responses an understanding both of behavioural and psychodynamic thinking (Hanko, 1999). They accepted, as a working hypothesis, a possible link between openly displayed behaviour and perhaps unrealised unconscious in what Corbett (2001, p. 77) describes as a 'gradual and organic way that feels natural, comfortable and confident'.

Waddell (1998) summarises the underlying rationale of such 'therapeutically affective' flexibility as understanding that problematic behaviour may express something in children, arising from unmet needs and experiences rooted in the *past* (such as being rejected, punished or not being valued), but also that something in the *present* situation (a fear of not managing a task or a perceived threat even in a mild and justified reprimand) may coincide with those experiences in the past and reactivate or maintain a now habitual pattern of behavioural reaction.

To supersede such earlier experiences, it will matter that something changes in the way in which such children can perceive themselves differently, such as experiencing themselves as valued in relation to others important to them. It is important that these others are not writing children off, but do in fact value them and recognise their efforts.

Using subjects as contexts of affective experience

Teachers can promote each other's awareness of the untapped dimension of the affective potential of subjects. Teachers who still keep 'subjects' separate from 'those basic themes which give form to life and learning' (Bruner, 1968), may hear from other colleagues of opportunities they found for 'education of the emotions' (Peters, 1974). For example, we may hear about how a colleague in the mathematics department asked his class, when teaching statistics, what it might 'feel like to be one of those statistics?' [...]

There is a wealth of teaching material for use across an effectively informed academic curriculum. Stories introduce children and young people to what Bettelheim (1985) referred to as the emotional conflicts in a world where bad things can happen, but where people can help each other in dealing with difficulties. Cleghorn (in Jeffries, 2002) describes his 'neo-Socratic' approach to the range of emotions we all experience, which can allow children to 'experiment' with their own problems, in the disguise of fictional or real characters, to express feelings, reduce anxiety, and learn how lives can be affected by understanding feelings – or by not doing so, as happens when inflicting pain and injustice by bullying.

New directions for professional development

Best (2001) sees the role of 'affective education' in provision for such experience in the curricular context and argues for its explicit encouragement as the task for the twenty-first century. The Elton Report saw such a curriculum for all as improving both the quality of pupils' education and the job satisfaction of their teachers. Encouraging a more imaginative curriculum that enables teachers to provide all children with meaningful personal experiences would clearly help to reconsider the currently conflicting curricular priorities. There are now some hopeful signs that this may happen.

The consultation paper on professional development (DfEE, 2000), hailed as a 'watershed in the history of the teaching profession' (Mittler, 2000, p. 146), emphasised the importance of a school culture that places the responsibility for its Pupils' emotional development on all teachers, as did other official documents such as *Promoting Children's Mental Health* (DfES, 2001a) and *Inclusive Schooling* (DfES, 2001b). The DfEE/DoH had referred, at their joint Healthy Schools – Healthy Teachers conference (DfEE/DoH, 1999), to the importance of all teachers being emotionally competent. After revisiting Elton, and taking stock of our better understanding of how children's emotional and social realities can be used as a fertile source of new learning experiences, we may indeed see also the curricular tempest as 'full of noises, sounds and sweet airs, that give delight and hurt not', so that pupils may not even consider indiscipline, as Elton suggested, and their teachers not even consider exclusion.

References

Barrow, G. (2002) *Delivering Effective Behaviour Support in Schools*. London: David Fulton.

Baxter, J. (1999) 'The place to be', *Young Minds Magazine*, 42, 12–14.

Bennathan, M. and Boxall, M. (2000) *Effective Intervention in Primary Schools – Nurture Groups* (second edition). London: David Fulton.

Best, R. (2001) 'Education and integrity – the role of affective education'. Paper presented to the Eighth Annual Conference on Education, Spirituality and the Whole Child. Roehampton, 2001.

Bettelheim, B. (1985) *The Uses of Enchantment*. Harmondsworth: Penguin.

Bowlby, J. (1969) *Attachment and Loss: Vol. 1*. London: Hogarth Press.

Bruner, J. (1968) *Toward a Theory of Instruction*. New York: Norton.

Claxton, G. (1997) *Hare Brain – Tortoise Mind: Why intelligence increases when you think less*. London: Fourth Estate.

Cooper, P., Arnold, R. and Boyd, E. (2001) 'The effectiveness of Nurture Groups: preliminary research findings', *British Journal of Special Education*, 28 (4), 160–166.

Cooper, P., Drummond, M.J., Hart, S., Lovey, J. and MeLaughlin, C. (2000) *Positive Alternatives to Exclusion*. London: Routledge Falmer.

Corbett, J. (2001) *Supporting Inclusive Education – A Connective Pedagogy*. London: Routledge Falmer.

Daniels, H. (ed.) (1993) *Charting the Agenda: Educational Activity after Vygotsky*. London: Routledge.

Daniels, H. (1996) 'Back to basics', *British Journal of Special Education*, 23 (4), 155–161.

DES (Department of Education and Science) (1989) *Discipline in Schools* (The Elton Report). London: DES.

DfEE (Department for Education and Employment)/DoH (Department of Health) (1999) *Brochure to Healthy Schools Healthy Teachers Conference*. London: DfEE.

DfEE (Department for Education and Employment) (2000) *Professional Development for Teaching and Learning – Consultation Document*. London: DfEE.

DfES (Department for Education and Skills) (2001a) *Promoting Children's Mental Health within Early Years and School Settings*. London: DfES.

DfES (Department for Education and Skills) (2001b) *Inclusive Schooling*. London: DfES.

Dowling, E. and Osborne, E. (1994) *The Family and the School: A Joint Systems Approach to Problems with Children* (second edition). London: Routledge.

Erikson, E.H. (1964) *Childhood and Society*. Harmondsworth: Hogarth with Pelican.

Fletcher-Campbell, F. (2001) 'Issues of inclusion: evidence from three recent research studies', *Emotional and Behavioural Difficulties*, 6 (2), 69–89.

Frederickson, N. and Cline, T. (2002) *Special Educational Needs, Inclusion and Diversity*. Buckingham: Open University Press.

Griffiths, F. (2002) *Communication Counts – Speech and Language Difficulties in the Early Years*. London: David Fulton.

Hanko, G. (1985) *Special Needs in Ordinary Classrooms – An Approach to Teacher Support and Pupil Care*. Oxford: Basil Blackwell.

Hanko, G. (1999, reprinted 2001) *Increasing Competence through Collaborative Problem-Solving – Using Insight into Social and Emotional Factors in Children's Learning*. London: David Fulton.

Hanko, G. (2002a) 'The emotional experience of teaching: a priority for professional development', in P. Gray (ed.) *Working with Emotions*. London: Routledge Falmer.

Hanko, G. (2002b) 'Promoting empathy through the dynamics of staff development: what schools can offer their teachers as learners', *Pastoral Care in Education*, 20 (2), 12–16.

Hanko, G. (2002c) 'Making psychodynamic insights accessible to teachers as an integral part of their professional task', *Psychodynamic Practice*, 18 (3), 375–389.

Head, C., Kane, J. and Logan, N. (2003) 'Behaviour support in secondary schools: what works for schools?', *Emotional and Behavioural Difficulties*, 8 (1), 33–42.

Jeffries, S. (2002) 'I giggle, therefore I am', *The Guardian*, 12.3.02.

King, A. and Chantler, Z. (2002) 'The Western Primary School "Quiet Room" project', *British Journal of Special Education*, 29 (4), 183–188.

Kolvin, I., Garside, R.E., Nicol, A.R., Macmillan, A., Wolstenholme, E. and Leitch, I.M. (1982) *Help Starts Here*. London: Tavistock.

Laslett, R. (1982) *Maladjusted Children in the Ordinary School*. Stratford-upon-Avon: National Council for Special Education, Developing Horisons Series.

Marshall, C. (1998) 'Interview', *Special!* Autumn, 16–21.

Mittler, P. (2000) *Working Towards Inclusive Education*. London: David Fulton.

Morris, B. (1991) 'The nature and role of educational therapy', *The Journal of Educational Therapy*, 3 (3), 5–14.

Mosley, J. (1993) *Turn Your School Round*. Wisbech: Learning Development Aids (LDA).

Newton, C. and Wilson, D. (1999) *Circles of Friends*. Dunstable: Folens.

Norwich, B. (1996) 'Special needs education or education for all? Connective specialisation and ideological impurity', *British Journal of Special Education*, 23 (3), 100–103.

O'Connor, T. and Colwell, J. (2002) 'The effectiveness and rationale of the "nurture group" approach to helping children with emotional and behavioural difficulties remain within mainstream education', *British Journal of Special Education*, 29 (2), 96–100.

Osborne, E. (1998) 'Learning cultures', in: B. Davou and F. Xenakis (eds) *Feeling, Communication and Thinking*. Athens: Papazissis Publishers.

Parsons, C. and Howlett, K. (1996) 'Permanent exclusions from school: a case where society is failing its children', *Support for Learning*, 11 (3), 109–112.

Peters, R.S. (1974) 'The education of the emotions', in R.S. Peters (ed.) *Psychology and Ethical Development*. London: Allen & Unwin.

Place, M., Reynolds, J., Cousins, A. and O'Neill, S. (2002) 'Developing a resilience package for vulnerable children', *Child and Adolescent Mental Health*, 7 (4), 162–167.

Quinton, D. (1987) 'The consequences of care', *Maladjustment and Therapeutic Education*, 5 (2), 18–29.

Renwick, F. and Spalding, B. (2002) 'A Quiet Place Project: an evaluation of early therapeutic intervention within mainstream schools,' *British Journal of Special Education*, 29 (3), 144–149.

Riley, K. and Rustique-Forrester, E. (2002) *Working with Disaffected Students*. London: Paul Chapman.

Robinson, G. and Maines, B. (1994) 'Who manages pupil behaviour? Assertive Discipline – a blunt instrument for a fine task', *Pastoral Care in Education*, 12 (3), 30–35.

Rutter, M. (1991) 'Pathways from childhood to adult life: the role of schooling', *Pastoral Care in Education*, 9 (3), 3–10.

Schore, A. (1994) *The Neurobiology of Emotional Development*. Hillsdale, NJ: Erlbaum.

Siegel, D. J. (1999) *The Developing Mind: Towards a Neurobiology of Interpersonal Experience*. New York and London: The Guildford Press.

Spalding, B. (2000) 'The contribution of a "Quiet Place" to early intervention strategies for children with emotional and behavioural difficulties in mainstream schools', *British Journal of Special Education*, 27 (3), 129–134.

Stirling, M. (1992) 'How many pupils are being excluded?' *British Journal of Special Education*, 19 (4), 128–130.

Visser, J, Cole, T. and Daniels, H. (2002) 'Inclusion for the difficult to include', *Support for Learning*, 17 (1), 23–26.

Vygotsky, L. (1978) *Mind in Society*. Cambridge, MA: Harvard.

Waddell, M. (1998) *Inside Lives: Psychoanalysis and the Growth of Personality*. London: Tavistock.

Watson, A. (1999) 'Building self-esteem in primary school children', Annual Review. London: The National Pyramid Trust.

Winnicott, D. (1965) The Maturational Process and the Facilitating Environment. London: Hogarth.

Part IV

Curriculum subjects, classroom organisation and inclusion

Chapter 12

Inclusive practice in English secondary schools

Lessons learned

Lani Florian and Martyn Rouse

Introduction

Schools in England face dilemmas about how they should respond to two conflicting demands from government. The first demand is for higher academic standards and second is the call for the inclusion of children with special educational needs in mainstream schools. For some schools these demands are incompatible, but for others, policies and practices that support inclusion are emerging as the means by which they may be able to raise academic standards for all children. This chapter considers how some of these schools have been able to respond to these different demands.

[...]

Effectiveness, inclusion and special educational needs

The emergence of these potentially competing strands in the current policy agenda is mirrored in two parallel areas of educational research; *school effectiveness and school improvement* on one hand and *inclusion* on the other (Slee and Weiner, 2001). The extent to which either of these fields of research has been informed by the other is questionable and when researchers with an interest in special needs and inclusion have engaged with school effectiveness research it has been to challenge its ideological, political or methodological stance (e.g. Brown *et al.*, 1995; Slee *et al.*, 1998). These are serious questions because much of the work on school effectiveness has failed to recognise the significance of the context in which schools operate, particularly with regard to diversity. And yet, as Ainscow (1991, 1999) argues, there are strong reasons for each of these traditions to be better informed about the other because they are both concerned with the ways in which schools and classrooms might be improved for the benefit of all learners.

According to Teddlie and Reynolds (2000), the school effectiveness movement has evolved through a number of stages since it first began to question the widespread assumption arising from the work of Coleman *et al.* (1966) and Jencks *et al.* (1972), that 'schools make no difference'. Researchers in many countries have been investigating the factors which make some schools more effective than others and the resulting literature on school effectiveness has been extremely influential on education policy in many countries. Not only does it describe the characteristics of effective schools, but it also provides the basis for an increasingly sophisticated and nuanced approach to school improvement. Unfortunately, in borrowing these ideas, policy makers have tended to focus only on academic achievement and underestimate the complexity of improving schools, preferring 'quick fix' solutions and approaches based on simplistic assumptions derived from management and systems theory. The reality of schools is far more complex than such 'bullet point' solutions would imply.

Although the effective schools and school improvement literature has only begun to influence the special needs debate during the past decade (Ainscow, 1991; Rouse and Florian, 1996; Lipsky and Gartner, 1997), it raises important issues for those who are struggling to create more inclusive schools because it suggests ways in which schools themselves, through the development of their own policies and practice, might become more effective at meeting the learning needs of *all* children. Such approaches require a re-conceptualisation of the special needs task so that it might emerge from being concerned only with students' cognitive, emotional or pathological problems to being seen as part of the process of school improvement. In turn, this entails the adoption of ecological perspectives which recognise, as Skrtic (1988) does, that it is the structure of schools as organisations rather than differences between individual pupils that creates special educational needs. This is not to move from blaming students for their failure to blaming their teachers or schools, but rather to acknowledge that human strengths and weaknesses can only be understood in the context in which they occur. Context is a significant factor in the construction of personal identity and the feelings that students have about themselves as learners.

[...]

Much research in special education has focused on teaching methods in an attempt to demonstrate the efficacy of individualised approaches, such as precision teaching, direct intensive structured teaching and skills-based instruction with particular 'types' of pupils (McDonnell et al., 1997). These strategies have been successful in segregated settings where teacher–pupil ratios are often lower than in mainstream schools. The difficulties of implementing them in mainstream classrooms where teacher–pupil ratios are larger and, it is argued, where pedagogy is based on a different understanding of how children learn, has contributed to the belief that mainstream schools may not be the best learning environment for pupils with difficulties. Indeed, there are those who would argue that the full inclusion of all students with special educational needs is impossible because mainstream schools do not have the will, capacity or resources to do the job (Kauffman and Hallahan, 1995). It is suggested that many mainstream teachers have negative attitudes about including pupils with special educational needs (SEN) because they lack knowledge about teaching such children (Scott *et al.*, 1998). However, too much of the debate about inclusion that appears in the special education literature has been detached from broader discussions about teaching and learning. Indeed, some of it has been conducted with little knowledge of the progress made around the world in developing inclusive learning environments. In addition, it seems uninformed by the debate about whether or not there is such a 'special pedagogy' that has evolved in segregated settings that is different from pedagogy in mainstream classrooms and therefore unavailable outside special settings (Lewis and Norwich, 2001).

Equally, much work in school effectiveness and school improvement has been too narrowly focused on academic outcomes and has ignored issues of disadvantage, diversity and equity (Slee and Weiner, 2001). Rarely has it questioned the purpose and nature of schooling or considered the ways in which it may have contributed to exclusionary pressures within schools by distorting the tasks that are considered important.

Lessons learned

[. . .]

Our earlier work (Rouse and Florian, 1996) attempted to link the growing evidence from the research into effective schools with the largely descriptive accounts of the development of inclusive schools. We argued that inclusion has much in common with the movement towards effectiveness, in that they are both concerned with school improvement. However, we acknowledge the view held by many that the quest for (academic) excellence in schools may be incompatible with the extension of the principle of equity and universal access. The clash between the principles that underpin market-based reforms and the principles that underpin the development of inclusive education have produced a set of tensions between such notions as inclusion and exclusion, individuals and groups, producers and consumers and equity and excellence. Our 1997 study suggested that many schools committed to the development of inclusive practice have been able to mediate these tensions and work creatively and successfully in the current climate. These schools do not see the tensions as bipolar, either/or opposites from which they have to choose one extreme or the other. Instead, they have found pragmatic ways to mediate the potential for conflict (Rouse and Florian, 1997). A fundamental question arising from this apparent tension between equity and excellence is how can a school become both equitable (i.e. inclusive) as well as being excellent (i.e. effective as defined by policy makers and school effectiveness researchers)?

More recently our work has focused on identifying strategies which seem successful in enabling secondary schools to extend inclusive practice. It has involved ongoing work with representatives from a group of eight secondary schools who meet regularly to discuss their practice, studies of classroom practice and evaluations of inclusive education projects.

Pedagogy and inclusion

As considered previously, the debates about pedagogy continue, but there appears to be some general agreement across the strands of the inclusion literature about the efficacy of a number of teaching strategies thought to promote inclusive practice. These include cooperative learning, peer-mediated instruction and collaborative teaching, strategies which have been used successfully in both special and main-stream classrooms, although not necessarily to address individual learning problems. The problem is that relatively little is known about the ways in which these and other techniques work (or do not work) in the context of a national (or core) curriculum and the demand for higher standards in classrooms which include pupils with a wide range of learning needs. Furthermore, there has been little considera-tion in the literature about whether such strategies are equally appropriate across all phases of education, with different size classes and in all subjects of the curriculum.

In an attempt to investigate inclusive practice in secondary schools more fully we conducted a survey of 268 teachers in five schools with a long-standing commit-ment to inclusive practice (Florian and Rouse, 2001). We were interested in what subject specialist teachers had to say about the strategies recommended in the inclu-sion literature. A list of 44 teaching strategies mentioned in the literature as helpful in promoting inclusive practice was constructed. These strategies were then organ-ised under the broad headings of: differentiation strategies, cooperative learning strategies; classroom management strategies; teaching social skills.

Teachers reported a high degree of familiarity with and use of these strategies, however, there was variation between teachers of different subjects in the extent to which they use some of the strategies. These differences between subjects could be a function of any number of factors, including the nature and status of knowledge in a particular subject domain and whether the teachers perceive learning their subject as being related to prior learning. Mathematics and modern foreign lan-guages tend to be seen as sequential while the humanities and English are much less so (Hallam and Ireson, 1999). The training of teachers is organised on a sub-ject basis and most secondary schools are organised into subject departments which have different histories, varying degrees of autonomy and different priorities. All these factors produce a range of subject and department 'cultures' that may have an impact upon teacher practice and their views about what works in promoting inclusion. These differences in the use of various teaching strategies between sub-jects have implications for the nature and organisation of learning support within and across inclusive settings.

We found no apparent difference between schools with respect to teachers knowledge about practice, although teachers in schools with more experience in mixed ability teaching made more suggestions about what works. That they may not be able to engage in a practice is different from not knowing how to do it and some teachers made this comment when filling out the questionnaire. Clearly, organisational arrangements and resource constraints were factors that determine whether certain strategies were or were not used. For instance, it would not be possible to make use of information and communication technology if the hardware was not available.

Moreover, the schools varied with respect to the extent they engaged in streaming or setting from none at all to setting in specific subjects from particular year groups (i.e. modern foreign language in Year 8), to setting for all subjects at Key Stage 4. In one school with a policy of setting, pupils with severe learning difficulties were included in the top set at Key Stage 3, to facilitate group work, but not at Key Stage 4 because, as one teacher explained 'everything is exam based so the curriculum is not appropriate'. [...]

Whole class teaching

In addition to the survey, eight teachers of five different subjects were observed and interviewed. Each teacher was observed on several sessions for the equivalent of two full teaching days arranged so that follow-up interviews could be held as soon after the observation as possible, often the next period. A total of 48 observations and 24 interviews were conducted. The teachers also kept 'Inclusion Journals' where they reflected on their practice. The aim was to see if we could confirm and or elaborate on Jordan and Stanovich's (1998) idea that teachers in inclusive classrooms 'use knowledge about the cognitive, social, emotional and self-concept characteristics of each individual in order to adapt their practice to reach [their lesson] objective' (p. 34). We read each teacher's journal and listed the themes which seemed to characterise the entries. These were then matched against the themes which emerged from the observations and interviews and the data obtained from the open-ended interview questions.

Overall, the teachers we observed were skilled in whole class teaching, presenting one lesson but offering a choice of tasks and varying expectations with respect to individual pupils. What enables these teachers to include pupils with a wide range of learning abilities seems to be the way in which they embed a responsiveness to individual need within the process of whole class teaching, a finding consistent with the Jordan and Stanovich (1998) study of inclusive practice. Teachers are constantly evaluating their performance and revising what they do in response to pupil reactions. Our observations and scrutiny of the teachers' journals highlight the fluidity and pragmatism of teachers' thinking about inclusive practice. Planning for mixed ability teaching extends beyond what individual pupils will be doing during a lesson and these plans are constantly under review during lessons in the light of pupil responses.

Teachers' knowledge and practice

There are two aspects to the debate about what teachers need to know and be able to do to sustain inclusive practice in their classrooms. The first concerns what teachers working in inclusive settings need to know about special education practice in order to include pupils who experience difficulties in learning. The second aspect is about whether successful inclusion is only about 'good teaching'.

Clearly it is impractical for every teacher to know about the educational implications of all disabilities and learning difficulties. [. . .] Equally, the often quoted view that 'good teaching is good teaching wherever it occurs' may not stand up to close scrutiny when differences in the use of various teaching strategies across the various subjects of the secondary curriculum and the limits of mixed ability teaching are probed. We would suggest that teachers in inclusive settings are first teachers of their subject, but are capable of being responsive to the individuals they face. They are helped in this task through the frequent use of personal planners that emphasise pupil involvement in their own target setting and systems of monitoring learning that are formative in their nature.

The learning support departments in these schools are able to provide specialist knowledge on a 'need to know' basis, but more importantly they support the process of meeting 'individual need' through co-teaching arrangements and curriculum differentiation. The key point is that it is the subject teacher who is responsible for the learning of all children. Obviously this has implications for the role of learning support and the ways in which special expertise is deployed.

[. . .]

Although the teachers expressed concern about their own capacity with respect to mixed ability teaching, they viewed the learning support departments in their respective schools as sources of knowledge and support for teaching and learning.

A redefined role for learning support assistants (LSAs) means that they are reallocated from working directly with individual children to being reassigned to subject departments. There are several advantages to such an arrangement. First, it enables LSAs to learn more about the subject in which they are supporting. Second, it makes it easier for them to be part of the planning process with teachers. Third, it means they are a resource for all children in the class and it also 'unhooks' the LSA from the individual child, creating more opportunity for meaningful inclusion and reducing the child's dependency on a particular adult.

A number of other innovations in pupil support were noted as having a positive impact on inclusion. Rather than working within the traditional special education model of pulling pupils out for individual support, individual tuition is provided in creative ways. For example, in some schools learning support personnel provide help with learning tasks, through structures such as lunchtime or after school 'homework clubs', which are available for all pupils. This is particularly important for homework (or the failure to do it) is often a reason why relationships between teachers and certain students become strained.

Connecting with the school

The schools in our research have made real progress in enabling all pupils to take part in extra-curricular activities, including school visits and trips, choirs, music, drama, sport and IT clubs. [...] A parent interviewed in one school underscored how important participation in extra-curricular activities was to the process of inclusion and its effect on pupils:

> Harry has higher self-esteem now. The trip on the barge was fabulous. For him to have the confidence to go was a real breakthrough. For me, I couldn't have been happier than if I won the pools. You see he was never allowed to go on any trips in his primary school.
>
> (Parent, Year 9 pupil with 'special needs')

Emotional well-being

Teachers' concerns for the emotional well-being of pupils influences their decisions about practice. The observations of teachers, their journal entries and comments made during interviews reflected a finely tuned sensitivity to issues of particular importance in adolescence. Personal privacy, friendship and belonging were of particular concern. As one teacher reflected in her journal:

> I noticed that Brian was very much left out of the small group discussions, because the boys with whom he was working were able to write down their answers much quicker than Brian could. I scribed for Brian while the LSA was working with Robert. I reminded the other boys several times that it was important that they waited for Brian and included him in the discussion. Brian' high desk (to cope with his wheelchair) acts a physical barrier when the boys huddle up to do a group activity, and Brian is physically unable to huddle with them. Disappointed that despite all the work we have recently done on disability and prejudice that the boys in my tutor group unwittingly exclude Brian. This is now something I need to discuss further with them.
>
> (Humanities teacher)

Teachers' concerns with respect to pupil friendship and participation is consistent with other research on inclusive practice. Chang (1984) reported that pupils with SEN were often classified as unpopular by their peers. Martin et al. (1998) noted that pupils with SEN 'often experience significant barriers to their social inclusion' (p. 149). Although they do not say it directly, these researchers seem to suggest that friendship among pupils will not necessarily occur without some kind of intervention, a finding supported by other research (McGregor and Vogelsberg, 1998).

Shifting concepts of inclusion

Finally, we found a shift in teacher concern from individual pupil progress in the curriculum at the end of Key Stage 3 (Year 9) to group performance on national examinations, the General Certificate of Secondary Education (GCSE), in Key Stage 4 (Year 11). That teachers shift their concern from individual pupil progress to group performance on examinations was clearly evident in their practice, discussions and reflections. Field notes and journal entries were filled with references to examinations. As one teacher stated: 'the GCSE requires a lot of essays so a lot of teaching is focused on how to write an essay'. In this school the department has developed procedures such as the use of 'writing frames' to support all pupils with these tasks.

The pressure of examinations is also felt by the pupils. There were many anxious questions about revision. Pupils were not observed to take the easy way out when offered a choice of task or activity. They seemed to understand the need to challenge themselves and this was confirmed by teachers during the interviews. As one pupil told us:

> When I came here (from a special school) they didn't think I could get any GCSEs but now they think I can get them. Before I came to this school I was ungraded but now I think I will pass.
>
> (Year 11 pupil with 'moderate learning difficulties')

The point here is that many pupils, and their parents, who previously would not have had the chance to take these examinations want to be included. These schools are enabling this to happen in a meaningful way.

Discussion

Proponents of inclusive schooling have attempted to develop practice in a number of ways. One has looked at ways in which knowledge and practices developed in special settings can be transferred to the mainstream through arrangements such as outreach work from special schools or support from external specialist services, another has attempted to build on the work of those in the school improvement field by extending the definition of 'all' pupils to include pupils with learning difficulties, disabilities and other special educational needs. This latter approach entails reconceptualising difficulties in learning as dilemmas for teaching in order to provide insights into ways in which practice might be improved for the benefit of all (Hart, 1996, 2000; Clark et al., 1999).

The evidence from our research is that teachers who create inclusive classrooms often do not distinguish between 'special' and other pupils. They often hesitated when answering questions about SEN pupils because they had to remind themselves who these pupils were. This is not because these teachers were not interested in meeting their learning needs, but they had adopted a problem solving approach to inclusion. Our investigations suggest that these teachers tend to be pragmatic rather than 'pure' in their views of what works. They appear to be utilising both special and school improvement approaches to inclusion.

When they have access to a wide variety of support and teaching strategies, inclusive schools can also be effective schools as defined by current criteria. Whilst it cannot be claimed that any improvement in examination results was directly brought about by moves to inclusion, the view was expressed in interviews with teachers that the greater levels of curriculum support has enabled more effective teaching and learning strategies to be employed.

Such claims need to be interpreted with caution and more evidence would be required before we could claim that teaching methods have changed because of inclusion. What is clear is that according to the teachers and the evidence from the examination results, inclusion has not had a negative impact on the achievement levels of other pupils. However, it is still the case that the quickest and easiest way to improve the percentage of children getting the highest grades would be to remove those children with special educational needs altogether. In secondary schools we have been working with the percentage of GCSE A–C passes would be increased by at least 5 per cent if the pupils with special needs were removed from the school and, therefore, the analysis of examination results. That these schools have not done this is a testament to their commitment to inclusive practice. Fortunately, the government has now recognised that there are exclusionary forces at work in the way examination results are published and they have proposed new ways of acknowledging achievement through the adoption of so-called 'value added' measures that will be more sensitive to children's starting points. This should provide a more inclusion-friendly policy context in which to operate.

We would propose that closer links between researchers who study inclusion and those who study school effectiveness and school improvement could prove to be mutually beneficial. A merging of these traditions may help schools to resolve some of the dilemmas that schools and teachers currently face. It might be beneficial to those with an interest in inclusive education by providing a better evidential base to inform the development of practice. It is clear that more robust and yet sensitive research designs are required to be able to explore what is happening in schools that are struggling to be more inclusive. It might also help researchers in the school effectiveness tradition to be more aware of issues of diversity and may encourage them to incorporate a broader range of outcome indicators than are currently employed.

Finally, we would argue that it is the process of becoming inclusive that makes some schools better for all children and as a result a more popular choice for parents. We would propose a conceptualisation of inclusive schools as those that meet the dual criteria of enrolling a diverse student population *and* improving academic standards for all pupils. Such schools have been struggling to resolve conflicting demands for more than a decade, but their results are beginning to speak for themselves. They have demonstrated that the inclusion project is not only possible, but it is of benefit to all. [...]

References

Ainscow, M. (Ed.) (1991) *Effective Schools for All* (London, David Fulton).
Ainscow, M. (1999) *Understanding the Development of Inclusive Schools* (London, Falmer Press).
Brown, S., Duffield, J. and Riddell, S. (1995) School effectiveness research: the policy makers tool for school improvement?, *European Educational Research Association Bulletin*, 1(1), pp. 6–15.

Chang, H. (1984) *Adolescent Life and Ethos: An Ethnography of a U.S. High School* (London, Falmer Press).

Clark, C., Dyson, A., Millward, A. and Robson, S. (1999) Inclusive education and schools as organisations, *International Journal of Inclusive Education*, 3(1), pp. 37–51.

Coleman, J.S., Campbell, E., Hobson, C., Mcpartland, J., Mood, A., Weinfeld, R. and York, R. (1966) *Equality of Educational Opportunity* (Washington, DC, Government Printing Office).

Florian, L. and Rouse, M. (2001) Inclusive practice in secondary schools, in R. Rose and I. Grosvenor (Eds) *Doing Research in Special Education* (London, David Fulton).

Hallam, S. and Ireson, J. (1999) Pedagogy in the secondary school, in P. Mortimore (Ed.) *Understanding Pedagogy and Its Impact on Learning* (London, Paul Chapman).

Hart, S. (1996) *Beyond Special Needs: Enhancing Children's Learning through Innovative Teaching* (London, Paul Chapman).

Hart, S. (2000) *Thinking Through Teaching: A Framework for Enhancing Participation and Learning* (London, David Fulton).

Jencks, C.S., Smith, M., Ackland, H., Bane, M.J., Cohen, D., Ginter, H., Heyns, B. and Michelson, S. (1972) *Inequality: A Reassessment of the Effect of the Family and Schooling in America* (New York, NY, Basic Books).

Jordan, A. and Stanovich, P. (1998) Exemplary teaching in inclusive classrooms, paper presented at the *Annual Meeting of the American Educational Research Association* (San Diego, CA, April).

Kauffman, J.M. and Hallahan, D.P. (Eds) (1995) *The Illusion of Full Inclusion: A Comprehensive Critique of a Current Special Education Bandwagon* (Austin, TX, Pro-Ed).

Lewis, A. and Norwich, B. (2001) A critical review of systematic evidence concerning distinctive pedagogies for pupils with difficulties in learning, *Journal of Research in Special Educational Needs* [online at http://www.nasen.org.uk] (Tamworth, National Association for Special Educational Needs).

Lipsky, D.K. and Gartner, A. (1997) *Inclusion and School reform: Transforming America's Classrooms* (Baltimore, Paul H. Brookes).

McDonnell, L., McLaughlin, M. and Morison, P. (Eds) (1997) *Educating One and All: students with disabilities and standards-based reform* (Washington, DC, National Academy Press).

McGregor, G. and Vogelsberg, R.T. (1998) *Inclusive Schooling Practices: Pedagogical and Research Foundations* (Baltimore, Paul H. Brookes).

Martin, J., Jorgensen, C.M. and Klein, J. (1998) The promise of friendship for students with disabilities, in C. Jorgensen (Ed.) *Restructuring High Schools for All Students: Taking Inclusion to the Next Level*, pp. 209–232 (Baltimore, Paul H. Brookes).

Rouse, M. and Florian, L. (1996) Effective inclusive schools: a study in two countries, *Cambridge Journal of Education*, 26(1), pp. 71–85.

Rouse, M. and Florian, L. (1997) Inclusive education in the marketplace, *International Journal of Inclusive Education*, 1(4), pp. 323–336.

Scott, B.J., Vitale, M.R. and Masten, W.G. (1998) Implementing instructional adaptations for students with disabilities in inclusive classrooms: a literature review, *Remedial and Special Education*, 19(2), pp. 106–119.

Skrtic, T. (1988) The organisational context of special education, in E.L. Meyen and T.M. Skrtic (Eds) *Exceptional Children and Youth: An Introduction* (Denver, CO, Love).

Slee, R. and Weiner, G. (2001) Education reform and reconstructions as a challenge to research genres: reconsidering school effectiveness research and inclusive schooling, *School Effectiveness and School Improvement*, 12(1), pp. 83–98.

Slee, R., Weiner, G. and Tomlinson, S. (Eds) (1998) *School Effectiveness for Whom? Challenges to the School Effectiveness and School Improvement Movements* (London, Falmer Press).

Teddlie, C. and Reynolds, D. (2000) *The International Handbook of School Effectiveness Research* (London, Falmer Press).

Chapter 13

The evolution of secondary inclusion

Jacqueline Thousand and Richard L. Rosenberg

Discussions about inclusion provoke strong and differing opinions among educators, families, community members, and policymakers. Nevertheless, across North America, a growing number of children with disabilities are being included as fully participating members of elementary, middle school, and secondary classrooms. School district data reveal not only an increase in the number of students involved in general education, but also an expansion of the range of disabilities involved. In the United States today, students in every disability category – at all levels of severity and at every grade level – are being educated effectively in inclusive settings (National Center on Educational Restructuring and Inclusion (NCERI), 1995; Villa and Thousand, 1995; Falvey, 1996; Stainback and Stainback, 1996).

Through these demonstrations, conceptual foundations and promising practices for inclusive schooling have emerged. Despite knowledge about key factors of inclusive schooling and the reported benefits to students and educators (NCERI, 1995; Villa and Thousand, 1995; Villa et al., 1996), there remains a scarcity of inclusive education programmes at the secondary level (NCERI, 1994). In a recent national study of teacher and administrator perceptions, results indicated that although educators with experience in inclusive schooling favoured education of children with disabilities in general education, middle and high school educators were less positive overall in their responses than their elementary-level counterparts (Villa et al., 1996). Furthermore, time to collaborate and administrative support were the most powerful predictors of positive attitudes. Villa et al. speculated that the middle and high school results reflect increased complexities in managing heterogeneous experiences in middle and high schools, 'settings where students have multiple classes and where scheduling time for adults to collaborate is a greater challenge' (p. 40).

We acknowledge that middle and high schools are different from elementary schools in many ways. We further acknowledge that there is at least a perception that structuring inclusive experiences is more difficult with adolescents in secondary settings. This perception is based, at least in part, on the assumption that the secondary schools in which students are included will retain the same organizational structures and curricular and instructional practices. Those of us who have attended and taught in public high schools in North America have a particular view – paradigm (Kuhn, 1970) – of a 'typical' secondary school. This paradigm includes teachers working alone in their content areas; a lockstep, grade-by-grade curriculum; an emphasis on individualistic and competitive student output and grading; classes scheduled in 50-minute time blocks; students tracked by academic ability; learning occurring only within classroom walls for most students or in vocationally oriented sites for other students; and separation of special education students and their teachers in their own tracks or classes. As Kuhn described in his observation of scientific revolutions, people who hold a particular view or paradigm can become blind to evidence suggesting that this view no longer works, rings true, or is necessary. The paradigm can actually block people from seeing an emerging new view – in this context, inclusive secondary education for youth with disabilities. Fortunately, this blockage, or paradigm paralysis, can be overcome by means of an alternative paradigm.

Inclusive schools are schools in which all students and adults are welcomed, valued, and supported, and are learning together through common, yet fluid, activities and environments (Sapon-Shevin, 1992). In this chapter, we first offer an alternative 'Circle of Courage' paradigm of education derived from Native American culture (Brendtro et al. 1990, p. 34) that suggests ways to create inclusive high schools that welcome, value, support, and facilitate the learning of adolescents with differing abilities.

Circle of courage: a paradigm for inclusive schooling

Over the past decade, we have been involved in or have been witness to the questioning of community members about what they value as priority educational outcomes for students with and without disabilities. Many thousands of citizens across North and Central America, Western and Eastern Europe, Russia, China, Vietnam, and Micronesia have been asked, 'What outcomes, attitudes, dispositions, and skills do you want schooling to develop in youth by the time they leave high school?' Regardless of the respondents' divergent perspectives, vested interests, or locales, their answers are strikingly similar and tend to fall into one or more of four categories borrowed from Native American culture – belonging, mastery, independence, and generosity. There is little difference between what is identified as important for youth with identified educational challenges versus youth without educational challenges.

In traditional Native American cultures, the main purpose for existence as a society was to produce courageous youth by fostering their development in these four categories or dimensions, which together are referred to as the 'Circle of Courage'. Listed here are examples of some frequently identified outcomes that represent each of the four Circle of Courage dimensions:

- Belonging – experiencing personal development, achieving social competence, having friends, forming and maintaining relationships, getting along with others, and being part of a community.

- Mastery – being able to communicate, becoming competent in something, and reaching one's potential.
- Independence – engaging in problem solving, assuming personal responsibility and accountability for decisions, having confidence to take risks, and being a lifelong learner.
- Generosity – exercising social responsibility, being a contributing member of society, valuing diversity, being empathetic, and being a global steward.

A monumental effort to develop a statewide curriculum based on community values establishes the validity of the Circle of Courage paradigm for education. In the early 1990s, the Vermont State Department of Education asked 4,000 students, parents, educators, business people, and community members to identify what they considered to be core educational outcomes. A two-year endeavour yielded Vermont's Common Core of Learning (Vermont State Board of Education, 1993), and the 'modern' Common Core outcomes of personal development, communication, problem solving, and social responsibility interface and align with the ancient Circle of Courage goals of education.

[. . .]

Translating the new paradigm into practice

This section describes some of the emerging trends and best practices that can help secondary educators implement the new paradigm. 'Examined' are (a) leadership requirements in the restructuring of high schools; (b) improvements of curriculum, instruction, assessment, and campus social life; and (c) support systems for individual students.

Leadership requirements and restructuring

In every successful inclusive schooling effort, there is at least one administrator who is recognized as providing support for implementing the vision of a school that welcomes, values, and supports the education of diverse learners.

Researchers and practitioners agree that administrators must go beyond merely articulating a vision (Ambrose, 1987; Villa and Thousand, 1995; Villa et al., 1995). They must work to create consensus for that vision by listening to concerns and responding to the concerns with appropriate information (e.g. legal, ethical, data-based) in a variety of formats (e.g. readings, inservice presentations, coursework, newsletters, observations of colleagues and other schools that are practising inclusive schooling), which results in a common conceptual framework (i.e. a shared vision). Administrators need to understand that teachers' initial reluctance is not necessarily a permanent barrier to implementing a restructuring effort or any other innovation. McLaughlin (1991) found that teacher commitment to an innovation (e.g. inclusive schooling) often comes only after teachers have acquired competence in the new skills necessary to implement the innovation. This finding was corroborated by Villa *et al.* (1996), who found that general educators with experience educating students with learning disabilities or severe/profound disabilities were more positive in their attitudes toward inclusive practices than those without such experiences.

Another vital administrative role is the support of people as they go through the change process so as to avoid burnout. Littrell *et al.* (1994) found that the most important dimension was that of emotional support. Administrators provide such support effectively when they maintain open communication, show appreciation, take an interest in teachers' work, and consider teachers' ideas Littrell *et al.* (1994) also found that administrators need to provide appraisal support by affording teachers frequent and constructive opportunities to appraise their own work so as to link their instructional practices to the inclusion vision.

Administrators also must offer instrumental support (i.e. providing necessary materials, space, resources, and time for teaching and nonteaching duties).

Informational support – that is, arranging for teachers to attend desired in-service activities that model the relevant instructional practices necessary for meeting diverse needs in inclusive classrooms – is important as well.

The administrator who is successful at accomplishing the management of change is one who fosters and supports collaborative partnerships. In fact, Villa *et al.* (1996) found more positive attitudes toward inclusive schooling where there was collaboration, training to learn how to collaborate, and time for people to collaborate during the school day.

Specific restructuring examples

The effectiveness of block scheduling and heterogeneous grouping to accomplish detracking has been documented in the literature on school restructuring. An increasing number of secondary schools are reorganizing the school day by dividing daily schedules into longer blocks of time. Instead of teaching six periods each day, teachers might, for example, teach two blocked periods as part of a cross-disciplinary team and one traditional period outside of the team. Through block scheduling of core curriculum classes, (a) the teacher : student ratio is reduced, in some cases from 180 to 80 students per teacher (Sizer, 1992); (b) the number of transitions students must experience is minimized; and (c) opportunities and time for more personalization of instruction are increased for all students. Further, the same block team may keep students as a cohort for more than one year, further allowing students and teachers to know one another and stay in meaningful relationships focused on goal achievement for extended periods of time. This team relationship more realistically reflects the kind of work environment that high school graduates are going to face in the next century – short-term project work in which people enter, form relationships, and exit. The old six-period school day, by contrast, reflects the work environment of the factory: the past, not the future.

When special educators and other support personnel, such as school counsellors, paraprofessionals, and administrators, are added to the block-scheduled team, students with disabilities, as well as all of the students in the cohort, are provided with additional personal attention, advisement, and support. The goal is to erase the negative special education labels placed on students and their teachers as well as to change the paradigm that only 'specialists' can work with students with exceptional labels. Finally, in such blocked-team configurations, when academic or social/ emotional challenges arise, early intervention by the more closely knit team of educators and learners can increase capacity for finding solutions and avoid failure and feelings of failure on the part of educators and students. The scenario just described has been implemented successfully in a large, urban Los Angeles County high school (Falvey et al., 1997).

Secondary educators also are acknowledging the need to group students heterogeneously in order to accomplish detracking. The effectiveness of the practice of ability grouping at the secondary level, referred to as 'tracking,' has not been substantiated in the research literature and, in fact, has resulted in negative outcomes for many students (Oakes, 1985; Sapon-Shevin, 1994). It is common knowledge that in tracked schools, students who end up in bottom track classes often experience diluted curricula and limited opportunity to experience courses (e.g. algebra) that are prerequisites for post secondary opportunities. For adolescents to be prepared to operate within the larger, complex heterogeneous community into which they will enter as adults, they need detracked high school experiences that reflect the range of abilities, multiple intelligences (Gardner, 1983), ethnicities, languages, economic levels, ages, and other human dimensions within a community. A school in which teachers group students heterogeneously allows all students to have equal access to the core curriculum, which the community has identified as important for future career and adult life success.

Curriculum, instruction, assessment, and campus life considerations for secondary inclusion

A paradigmatic shift regarding what constitutes curriculum

Historically the concept of including students with disabilities at the secondary level was often challenged due to the strong 'academic' nature of the high school curriculum. The value of subjects such as history, science, and advanced mathematics was typically questioned for students with significant disabilities, who were thought to benefit the most from an alternative, functional curriculum (Brown et al., 1990). Such rigorous content was also questioned for students with mild disabilities and economic disadvantages, who instead were offered simplified or 'watered down' versions of the core curriculum (Levin, 1988). Fortunately, the paradigmatic shift toward restructuring high schools to embrace broad-based outcomes such as the mastery and application of the Circle of Courage and Vermont Common Core goals represents an opportunity for secondary teachers to generate a more flexible curriculum that promotes creativity in students, honours students' multiple and unique ways of knowing and showing their learning (Gardner, 1983), and encourages higher order outcomes for a greater number of youth.

A broad-based, creativity-oriented curriculum allows teachers to develop curricular units and activities that accommodate the characteristics of a more diverse array of youth while promoting a sense of community and common good within the classroom. For example, in a unit on the history of relations between the United States and Cuba, a lesson on the Cuban Missile Crisis might feature a role-play of the characters of the leaders involved in the crisis and the decisions they made. The role play could lead to a discussion of role models and peer pressure in students' lives. A student with disabilities might seize the moment to express frustration with the fact that she is allowed few decision-making opportunities in her own life. Lessons such as this enable students to be exposed to and to examine actual historical events and simultaneously consider contemporary and personal parallels.

Even with the shift from discipline-specific to Circle of Courage outcomes and increased appreciation of and attention to the variations in students' learning styles (Gardner, 1983), some students will still need personalized curricular modifications and/or human support to access the curriculum in general education settings.

In successful inclusive secondary schools, human support originates from a collaborative team consisting of teachers, specialists, paraprofessionals, the student and his or her peers, family members, and administrators (Thousand and Villa, 1992). The team members work together to determine (with the student, whenever possible) the amount and types of support needed for the student to meet his or her goals within the general education classroom. The degree of human support can range from minimal to intensive and can take the form of (a) consultative support one or two times per month; (b) 'stop-in' support one to three times per week from one or more of the team members; (c) peer support (e.g. classroom companion, peer buddies, peer tutors); (d) part-time daily in-class support from one or more team members; (e) team-teaching arrangements in various subject areas and for various parts of the day; or (f) daily part-time or full-time in-class staff (e.g. paraprofessional) support.

Access to the general education curriculum also can be facilitated through modifications of the curriculum itself. Specific curricular modifications have been outlined by Giangreco and Putnam (1991) as follows: curriculum as is (no modification necessary); physical assistance, as necessary (peer or adult assists); material adaptations (changing or substituting instructional materials); multilevel outcomes (same activity with different expectations for mastery); and goals outside of the content area (a focus on social, communication, or life skills during content-area activities). For some students, then, curricular modification involves going beyond mastery of specific academic content. To illustrate, a science teacher might not be expected to ensure that a student with a significant disability demonstrates an understanding of the periodic table of elements, which may be considered necessary for some other students in the class. Instead, for the student with disabilities, the teacher might be expected to teach the student to properly handle materials and to follow three-step directions from a peer partner in a lab situation. For each classroom activity, curricular modifications should be considered. Clearly, the more interactive and hands-on the activity, the less likely it will be that any major modification will be necessary.

[...]

Instruction for motivation: active learning and multiple intelligences theory application

As teachers determine what to teach on the basis of desired student outcomes, they must determine how to ground their teaching in student motivation and learning styles theories, such as multiple intelligences theory (Gardner, 1983).

Student motivation is enhanced when teachers promote active learning strategies as opposed to instructional strategies such as whole-class lectures, which relegate students to being passive learners. Active learning allows students to be shapers of their own learning processes. Enhancing active learning for students means that teachers seek and use student input into curricular and instructional decisions. Students participate with teachers to identify problems, learning strategies, and desired educational outcomes. Active learning includes hands-on activities and student-to-student teaching, sharing, and collaborating to direct the course of learning under the guidance and support of the teacher.

Active learning also involves the engagement of students as (a) instructors (e.g. peer tutors, co-instructors with teachers, cooperative group members); (b) advocates for themselves and others (e.g. members of their own and classmates' Individualized Education Program (IEP) team, peer buddies, peer advocates, conflict mediators); and (c) decision makers (e.g. members of the school board, members of classroom and schoolwide discipline policy-making teams).

In understanding how to best teach students, we should capitalize on new information about how students best learn. Gardner (1983) introduced – and Armstrong (1987,1994) and others (e.g. Lazear, 1994) translated for educators – a model for thinking about how people learn by considering a range of learning styles that he called 'multiple intelligences'. Gardner's model assumes that all individuals possess capacity for knowledge, but each person acquires and expresses it in diverse ways.

An acknowledgement of diverse learning and expressive styles enhances a teacher's ability to provide academic content in ways that allow greater, student access to material and provides a way for students to demonstrate their knowledge more effectively. A teacher who is aware of the theory of multiple intelligences can support the active learning students by offering a variety of learning experiences. [...] Students can increase their own ability to process information through a number of intelligences by being encouraged to select a range of learning activities throughout the year.

An understanding of the processes of active learning and multiple intelligences aids a teacher in planning an array of instructional opportunities for student learning. However, these processes provide only a generic framework for success.

A more thorough knowledge of the individual skills and needs of students is necessary to ensure students' greatest learning potential.

[...]

Beyond academics: social life on campus

When adults in our society reflect on their lives during their high school years, few comment on the academic material they mastered. High school is a time of self-exploration, social activities and meaningful relationships. For students with disabilities, these nonacademic components of life in high school are just as critical. Screaming and cheering at football and basketball games, looking 'cool' at school dances, 'hanging' at fast-food restaurants, going on field trips with the science club, and owning the latest CDs are all part of feeling a sense of belonging in high school and of experiencing life as a teenager. A central – if not the most important – facet of high school life is that of developing and maintaining friendships.

Friendships provide nurturance, support, a sense of well-being, and a variety of communicative, cognitive and social skills for people with and without disabilities throughout childhood and adulthood (Grenot-Scheyer, 1994). Bishop *et al.* (1996) stated that the necessary components for friendship development include physical proximity; opportunities for interaction: awareness of friendship; and respect for diversity, time, reciprocity of relationships and specific skills that support interactions. Students with and without disabilities need a range of physical and emotional supports from peers and thrive when these needs are met consistently and predictably. Students with significant disabilities are no different and experience the same Circle of Courage needs for intimacy and belonging, support and meaningful contribution to the lives of others. Teachers and other adults play a vital role in facilitating relationships for youth. Perhaps the most important contribution teachers make in the lives of youth with disabilities is affording them opportunities for personal interactions, facilitating social skill development, and, most of all, listening to their wants and needs, successes and failures, and joys and sorrows.

[...]

Processes for supporting individual students

Teachers who have the broad understanding of the array of instructional arrangements, resources, curricular adaptations and individualized support staff (e.g. paraprofessionals, volunteers) that can be orchestrated to support secondary students, still need a process to translate this understanding into specific actions for an individual student with special needs. Making Action Plans (MAPs; Falvey, Forest, Pearpoint and Rosenberg, 1995) is a process that has proven to be a family-friendly tool for gathering information about an individual child and translating that information into a plan for future student goals as well as day-to-day instruction.

The MAPs process is initiated when a team forms; it can include the student, peers, family members, friends, school staff, and anyone else the student wants on the team. With the help of a 'neutral' facilitator, the team addresses a sequence of key questions in order to visualize creative schemes, short-term outcomes and long-term goals for the student.

David's MAPs illustrates the process in action. His MAPs was initiated at the start of his sophomore year in order to identify and plan for the highest priority objectives for his secondary and post secondary life. Attending David's MAPs meeting were his family members (mother, father, brother and sister); two high school students (a football player and another friend); a counsellor from the Department of Rehabilitation; and his advisor/counsellor, who represented the school staff. Together, they addressed the following questions:

1   What is David's history?
2   What are dreams for David?
3   What are nightmares for David?
4   Who is David? What are David's strengths, gifts, and abilities?
5   What are David's needs? What do we need to do to address those needs?
6   What do we need to do to achieve the dreams and avoid the nightmares?

Specifically, what would David's ideal education look like to make dreams happen?

In his MAPs meeting of approximately 90 minutes, David made clear to his family and team members that his priority dreams were to have a job, live in his own apartment, and maybe marry and have a family some day. It was discovered that David enjoys sports and dancing. He wants to live close to his family, yet be on his own. Community college was identified as a possible postschool option. Job exploration is still needed. Thus far, David has worked at four different fast-food restaurants and no longer wants to work around food.

On the basis of the MAPs session, David's strengths were noted and IEP objectives were crafted that related to the global goals identified by David and his team in the session. The Individualized Education Program/General Education Matrix for David meshes the student's IEP goals with the classes, courses and other daily activities available to a student before, during and after school (Giangreco *et al.*, 1993). The matrix, when completed by a student's support team, suggests which classes or activities would most likely address priority objectives and helps in determining a student's schedule. Once the schedule is determined, the matrix also offers educators a quick overview of where, when, and in what classes priority objectives are to be addressed in the curriculum.

One final communication tool for facilitating support is the Inclusive IEP Adaptation Checklist, which represents what David's IEP team considers to be reasonable and needed accommodations to facilitate David's learning and success. This checklist, as well as David's Program-at-a-Glance, is shared with any and all of the adults or youth who support David. David also carries these summaries with him, so he can inform others and advocate for his interests and needs readily.

In summary, the vehicles for translating long-term dreams into specific goals and objectives, daily schedules, and individualized accommodations suggested in this section are based on at least three fundamental assumptions. The first is that the student of concern has a caring support team that meets regularly, communicates often and effectively with one another using these and other strategies, and holds the student's long-range dreams and nightmares in mind when making more short-term decisions with and on behalf of the student. The second assumption is that the student, peers and family members are included as team members at every step of the way (Villa and Thousand, 1996) and that their voices are heard and are as valued as the voices of the professionals (Thousand and Villa, 1992). The third assumption is that whatever process is used for planning for the future (e.g. MAPs), it must be dynamic; that is, priorities – dreams and nightmares – are reexamined regularly.

Discussion and conclusions

For decades, researchers, policymakers and educators have been discussing school reform. Rhetoric has been rampant as individuals with differing positions have attempted to bolster their positions with respect to needed changes. Despite all of this talking, most secondary schools have changed little and continue to operate out of the all-too-familiar exclusionary paradigm, in which (a) there is a narrow view of intelligence; (b) assessments are used to rank-order students and schools as well as to label and sort students; and (c) to be named 'special' likely means an invitation to leave the 'mainstream'.

Wiggins (1992) has reminded us that we will not successfully restructure schools to be effective until we stop seeing diversity in students as a problem – that is, until we give up our exclusionary paradigm. And there appears to be evidence that this can and will happen if educators jump in and try out inclusive alternatives. In the study of attitudes toward inclusion referred to in the opening of this chapter (Villa et al., 1996), it was found that educators – including secondary educators, who had actually tried including students with disabilities in general education activities – overall did not see student diversity as a problem. In fact, teachers and administrators with experience in inclusive settings believed that the organizational structure and culture of the schools changed in a positive direction as a result of educating youth with disabilities in general education classrooms. Furthermore, they believed that (a) general and special educators are able to work as equal partners to provide education to a diverse group of students; (b) team teaching results in general and special educators' feeling successful in meeting student needs; (c) general educators acquire a belief in the feasibility of educating all students together; and (d) inclusive schools are more democratic because decision making is shared among administrators, teachers, students, support personnel and other community members. Taken together, these results suggest that the presence of youth with disabilities in secondary classrooms, in fact, represents a gift to school restructuring. Their presence both requires and pushes implementation of the educational goals, theories and best practices which simultaneously define and support a Circle of Courage paradigm of schooling and which have the potential of benefiting all students in the school community.

As a final exercise, we invite the reader to consider the potential impact of adopting a Circle of Courage paradigm and the outcomes of belonging, mastery, independence and generosity for secondary students in inclusive settings. We further invite the reader to consider the impact of this paradigm if applied to the adults of the school as well. If schools in which everyone – including the educators of the school – is welcomed, valued, supported, and learning together (i.e. inclusive schools) were to adopt a Circle of Courage curriculum for adults as well as students, what might be the impact on educators? We speculate that educators would experience enhanced personal and professional well-being and development, for the following reasons. First, a focus on belonging would foster the seeking out and celebration of the diversity and unique talents and interests of educators as well as increased emphasis (and time for) collaborative and joint creative problem solving. Attention to mastery and independence would encourage school personnel to acquire new skills in instruction and assessment, as well as developing a curriculum that accommodates greater diversity in student learning styles and abilities. Independence would further develop from collective risk taking, problem solving, and the modelling of lifelong learning for students. Finally, replacing professional isolationism (i.e. teaching alone) with a spirit of generosity would foster increased sharing of skills, resources and perceptions – and the development of a genuine community of adult learners.

Of course, these proposed adult outcomes are speculative at this point, but so was the feasibility and the anticipated positive outcomes of inclusive education just a decade ago (NCERI, 1994, 1995). Being speculative and holding out a vision, nevertheless, is the starting point to any change process (Ambrose, 1987). In the words of Oscar Hammerstein II from the 1949 musical South Pacific hit song 'Happy Talk': 'You gotta have a dream. If you don't have a dream, how ya gonna make that dream come true?' (Williamson Music, 1981, pp. 42–44).

References

Ambrose, D. (1987). *Managing Complex Change*. Pittsburgh: Enterprise.

Armstrong, T. (1987). *In Their Own Way*. Los Angeles: Jeremy P. Tarcher.

Armstrong, T. (1994). *Multiple Intelligences in the Classroom*. Alexandria, VA: Association for Supervision and Curriculum Development.

Bishop, K.D., Jubala, K.A., Stainback, W. and Stainback, S. (1996). Facilitating friendships. In S. Stainback and W. Stainback (Eds), *Inclusion: A guide for Educators* (pp. 155–169). Baltimore: Brookes.

Brendtro, L., Brokenleg, M. and Van Bockern, S. (1990). *Reclaiming Youth at Risk: Our Hope for the Future*. Bloomington, IN: National Educational Service.

Brown, L., Schwartz, P., Udvari-Solner, A., Kampschroer, E., Johnson, F., Jorgenson, J. and Gruenwald, L. (1990). *How Much Time Should Students with Severe Intellectual Disabilities*

Spend in Regular Education Classrooms and Elsewhere? Madison: University of Wisconsin, Department of Behavioral Studies.

Falvey, M.A. (1996). *Inclusive and Heterogeneous Schooling: Assessment, Curriculum and Instruction.* Baltimore: Brookes.

Falvey, M.A., Forest, M., Pearpoint, J. and Rosenberg, R.L. (1995). Building connections. In J.S. Thousand, R.A. Villa and A. Nevin (Eds), *Creativity and Collaborative Learning: A Practical Guide to Empowering Students and Teachers* (pp. 347–368). Baltimore: Brookes.

Falvey, M.A., Rosenberg, R.L. and Falvey, E.M. (1997). Inclusive educational schooling. In S. Pueschel and M. Sustrova (Eds), *Adolescents with Down Syndrome: Toward a More Fulfilling Life* (pp. 145–160). Baltimore: Brookes.

Gardner, H. (1983). *Frames of Mind.* New York: Basic Books.

Giangreco, M F. and Putnam, J. W. (1991). Supporting the education of students with severe disabilities in regular education environments. In L.H. Meyer, C.A. Peck and L. Brown (Eds), *Critical Issues in the Lives of People with Severe Disabilities* (pp. 245–270). Baltimore: Brookes.

Giangreco, M.F., Cloninger, C.J. and Iverson, V.S. (1993). *Choosing Options and Accommodations for Children (COACH): A Guide to Planning Inclusive Education.* Baltimore: Brookes.

Grenot-Scheyer, M. (1994). The nature of interactions between students with severe disabilities and nondisabled friends and acquaintances. *Journal of the Association for Persons with Severe Handicaps,* 19, 253–262.

Kuhn, T. (1970). *The Structure of Scientific Revolutions.* Chicago: University of Chicago Press.

Lazear, D. (1994). *Seven Pathways to Learning: Teaching Students and Parents about Multiple Intelligences.* Tuscon, AZ: Zephyr.

Levin, H. (1988). *Accelerating the Education of All Students.* New Brunswick, NJ: Rutgers University, Center for Policy Research in Education.

Littrell, P.C., Billingsley, B.S. and Cross, L.H. (1994). The effects of principal support on special and general educators' stress, job satisfaction, school commitment, health, and intent to stay in teaching. *Remedial and Special Education,* 15, 297–310.

McLaughlin, M.V. (1991). The Rand change agent study: Ten years later. In A.R. Oden (Ed.), *Education Policy Implementation* (pp. 143–155). Albany: State University of New York Press.

National Center on Educational Restructuring and Inclusion (1994). National survey on inclusive education. New York: City University of New York, Graduate School and University Center.

National Center on Educational Restructuring and Inclusion (1995). National study on inclusion: Overview and summary report. New York: City University of New York, Graduate School and University Center.

Oakes, J. (1985). Keeping track: How schools structure inequality. New Haven, CT: Yale University Press.

Sapon-Shevin, M. (1992). Celebrating diversity. In S. Stainback and W. Stainback (Eds), *Curriculum Considerations in Inclusive Classrooms: Facilitating Learning for All Children* (pp. 19–36). Baltimore: Brookes.

Sapon-Shevin, M. (1994). *Playing Favorites: Gifted Education and the Disruption of Community.* Albany: State University of New York.

Sizer, T. (1992). *Horace's School: Redesigning the American High School.* Boston: Houghton Mifflin.

Stainback, S. and Stainback, W. (1996). *Inclusion: A guide for Educators.* Baltimore: Brookes.

Thousand, J. and Villa, R. (1992). Collaborative teams: A powerful tool in school restructuring. In R.A. Villa, J.S. Thousand, W. Stainback and S. Stainback (Eds), *Restructuring for Caring and Effective Education: An Administrative guide to Creating Heterogeneous Schools* (pp. 73–108). Baltimore: Brookes.

Vermont State Board of Education (1993). *Vermont's Common Core of Learning: The Results We Need from Education*. Montpelier: Author.

Villa, R.A. and Thousand, J.S. (Eds) (1995). *Creating an Inclusive School*. Alexandria, VA: Association for Supervision and Curriculum Development.

Villa, R.A. and Thousand, J.S. (1996). Student collaboration: an essential for curriculum delivery in the 21st century. In S. Stainback and W. Stainback (Eds), *Inclusion: A Guide for Educators* (pp. 171–191). Baltimore: Brookes.

Villa, R.A., Thousand, J.S. and Rosenberg, R.L. (1995). Creating heterogeneous schools: a systems change perspective. In M. Falvey (Ed.), *Inclusive and Heterogeneous Schooling: Assessment, Curriculum, and Instruction* (pp. 395–414). Baltimore: Brookes.

Villa, R.A., Thousand, J.S., Meyers, H. and Nevin, A. (1996). Teacher and administrator perceptions of heterogeneous education. *Exceptional Children*, 63, 29–45.

Wiggins, G. (1992). Foreword. In R. Villa, J. Thousand, W. Stainback and S. Stainback (Eds), *Restructuring for Caring and Effective Education: An Administrative Guide to Creating Heterogeneous Schools* (pp. xi–xvi). Baltimore: Brookes.

Williamson Music (1981). South Pacific vocal selections. New York: Hal Leonard.

Chapter 14

An inclusive pedagogy in mathematics education

Claudie Solar

[...]

Why an inclusive pedagogy?

The need for an inclusive pedagogy in mathematics education emerges from different viewpoints on the status of girls and women in mathematics. Recent researches indicate that women are succeeding as well as men in mathematics (Hanna, 1989; Baudelot and Establet, 1992; IAEP, 1992; Lafortune and Kayler, 1992), yet they participate much less in mathematics-related careers. Because of inequities in the workplace, the success of girls in school does not translate into the progress of women at work (Baudelot and Establet, 1992). For example in Canada, only 6 per cent of university mathematics professors are women despite the fact that women make up 18 per cent of the overall university professoriate (Mura, 1990). Just because women can succeed in mathematics does not ensure that they will choose to pursue careers in this field. They also need to believe that they can succeed, and want to succeed. Some researches in Canada indicate that girls have less confidence in their skills than boys (Lemoyne, 1989), that girls tend to attribute success more to hard work than to abilities (Mura *et al.*, 1986), and that both boys and girls believe that men are superior in mathematics (Lafortune, 1989). Confronted with a mathematical problem that cannot be solved immediately, girls are more likely than boys to experience the situation as a threat (Lemoyne, 1989). Another explanation for the lack of participation of women in mathematics may be the importance most girls give to a feminine self-image (Holmes and Silverman, 1992). If they also hold stereotypical images of mathematicians and scientists (Lafortune and Kayler, 1992), the conflict between these images and their desired self-image may deter them from seeking mathematical or scientific careers.

[...] Changing the situation may call for a global approach in which men and boys need to be involved as well as women and girls. Schools can play an important role in encouraging women in mathematics. Teachers may use a pedagogy which takes the aspects mentioned previously into account in the convergence between gender and mathematics education. Such a method can draw from feminist pedagogy the aspects that deal with the promotion of women and that can be applied to a co-educational mathematics class. It can also draw from an analysis of discriminatory classroom practices. The resulting pedagogy may be called an inclusive pedagogy for it should encompass women not only as a social class but also as diversified socio-economic and ethnocultural classes. It should also take into account the diversity of men and break away from the stereotyped male norm.

'Feminist pedagogy' combines two words into one expression and its meaning depends on the meaning given to each word. Let us first consider 'feminism'. On the one hand, most dictionaries or encyclopaedias define feminism as a doctrine or a set of ideas. On the other hand, most definitions given by feminists tie these ideas to the arena of politics (Solar, 1988). Feminism, for them, links thought and action, weaves theory and practice, connects experience and education. In this perspective, feminism is closely related to the notion of 'praxis' (Freire, 1974) and is defined as the frame of reference on which individuals, women in particular, build their actions in order to transform the social division of the sexes. This is a broad definition that allows different feminist perspectives ranging from the more equalitarian to the more radical (Descarries-Bélanger and Roy, 1988).

'Pedagogy' deals with knowledge as well as its transmission, and can be viewed as a generic expression which defines the field of inquiry dealing with educational situations (Best, 1988). Feminist pedagogy can thus be defined as 'the science that studies the teaching, learning, knowledge and educational environment from a feminist perspective' (Solar, 1992a, p. 267; translation by the author). And the analysis of feminist pedagogies as developed through classroom practices in Women's Studies or Feminist Studies would provide some guidelines to describe them.

[…]

A survey of the literature on feminist pedagogy reveals three different approaches. First, there is the approach that deals with the teaching of a specific discipline. The second approach is related to the personal experience of teachers in Women's Studies courses. Because sharing experiences is valued in feminist perspectives and is perceived as a way to construct knowledge, many writers illustrate their theoretical analysis of classroom practices with personal experience. The third approach focuses on a theorization of feminist classroom practices either by comparing these practices with other pedagogies such as the consciousness-raising pedagogy of Freire, or by using a feminist analysis of the oppression of women or the experience of teachers (see Culley and Portuges, 1985).

Many feminist scholars refer to consciousness-raising pedagogy because of its ties to situations of oppression experienced by women. Sometimes, it is referred to as radical pedagogy (Thorne, 1984), critical pedagogy (Nemiroff, 1988) or liberation pedagogy (Maher, 1987). These pedagogies are viewed as belonging to the theory of liberatory education (Nemiroff, 1988) or to critical theory in education (Weiler, 1988): 'Critical education theory, as its name implies, rests on a critical view of the existing society, arguing that the society is both exploitative and oppressive, but also is capable of being changed' (Weiler, 1988, p. 5). Weiler further argues that 'feminist educational critics (…) want to retain the vision of social justice and transformation that underlies liberatory pedagogies' (Weiler, 1991, p. 450).These approaches emphasize the need to break the silence that confines the oppressed to make them active participants in their learning process, to use material relevant to them in such a way that they become empowered by the process. 'Feminism is about social change; it is a politic of transformation' write Briskin and Coulter (1992, p. 249). 'Feminist pedagogy, like the radical pedagogy Freire developed for teaching literacy to peasants in Latin America, seeks to break through silence and passivity and to empower subordinate groups' (Thorne, 1984, p. 6). From consciousness-raising pedagogy or liberation pedagogy, feminist pedagogy retains in particular the following four dialectical aspects:

- silence/speech
- passivity/active participation
- powerlessness/empowerment
- omission/inclusion

(Solar, 1992a, p. 273; translated by the author)

[…]

Gilligan's book, *In a Different Voice* (1982), has had an important impact on the definition of pedagogical settings for women. It sustains the pedagogical perspectives of cooperation and sharing (Shrewsbury, 1987), and promotes interactive pedagogical practices (Maher, 1987) in order to respect women's preference for interaction and interdependence rather than isolation and independence.

> A feminist pedagogical approach seeks to incorporate the affective, emotional and experiential into the learning process and to replace the competitiveness of the classroom interaction with communal, collective and cooperative ways of learning.
>
> (Briskin, 1990, p. 23)

Belenky *et al.* (1986) contribute to the definition of feminist pedagogy in studying *Women's Ways of Knowing* and women's relationship to knowledge. Because knowledge omitted women, women's lives, women's experiences and women's contributions in the past, it has now become a central part of the educational process. Women need to be connected to meaningful knowledge. As a result, they may have to overcome some inner conflicts to construct their knowledge (Bolli, 1985).

[…]

Feminist pedagogies draw from different feminist theories, liberatory pedagogy and humanistic education. An analysis of recurrent themes found in feminist pedagogy literature has given rise to the following list of characteristics:

1 breaking the silence and giving all women the right to speak;
2 creating an appropriate learning climate for women, that is, a climate where competition is reduced and cooperation encouraged;

3   changing the power distribution in the classroom in order to counteract domination and hierarchy;
4   sharing feminist knowledge that ties in with women's lives;
5   valuing intuition and emotions as opposed to rationality and objectivity;
6   taking experience as a source of knowledge;
7   demystifying the construction of knowledge, its political value and the way women relate to it;
8   revealing the omission of women and constructing a women's collective memory;
9   working towards social change and giving women the means to do so;
10 transmitting the necessary intellectual tools to build up a feminist critique;
11 using verbal and written language which respects the experience and diversity of women;
12 working towards the transformation of education (Solar, 1992a, p. 277; translated by the author).

[...]

If the characteristics of feminist pedagogy are analysed further and juxtaposed with the four dialectical aspects, then it is possible to classify them with respect to these aspects. Even though certain characteristics may belong to more than one aspect, Figure 14.1 provides a new schema of the characteristics of feminist pedagogy and sets out four main aspects that make it easier to grasp and work with them.

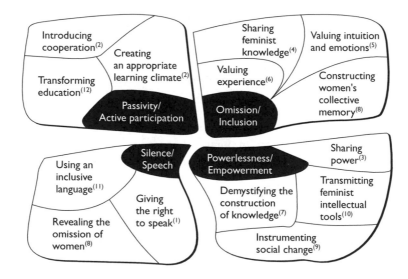

Figure 14.1 Characteristics of feminist pedagogy. © Claudia Solar, University of Ottawa. Design Martine Clément.

The table of characteristics of feminist pedagogy offers a frame of reference for constructing feminist pedagogical approaches (numbers in parenthesis refer to the number of the characteristic). Before applying it to mathematics education, let us consider what a favourable climate for learning mathematics entails. For that, we will turn to non-discriminatory classroom practices.

Inequity in the classroom

[...]

Discriminatory classroom interaction

Sexism

'Sexism in general classroom interaction is evident in sex-differentiating feedback, differentiating when giving attention and the oppourtunity to speak in the classroom, or by asking men the more complex and difficult questions' (Solar, 1992b, p. 53). This happens, for example, when teachers and professors let boys or men monopolize class time and take more than their share of their attention. It happens also when girls and women are asked fact-based questions while boys and men are asked more complex and difficult questions (Solar, 1992b, p. 53).

Sadker and Sadker (1985, p. 56) report that, in American schools, 'boys are eight times more likely to call out answers than girls; teachers are twice as likely to have extended conversations with boys than with girls; teachers are twice as likely to give detailed instructions for specific tasks to boys than to girls and that in fact they often do the task for girl'. If we combine these data with researchers' findings on gender and mathematics education, such as Fennema's findings about teachers' beliefs about the success of males' and females' in mathematics (Fennema *et al.*, 1990) or Leder's findings about teachers giving attention to males in mathematics classes (Leder, 1990b), then we have some kind of evidence of sexist classroom practices in mathematics education. This creates a chilly climate for women (Hall and Sandler, 1982).

Ethnocultural discrimination and racism

Ethnocultural discrimination and racism occur in the classroom when teachers and professors exhibit ethnocultural and race-differentiated feedback and attention. Discrimination is evident when professors favour a white, western, male perspective in curricular materials. It exists, for example, when there is an omission of the perspectives of aboriginal people (Solar, 1992b, p. 55). Examples of this can be found when there is impatience with students whose first language is not the official language, or when commenting on a student's academic difficulties by referring to his or her cultural or racial background (Solar, 1992b). Evidence of discrepancy in performance in mathematics education within ethnic groups has been reported (Reyes *et al.*, 1988; Secada, 1992) and raises the question of ethnocultural and gender equity.

Heterosexism

Heterosexism can be seen in the classroom through stereotyped heterosexual behaviour, attitudes and assumptions that are based on the heterosexuality, as well as through the exclusion of individuals on the basis of their homosexuality (Solar, 1992b, p. 57). This aspect of general discriminatory classroom interaction might sound, for some, far removed from the mathematics classroom. However, mathematics is a discipline which has its own code of conduct. If we look closer, we might find that the mathematical culture is not attractive to homosexual people, that real life mathematics situations (such as those using statistics for example) never reveal this aspect of life, and that some mathematical humour often refers to a heterosexual context.

Other forms of discrimination in the classroom

The other forms of discrimination in the classroom relate to teachers' and professors' assumptions about religion, age, class or disability. This type of discrimination manifests itself by 'becoming impatient or not paying attention to certain students; commenting on students' academic difficulties referring to their age or disabilities, or assuming a student will be unable to do an assignment because of a disability; preventing students from writing essays on specific issues related to age, religion, class differences and disabilities' (Solar, 1992b, p. 59). Here also, the language and humour prevalent in the mathematics classroom ignore women's differences, therby often resulting in disparaging comments. This aspect of discrimination in the mathematics classroom might become a bit more evident if we consider the prevailing beliefs tying mathematical creativity and success to youth – a mathematical genius has to discover a new theorem by age 19; one does not learn mathematics in adulthood (see Lee, 1986). Further, mathematics is commonly equated to intelligence but disability is not. This construct makes mathematics sound inaccessible to people with disabilities.

Stereotypes

As we have seen in general discriminatory classroom interaction, the manifestations of discrimination are very much tied to stereotypes. Stereotypes are 'standardized, often caricaturized, images or conceptions of people which assign specific abilities, characteristics and roles in society according to sex, race, ethnicity, class, religion, sexual orientation, age or disability' (Solar, 1992b, p. 61). Stereotyping in schools and the construction of gender though school are a well-documented area.

In the mathematics classroom, stereotypes can be found in course material that depicts only male mathematicians; only males doing scientific experiments; only males occupying jobs requiring a good mathematical background – usually as scientists; only women and women of colour occupying second-order positions or lower status occupations. It is also found in course material in which females are omitted. Stereotypes are revealed through teachers' low expectations for women in general, older women, members of visible and ethnocultural minorities and women with disabilities. Stereotyping manifests itself when Asian women, but not Black women, are expected to do well in mathematics. It also manifests itself through humour.

Language

Since the late 1970s, discrimination through language has attracted considerable attention. Discriminatory language refers to

> the explicit and implicit elements of language which convey an inferior status to individuals according to their sex, race, ethnicity, class, religion, sexual orientation, age or disability, with demeaning or derogatory implications. [It also refers to] distorted and disparaging racist or sexist attitudes [which] are transmitted through the language structure, grammar, lexis and power dynamics of communicative behaviour.
>
> (Solar, 1992b, p. 65)

This form of discrimination is present in the mathematics classroom, for language is the main vehicle for communication. It might manifest itself through using a generic masculine language, always referring to a mathematician as a man, using a language which universalizes experience and ignores the differences between people and cultures, and making racist and sexist puns and jokes, including heterosexual innuendos (Solar, 1992b, p. 65).

With respect to language and aggressiveness in mathematical instruction, Damarin writes:

> Our vocabulary reflects goals of *mastery* and mathematical *power*. We teach students to *attack* problems and to apply *strategies*. Our instructional strategies include *drill* and the use of many forms of *competition*. We are advised to *torpedo* misconceptions and to build concept *hierarchies*. In short, the ways we think about, talk about, and act out our roles as teachers of mathematics are heavily influenced by the masculine roots of the subject.
>
> (Damarin, 1990, p. 145)

Bouchard (1989) penned an interesting analysis of humour which she entitled *Pour ne plus mourir de rire* (Not to die laughing anymore). She analysed puns and jokes circulating in schools. She found that, among approximately 150 sexist puns, 35 per cent negated women as subjects, 27 per cent related to women's lack of intelligence and 8 per cent associated women with animals in a disparaging way. Women are referred to as objects, in particular sexual objects. Jokes also tend to trivialize violence. This work reveals that sexist and racist humour is directed towards people holding an inferior status in society and plays an important role in maintaining them in this situation. The negation of women's intelligence in humour, often combined with racist undertones, has to be viewed as an important side of classroom interaction. Humour is part of the climate within which girls and women study and work, and often contributes to the construction of a male environment.

[...]

Discriminatory nonverbal behaviour

Discriminatory nonverbal behaviour is a 'behaviour that communicates, without using words, different expectations and judgements on the interests, abilities and achievements of people according to their sex, race, ethnicity, class, religion, sexual orientation, age or disability'(Solar, 1992b, p. 63). Many mathematicians, especially women, have experienced this: people not knowing what to say when discovering you are a mathematician or, on the contrary, finding you suddenly interesting. This is generally not seen through language but through nonverbal behaviour. In the classroom, this behaviour manifests itself through 'adopting a closed and indifferent posture when interacting with girls, women or persons of racial or ethnocultural minorities but being open and alert with white boys and men [in a white context]; gravitating towards the area of the classroom where most men and boys are sitting; looking at course notes while women or certain students are speaking' (Solar, 1992b, p. 63).

Discrimination in the curriculum

Discrimination in the curriculum can be defined as

> exclusion or stereotypical representation of women, racial and ethnic minorities, aboriginal peoples, lesbians and homosexuals, people with disabilities, and older women in the curriculum. [A discriminatory curriculum] ignores the experiences, contributions, perspectives and values of members of any of these groups and [...] reinforces racist and sexist attitudes and stereotypes.
>
> (Solar, 1992b, p. 67)

This form of discrimination can be found in instructional materials, textbooks and other publications used in courses, as well as in the adherence to perspectives that exclude members of these groups. It omits important achievements, issues, and contributions of women, people with disabilities, minorities and different ethnocultural groups in course content, and underestimates the assumptions and premises on which theories are constructed. Ignoring these assumptions and premises in mathematics, or in any other science, leads to the assumption, held by most mathematicians and non-mathematicians, that mathematics is neutral and that its teaching is value-free. In fact, one can easily see that real-life mathematics situations in textbooks draw more from the public world of men than from the private world of women, as O'Brien pointed out (1990), and it is only recently that books on the history of mathematics do mention some women mathematicians.

Towards an inclusive pedagogy in mathematics education

At the beginning of this chapter, feminist pedagogy was defined as dealing with the teaching, learning, curriculum and educational environment from a feminist perspective. Here, the context is mathematics education. Let us now see how feminist pedagogy and non-discriminatory classroom practices can be combined to provide guidelines for an inclusive pedagogy in mathematics education.

Teaching

There is abundant evidence that teachers and professors do interact differently with their female and male students, in mathematics education as well as in other subject areas (see Fennema and Leder, 1990; Lafortune and Kayler, 1992; Leder, 1992; Solar, 1992b). Discrimination in teaching mathematics is pervasive and from the earlier discussion on non-discriminatory practices, we can say that when a mathematics teacher or professor manages to respect all students by

- paying attention to all of them;
- having high expectations for them;
- using inclusive language;
- avoiding stereotypes;
- forbidding sexist and racist humour;
- referring to the contributions of women in the ancient and contemporary history of mathematics, wherever possible;
- using real life situations related to women's lives;
- using problems and pedagogical settings that require students to speak of the process they follow to solve them and bring them to realize that there is neither a single solution to most problems nor one single way to solve them,

then the professor is working toward closing the gap between women and mathematics.

Learning

There is also evidence that girls and women do not share an 'equal opportunity to learn mathematics' with their male counterparts (Fennema, 1990, p. 2). The literature on feminist pedagogy and classroom discriminatory practices provides an indication of how the situation can be improved. Hence,

- when boys and girls, men and women are able to share their thinking and their understanding of mathematics;
- when the problems they have to solve also include mathematical situations that women confront in real life;
- when stereotypes, sexist language and humour are banished from the class by the teacher or professor;
- when mistakes or faults are taken as a springboard to learning;
- when cooperation is valued and encouraged;
- when the way mathematics has been constructed and its use in society are part of the curriculum;
- when women mathematicians and scientists are made visible,

then students may learn that mathematics is accessible to all of them and might develop a positive attitude towards it. This type of learning should help girls and women to be more autonomous and independent in their learning and use of mathematics, as Fennema and Peterson advocate (1985).

Curriculum

Less has been said on the mathematics curriculum, but if 'mathematics is a unique product of human culture' (Fennema, 1990, p. 2) and if mathematics has been a male construct until now (Mura, 1986), then the mathematics curriculum, just like any curriculum, is a male curriculum that needs to be revised (Solar and Lafortune, 1994). It is time to examine the school mathematics curriculum to see how it is built up into a male science in the mind of both males and females, how it serves men more than women, and how it should be changed to be balanced. Whatever the present situation, we already know that when the mathematics curriculum

- includes women in its history, ancient and contemporary;
- includes mathematical situations experienced mainly by women;
- excludes material which is stereotypical, sexist or racist;
- includes aspects of mathematics which are more related to women's lives;
- presents mathematics as a process rather than a set of rules,

then mathematics is more inclusive of women.

Educational environment

The educational environment is a difficult concept to grasp and a difficult area to change. It includes the climate and goals of the school, teachers' beliefs and expectations as well as those of learners, peer values and pressure as well as family values and pressure, and finally, the culture of a society in which women are still second-class

Top-left quadrant:

Teaching
Having high expectations for all women
Using pedagogical approaches that encourage participation
Introducing cooperation
Asking women high cognitive-level questions

Learning
Sharing the thinking process
Sharing the understanding of mathematics
Learning cooperatively

Curriculum
Having women participate in defining the content

Educational environment
Allowing women to participate in defining their learning process
Having women participate in defining the goals of the shool
Addressing the issue of gender differences

Passivity / Active participation

Top-right quadrant:

Teaching
Paying attention to all students regardless of sex, race, age, etc.
Monitoring speech in order to include women
Using examples which relate to women
Describing mathematicians and scientists as both males and females
Valuing intuition and emotions

Learning
Solving problems that deall with women's situations
Receiving feedback and learning from mistakes

Curriculum
Referring to the contributions of women
Using situations related to women's lives
Using non-stereotypical material
Including ethnomathematics
Revealing the omission of women

Educational environment
Including and valuing women
Making women visible

Omission / Inclusion

Silence / Speech

Bottom-left quadrant:

Teaching
Using inclusive language
Forbidding sexist and racist humour
Using pedagogical settings that make it easier for students to speak
Limiting extended conversations with male students

Learning
Speaking about the learning of mathematics
Giving time for women to respond

Curriculum
Explaining the construction of mathematics and its use in society

Educational environment
Valuing women's contributions and concerns
Setting school goals which include women
Using inclusive language

Powerlessness / Empowerment

Bottom-right quadrant:

Teaching
Avoiding stereotypes
Naming differences and explaining them
Giving women the time and means to learn
Letting women solve problems by themselves
Praising women's achievements
Sharing power

Learning
Demystifying mathematics: more then one solution and more than one process
Receiving appropriate feedback and instructions
Learning about women's participation in mathematics and science

Curriculum
Demystifying mathematical construct
Mathematics as a process, not a set of rules
Including the lives of women scientists
Including women's perspectives

Educational environment
Creating a warm and supportive climate
Working out beliefs anout men and women
Denouncing stereotypes

Figure 14.2 Inclusive mathematics education. © Claudie Solar, University of Ottawa. Design Martine Clement.

citizens, even though tremendous changes have already taken place in many countries. This is why changing the educational environment requires everyone, regardless of their discipline and role in the education of women and men, to contribute to the eradication of discrimination. I believe that these directions in teaching, learning and the curriculum are conducive to an educational environment which is inclusive of women and minorities.

A step further

In this present effort to construct a model of inclusive mathematics education, I have tried to combine the elements of feminist pedagogy, non-discriminatory classroom practices and guidelines for an inclusive pedagogy in mathematics education. This process leads to the table presented in Figure 14.2.

This table should be viewed as an attempt to schematize what could be, in a mathematics classroom, the characteristics of an inclusive pedagogy. It is neither complete nor immutable. [...]

Conclusion

Discrimination in mathematics education is a complex situation, and eliminating it is a complex problem to solve. For more than twenty years now, researchers have been studying its diverse manifestations. Its complexity has often required the problem to be fragmented into smaller subproblems or sub-issues. With respect to this, Leder (1990a, p. 14) writes: 'The tendency to concentrate on one or perhaps a small set of variables, and to ascribe differences obtained to these variables alone, has at times given rise to unproductive and largely artificial controversies.' However, as she points out, the synthesis of the findings offers an integrative view of gender differences. In this chapter, I have also tried to combine different variables influencing women's learning in the mathematics classroom. This is done from a pedagogical perspective in which feminist pedagogy and non-discriminatory classroom practices are combined to define a frame of reference for an inclusive pedagogy in mathematics education. Such an inclusive pedagogy takes into account the complexity of the different manifestations of discrimination against women in their learning of mathematics, and its framework offers an alternative to this discrimination so that, in the future, women will be equal 'definers' of the mathematical domain.

References

Baudelot C. and R. Establet: 1922, *Allez les filles!*, Editions du Seuil, Paris.
Belenky M.F., B.M. Clinchy, N.R. Goldberger and J.M. Tarule: 1986, *Women's Ways of Knowing*, Basic Books, New York.
Best F.: 1988, 'Les avatars du mot "pédagogie"', *Perspectives* 18(2), 161–170.

Bolli M.: 1985, 'Femmes et savoir: mouvement d'approche', *Femmes et formation*, Université de Genève. Faculté de psychologie et des sciences de l'éducation (Pratiques et théorie, cahier No 38), pp. 11–24.

Bouchard P.: 1989, *Pour ne plus mourir de rire: études des plaisanteries sexistes*, Ottawa, Perspectives féministes No 18. Institut canadien de recherche sur les femmes.

Briskin L.: 1990, *Feminist Pedagogy: Teaching and Learning Liberation*, Ottawa, Canadian Research Institute for the Advancement of Women/Institut canadien de recherche sur les femmes. Feminist Perspectives Féministes. No 19.

Briskin L. and R. Coulter: 1992, 'Feminist Pedagogy: Challenging the normative', *Canadian Journal of Education/Revue canadienne de l'éducation*, 17(3), 247–263.

Culley M. and C. Portuges: 1985, *Gendered Subjects. The Dynamics of Feminist Teaching*, Boston, Routledge and Kegan Paul.

Damarin S.: 1990, 'Teaching mathematics: a feminist perspective', in L. A. Steen, ed., *Teaching and Learning Mathematics in the 1990's*, National Council of Teachers of Mathematics 1990 Yearbook, pp. 144–151.

Descarries-Bélanger F. and S. Roy: 1988, *Le mouvement des femmes et ses courants de pensée: essai de typologie*, Les documents de l'ICREF, No 19, Ottawa, Institut canadien de recherche sur les femmes/Canadian Research Institute for the Advancement of Women.

Fennema E.: 1990, 'Justice, Equity, and Mathematics Education', in E. Fennema and G. Leder, eds, *Mathematics and Gender*, New York and London, Teachers College, Columbia University, pp. 1–9.

Fennema E. and G. Leder, eds: 1990, *Mathematics and Gender*, New York and London, Teachers College, Columbia University.

Fennema E. and P.L. Petersen: 1985, 'Autonomous learning behavior: a possible explanation of gender-related differences in mathematics', in L.C. Wilkinson and C.B. Marrett, eds, *Gender-Related Differences in Classroom Interactions*, New York, Academic Press, pp. 17–35.

Fennema E., P. Peterson, T.P. Carpenter and C.A. Lubinski: 1990, 'Teachers' attributions and beliefs about girls, boys, and mathematics', *Educational Studies in Mathematics* 21, 55–69.

Freire P.: 1974, *Pédagogie des opprimés*, Maspéro, Paris.

Gilligan C.: 1982, *In a Different Voice. Psychological Theory and Women's Development*, Cambridge, London, Harvard University Press.

Hall R. and B. Sandler: 1982, *The Classroom Climate: A Chilly One for Women?*, Association of American Colleges, Project on the Status and Education of Women. Washington, DC.

Hanna G.: 1989, 'Mathematics achievements of girls and boys in grade 8: results from twenty countries', *Educational Studies in Mathematics* 20, 225–232.

Holmes J. and E.L. Silverman: 1992, *J' ai des choses à dire…Écoutez-moi!*, Ottawa, Conseil consultatif canadien de la situation de la femme (also available in English).

IAEP – International Assessment of Educational Progress: 1992, *Évaluation internationale du rendement scolaire en mathématique et en sciences chez les élèves de 9 ans et de 13 ans.* Mars 1991. Rapport préliminaire.

Lafortune L.: 1989, *Quelles différences? Les femmes et l' enseignement des mathématiques*, Montréal, Remue-ménage.

Lafortune L. and H. Kayler, en collaboration avec M. Barrette, R. Caron, L. Paquin and Solar C.: 1992, *Les femmes font des maths*, Montréal, Remue-ménage.

Leder G.C.: 1990a, 'Gender differences in mathematics: an overview', in E. Fennema and G. Leder, eds, *Mathematics and Gender*, New York and London, Teachers College, Columbia University, pp. 10–26.

Leder G.C.: 1990b, 'Teacher/student interactions in the mathematics classroom: a different perspective', in E. Fennema and G. Leder, eds, *Mathematics and Gender*, New York London, Teachers College, Columbia University, pp. 149–168.

Leder G.C.: 1992, 'Mathematics and gender. changing perspectives', in Grouws D., ed., *Handbook of Research on Mathematics Teaching and Learning*, New York, Macmillan, pp. 597–622.

Lee L.: 1986, 'Des épouvantails qui effraient les femmes. Les mythes en science', in L. Goulet and L. Kurtzman, eds, *L'école des femmes*, Montréal, Groupe interdisciplinaire pour l'enseignement et la recherche féministes, Université du Québec a Montréal, pp. 87–100.

Lemoyne G.: 1989, 'Les enjeux intellectuels de l'apprentissage des mathématiques', in L. Lafortune, ed., *Quelles différences?*, Montréal, Remue-ménage, pp. 53–70.

Maher F.A.: 1987, 'Toward a Richer theory of feminist pedagogy: a comparison of "Liberation" and "Gender" models for teaching and learning', *Journal of Education* 169(3), 91–100.

Mura R.: 1986, 'Regards féministes sur la mathématique', *Resources for Feminist Research / Documentation sur la recherche féministe* 15(3), 59–61.

Mura R.: 1990, *Profession: Mathématicienne. Etude comparative des professeur-e-s en sciences mathématiques*, Cahiers de recherche du GREMF, Groupe de recherche multidisciplinaire féministe. Université Laval, Cahier 36, Québec.

Mura R., R. Cloutier and M. Kimball: 1986, 'Les filles et les sciences', in L. Lafortune, ed., *Femmes et mathématique*, Montréal, Remue-ménage, pp. 101–136.

Nemiroff G.H.: 1988, *Beyond 'Talking Heads': 'Toward an Empowering Pedagogy of Women's Studies*, Windsor, Communication présentée aux Sociétés savantes, Association canadienne des études sur les femmes/Canadian Women's Studies Association.

O'Brien M.: 1990, 'Political, ideology and patriarchal education', in F. Forman, M. O'Brien, J. Haddad, D. Hallman and P. Masters, *Féminism and Education*, Toronto, Ontario Institute for Studies in Education, Centre for Women's Studies in Education, pp. 3–26.

Reyes L.H., Stanic G.M. and Lappan V.: 1988, 'Gender and race equity in primary and middle school mathematics classrooms', *Arithmetic Teacher* 35(8), 46–48.

Sadker M. and D. Sadker: 1985, 'Sexism in the classroom', *Psychology Today* 19(3), 54–57.

Secada W.G.: 1992, 'Race, ethnicity, social class, language and achievement in mathematics', in D.A. Grouws, ed., *Handbook of Research on Mathematics Teaching and Learning*, New York, Macmillan, pp. 623–660.

Shrewsbury C.M.: 1987, 'What is feminist pedagogy?', *Women's Studies Quarterly* 15(3, 4), 6–14.

Solar C.: 1988, *Les connaissances liées la transformation du cadre de référence dans la démarche féministe*, PhD dissertation, Montréal, Université de Montréal.

Solar C.: 1992a, 'Dentelle de pédagogies féministes', *Revue canadienne de l' éducation / Canadian Journal of Education* 17(3), 264–285.

Solar C. ed.: 1992b, *Inequity in the Classroom*, Montreal, Office on the Status of Women, Concordia University.

Solar C. and L. Lafortune: 1994, *Des mathématiques autrement*, Montréal, Remue-ménage.

Thorne B.: 1984, 'Rethinking the way we teach', in K. Loring, *Feminist Pedagogy and the Learning Climate*, Proceedings of the 9th Annual GLCA Women's Studies Association, Ann Arbor, Great Lakes Colleges Association. Women's Studies Program.

Weiler K.: 1988, *Women Teaching for Change. Gender, Class and Power*, Massachussets, Critical Studies in Education Series, Bergin and Garvey Publishers.

Weiler K.: 1991, 'Freire and a feminist pedagogy of difference', *Harvard Educational Review* 61(4), 449–474.

Chapter 15

Inclusion in music in the primary classroom

Mary Kellett

Introduction

In this chapter, I argue that the emphasis on performance-related musical activities in many primary schools can be a principal barrier to inclusion. Equating musicality with an ability to sing well or play an instrument can lead to low self-esteem and exclusionary practices. Inclusion is about equal access to the curriculum for *all* pupils (Allan, 1999; Visser *et al.*, 2002). We are increasingly aware that pupils whose first language is not English cannot have equal access to the curriculum unless we make appropriate adaptations and provide the right level of support. We do not, as readily, make the connection that pupils who do not play a musical instrument or experience difficulties singing 'in tune' (although this is a subjective value judgement in itself) can be similarly excluded if music lessons are heavily oriented towards performance elements (Kellett, 2000a). This chapter examines a teaching approach that fosters an inclusive musical environment by concentrating on a relatively neglected area of the music curriculum – listening and appraising. The approach (Kellett, 2000b) creates an environment where pupils' skills emanate from personal constructs (Kelly, 1955) thereby acquiring an 'expert status' that avoids feelings of inadequacy which frequently characterise self-perception regarding music in children who do not play an instrument. It was found that raising self-perceived musicality in this way re-motivated disaffected pupils most at risk of exclusion from music. The teaching approach also demonstrates how scaffolding (Vygotsky, 1962) can be used in a practical way to enhance pupils' learning in music. The scaffolding is offered at an individual level so that *all* pupils can benefit in an inclusive, nurturing environment.

Barriers to musical learning

Barriers to musical learning include low self-esteem, disaffection, short concentration spans and difficulties in verbal expression. In the context of this chapter, self-esteem is based on Lawrence's (1988) view that low self-esteem can interfere with learning and lead to pupils avoiding activities they associate with low self-esteem. This is frequently the case in music lessons where pupils who perceive themselves as unmusical become disaffected and avoid engagement with musical activity whenever possible. Children can have high self-esteem in some areas and low self-esteem in others, and this appears to be particularly pertinent to the music curriculum.

Listening to music is an active, perceptual experience requiring sustained concentration. Some pupils' responses are underestimated because of poor concentration span rather than lack of musicality and much potential goes undetected. Moreover, some children only communicate a fraction of their response to music because of the limitations of their language skills. This is a disquieting thought when one considers how many judgements and assessments are based on verbal responses. Many of these judgements also rely on adult (mostly white, Western) norms. The approach described in the study given here uses non-verbal stimuli to maximise, as well as partially scaffold, the verbal response. It moves away from the idea that there is likely to be a correct or incorrect response and values the raw child response for its intrinsic merit as a personal construct, referenced neither to adult criteria, pre-determined culture, nor the constraints of verbal competence.

The relationship between music and emotional response

Theoretical frameworks underpinning the concept of personal constructs in music stretch back over several decades and to studies that first explored the relationship between music and emotional response (e.g. Sloboda, 1991). Gregory and Varney (1996), contributing to a long-running debate, invited pupils from European and Asian backgrounds to listen to a variety of musical extracts from Western Classical, New Age and Indian Classical music and choose appropriate adjectives to match the mood of the music. Their results suggested that affective response to music was determined more by cultural tradition than the inherent qualities of the music. Most research on music with young children uses the judgements of professional adult musicians to norm reference the child response. One of the few researchers who went some way towards valuing the child perspective was Ward (1984). Basing his work on Kelly's (1955) theory of Personal Constructs he measured musical response in 7-year-olds. Ward observed that children's verbal ability was an inadequate vehicle for their musical responses. Gilbert (1990) also examined the use of personal construct theory in her study of aesthetic development in music. She argued that response to music was dependent on replication theory and difficulties arose when the music was alien to the individual's experience. This has particular relevance to inclusive practices in the music classroom if cultural diversity is not acknowledged.

The study

The approach investigated ways in which 24 children (aged 6–8 years) respond to music, how they perceived themselves in relation to music, and how all of these factors affected their self-esteem regarding music. Initial measures of self-perceived musical skills and musical self-esteem were established for each pupil via orally administered self-assessments, adapted from Salmon (1995). Pupils were invited to put a mark on a horizontal line with 'not at all musical' at one end and 'very musical' at the other. These same assessments were used again at the end of the study to discover whether pupils showed any noticeable increase or decrease in self-perceived musicality. Observation and interview data were also collected to triangulate the findings.

For a period of one term music lessons were focused on listening skills. Each child was given her or his own set of 'choice cards'. The first set had 8 different colours, the second 8 different patterns (computer generated) and the third 8 different textures (bubble wrap, cotton wool, velvet, suede leather, shiny paper, chiffon, sacking and sandpaper). The class was divided into small groups and each week pupils listened to an extract of music, approximately one minute long, taken from a multicultural range of musical styles, with various mixes of voices and instruments. It was hoped that this wide variety would give children maximum scope for individual interpretation and the employment of personal constructs. Pupils were invited to tick which colour, pattern and texture they thought best matched the music and then discuss, within their groups, the reasons for their choices.

Before each session, pupils were reminded that they were the experts and there were no 'right or wrong answers'. In the first three weeks, only the colours and patterns were used. Initially the choice cards were given to pupils separately and the musical extract played for each type of choice activity. Over the weeks, pupils became increasingly familiar with the patterns and colours and were able to choose from two sets of cards on one playing. The texture choice cards were introduced at Week 4. This was the least successful of the activities and received quite a mixed response. Some children disliked the tactile nature of the task, particularly if the texture was rough or prickly. In the plenary, it became apparent that some pupils were making choices based on the colour or pattern of the material rather than the texture of it.

As the weeks progressed, pupils became more experienced at concentrated listening and began to show signs of wanting to expand their repertoire. Several requests came from them to create their own pattern rather than use the prescribed ones. This was an unforeseen and encouraging development because it demonstrated that children were interacting positively with the activities and wanting to take ownership of them.

A development in listening skills gradually became apparent. Initially, choices and comments were based on an emotional response to the music, for example 'the music felt warm so I chose this warm yellowy colour like the sun'. However, over the weeks, comments and observations began to focus on technical aspects of the music such as structure, tempo and texture demonstrating sophisticated levels of concentrated listening.

> I chose this pattern because there are different patterns in it but also they repeat and there were lots of little different patterns in the music that kept repeating.

I chose this pattern because it felt like the music kept going round and round and starting again.

This one because there's the same spaces between the dots and it keeps to the same spaces and the music sort of kept to the same beat all the time like if they walk along they're always walking the same speed.

The music felt like there were a lot of instruments playing, sort of deep, so I chose brown because it was the deepest colour except for black but black would have been wrong because it's too sort of loud.

The music was going up and down and in and different instruments were coming in at different times.

Pupils used the visual imagery of the patterns in a scaffolding process (Vygotsky, 1962) to help recognise and interpret what their language skills alone could not communicate. Some subtle changes of group dynamics were observed. Children who were normally reluctant to share their opinions for fear of being sneered at by more dominant characters in the group became increasingly confident about speaking out. Judgements, and the reasons given for judgements, appeared to be valued equally by all pupils irrespective of who volunteered it. More articulate children did not dominate discussion in the same way as was noticeable in other class discussions. In summary,

- the judgement choice activities led to an increase in focused concentration;
- there was a positive response from pupils to the activities;
- pupil responses revealed a development in listening skills;
- the non-verbal tasks provided a scaffold for verbal responses; and
- group social interaction was seen to improve.

A large majority of the class registered an increase in self-perceived musical listening skills. Some of the highest increases were from pupils who did not play an instrument and had initially assessed their musicality as low. This appears to suggest that these activities might be particularly successful with children who are at greatest risk of exclusion from the musical environment.

One-to-one interviews were undertaken with each pupil at the end of term. The interviews were semi-structured and designed to maximise the spontaneity of the child responses. Without exception, all 24 pupils thought the activities were enjoyable and the word *fun* was used frequently to describe them. All the pupils said they thought they had got better at listening to music. All pupils thought that the activities should be used with other children and some were particularly keen that their younger siblings should have the opportunity. Many asked if they would be able to do the activities again. All but one of the pupils reported that the choosing activities had encouraged them to listen more carefully.

Pupil comments indicated that a high level of concentration and sophisticated listening skills were developing without them being consciously aware of it. For example one girl, aged seven said, 'when it had lots of instruments all doing different things, it was hard to hear them all'. Without realising it, she was demonstrating that she had listened hard enough to discern more than one instrument playing and furthermore that she could recognise that these were different instruments. Her frustration was born out of not being able to discriminate the timbres well enough.

An illustrative case study

Pupils who have low self-esteem in music *and* experience difficulties in learning are particularly at risk of musical exclusion. A summary of one individual case study follows to illustrate the positive outcomes that can be achieved by shifting the emphasis away from performance-based musical activities.

Zak, aged 8, was registered as having special needs for reading and writing but responded well in all other aspects of learning, particularly mathematics and science. Historically, he had a negative attitude towards music, particularly if it involved singing which he described as 'boring and a waste of space'. Zak's loud voice and unreliable pitch provoked unkind comments from his peers resulting in a further lowering of his confidence related to music. Sadly, he had come to equate pitch with musicality. His disaffection led to disruptive behaviour in music lessons.

Emphasising the 'no right or wrong answer' and the 'child as expert' prelude to the activities was helpful to Zak, as was the assurance that he would not be 'doing singing'. The idea of choosing patterns and colours to match to music was intriguing enough to hold his attention in the first session. He concentrated hard on listening to the extract and seemed to enjoy choosing what he thought was the best colour and pattern match. In the second session, the extract was some African tribal singing and I wondered if he would be switched off by the fact that it was *singing*. However, he applied himself with equal concentration and I was particularly encouraged by his willingness to talk about his choices, which by implication meant talking about the music – the *singing*.

Zak participated fully in all the group sessions, examples of some of his contributions include the following:

> I chose this colour because it's sort of like the sun rising early in the morning, a Mexicoey colour.

> The singing kept doing the same again and again and this pattern sort of goes round and round again and again.

Over the ten weeks, he grew more confident and more adventurous in his comments:

> I chose this one because it was like lots of different things happening in the music in different ways like these squiggles here pointing in all different directions.

He made no attempt to be disruptive and even asked for extracts to be repeated on some occasions. Zak's perception of his own musicality changed greatly during

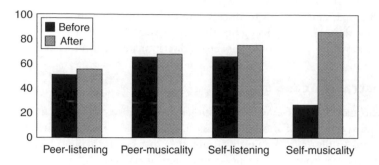

Figure 15.1 Zak's before and after self-assessment scores.

the course of the term project. Set out in Figure 15.1 are Zak's own self-assessment percentage scores taken at the beginning and end of the study. The four series represent,

- what Zak thinks his peers think about his listening skills;
- what Zak thinks his peers think about his musicality;
- Zak's own assessment of his listening skills;
- Zak's own assessment of his musicality.

The greater differentials were achieved in Zak's own judgements about himself and, most significantly, his own assessment of his musicality made a huge leap from 28 per cent to 86 per cent. Zak's post-study interview was also encouragingly positive:

T: How do you feel about yourself and music?
Z: I think I've got better at music. It's been fun choosing all the patterns and stuff. I think I'm good at that. I used to think I was rubbish at music 'cos I'm rubbish at singing and all that but I think I'm good at doing the patterns and stuff.
T: I've been wondering what you thought about the listening activities we've been doing in music?
Z: Good, yeah, not boring nor nothing.
T: What did you think about choosing the colours?
Z: Some of the yellows and light yellows were a bit boring but some of the blacks and dark yellows were quite good. It was sort of hard to match them to the music.
T: Did having to match them to the music make you listen harder to the music?
Z: Yes. Having to match the colours made me listen harder to the music. I prob'ly heard more things 'cos in some of the pieces there are a lot of things going on at the same time and if I just listened to it without having to choose something I might not hear them.
T: What did you think about the patterns?

Z: I liked them better. It was easier to choose. The music gave me ideas of what to choose in the patterns so I had to listen to the music before I could choose.

T: Do you think it would have been better if we'd just listened to the extracts of music without any choosing activities?

Z: If you'd played them without anything to look at and choose I might start looking around a bit and not listening as well.

T: What about the textures, the materials we felt?

Z: They were good fun, but sometimes hard to choose.

T: And when we did all three choosing activities together?

Z: Difficult but I quite liked trying to do it.

T: How did you feel about drawing your own pattern to match the music?

Z: It was hard to draw your own I preferred it when I could choose one of the patterns you gave us.

T: Do you think I should try these listening activities with other children when they come up into my class?

Z: Yeah, I think they'd like doing them. Will we get to do them again too?

T: Would you like to do them again?

Z: They were a good idea. I liked it. We should definitely do it again.

There is always the danger of bias and/or unwittingly leading children, eager to please their teacher, in an interview situation. However, Zak does not present as the kind of child who would typically try to please his teacher, especially regarding an area of the curriculum which he had previously disliked and the interview could have been a golden opportunity for him to 'rubbish' the sessions. The benefits for Zak from the inclusive approach adopted were as follows:

- his self-esteem related to music was raised as measured by his own self-assessment;
- his perception of music broadened from its former equation with singing;
- he developed better concentration skills;
- the inclusive participation element heightened his listening skills and reduced his inclination to be disruptive.

Conclusions

In the study reported here, the greatest progress appeared to be made by less 'musical' children and those whose self-esteem related to music was low. It suggests that children who fare poorly in performance-related tasks can still achieve highly in listening-based tasks. Pupils who are traditionally viewed as 'hard to include' because of perceived learning difficulties or emotional and behavioural difficulties can benefit from this kind of scaffolded, inclusive approach to music teaching. It raises questions such as, have we got the right balance between performance and listening in primary music teaching and are we doing enough to promote equal opportunities in our music classes or are lessons biased in favour of 'musical' children? Such questions need to be posed if we are to foster a genuinely inclusive music-learning environment in schools. This will help to achieve optimum musical development and avoid early disaffection of pupils who perceive themselves as 'unmusical', regarding music as something that only musicians do (Small, 1984).

References

Allan, J. (1999) *Actively Seeking Inclusion: Pupils with Special Needs in Mainstream Schools*, London: Falmer Press.

Gilbert, L. (1990) Aesthetic development in music: an experiment in the use of personal construct theory, *British Journal of Music*, 7, pp. 173–190.

Gregory, A.H. and Varney, N. (1996) Cross-cultural comparisons in the affective response to music, *Psychology of Music*, 24, pp. 49–52.

Kellett, M. (2000a) Motivating the musically disaffected, in S. Clipson-Boyles (ed.) *Putting Research into Practice in Primary Teaching and Learning*, London: David Fulton.

Kellett, M. (2000b) Raising musical self-esteem in the primary classroom: an exploratory study of young children's listening skills, *British Journal of Music Education*, 17(2), pp. 157–181.

Kelly, G. (1955) *The Psychology of Personal Constructs*, New York: Norton.

Lawrence, D. (1988) *Enhancing Self Esteem in the Classroom*, London: Chapman.

Salmon, P. (1995) *Psychology in the Classroom*, London: Cassell.

Sloboda, J.A. (1991) Musical structure and emotional response: some empirical findings, *Psychology of Music*, 19, pp. 110–120.

Small, C. (1984, 2nd edition), *Music, Society and Education*, London: Calder.

Visser, J. Cole, T. and Daniels, H. (2002) Inclusion for the difficult to include, *Support for Learning*, 17 (1), pp. 23–26.

Vygotsky, L. (1962) *Thought and Language* (transl. Haufmann and Vakar), Cambridge, MA: MIT Press.

Ward, D. (1984) 'Personal construct theory: its application to research in music education and therapy', in M. Ross (ed.) *Artstrip*, Vol. 14, Exeter: University of Exeter Publications, pp. 197–209.

Part V

Lessons from learners about inclusive curriculum and pedagogy

Chapter 16

Lessons from learners about inclusive curriculum and pedagogy

Cedric Cullingford

Introduction

Recent research, through a series of ingenious experiments, has once again demonstrated the acute intelligence of the very young. They show powers of reasoning, perception and observation that are powerful and impressive. This should give us even more reason to explore what goes on inside young people's minds. Despite this we rarely listen to pupils, let alone hear them and let alone act on what we hear.

Perhaps this is because of the strong hold of the developmental (even sentimental) tradition of progressivism, that only slowly do we become as clever and reasonable as we now are, and that the young who look so sweet and naïve must be as limited as they look! Despite this, there are signs that people increasingly acknowledge that what is beyond observation, what goes on inside the mind, is worth exploring. The research indicated here is based on a series of lengthy interviews in which pupils, with confidence and prowess, respond to the opportunity to be listened to and analyse the experiences consistently and acutely.

The institution of the school looks very different from the pupil's point of view. Whilst all teachers can remember parts of what it was like to experience the daily highs and lows of contacts with other people, we tend to think that such recall highlights extremes. We are so busy with the immediate pressures that we do not have time to take in what school is like for pupils. The experience is different. It is more intense. It is more centred on people, and it is a battle for inclusion in a place where different forms of exclusion prevail, exclusion from knowing, from relationships and from success.

The curriculum: formal and hidden

The notion of the 'hidden' curriculum is well established but the very phrase hints at how it is viewed, as out of sight and essentially obscure. It is also a hint at the way that pupils look at the workings of the school so differently, with alternative meanings at once simpler and more profound. The simpler significances that they see in school derive from the fact that there are strong themes and clear rituals on which the institution depends. Certain matters are always the same, the same routines and discipline, the same teacher behaviours. The individual teacher feels his or her performance fluctuates, from good lesson to bad. To pupils they are essentially the same. These very interpretations of the diurnal experience are profound because they form pupils' views of the world and of their place in it both at present and in the future. The effect of school is not so much a matter of knowledge as a matter of character, conduct and attitude.

Pupils understand very well the significance of different subjects and of the core curriculum, because they are often told about it. All teachers are presumed to be enthusiastic for their particular subject but to accept the centrality of those that dominate the prime times of the school day. To pupils, however, the essential task is to guess what it is the teachers want. This means learning the particular requirements, when to work by themselves and when to collaborate, when neatness or correctness are the most important things. A great deal of mental activity is given over to adapting to what is required, so the underlying purpose of a subject or of its excitement is rarely addressed. Instead, pupils feel they are submitting to requirements. They understand what are the 'main' subjects but do not know why.

> Probably Maths and English...I don't know really, they always sound as though, sort of like, and English are your main subjects and that...
>
> (male, year 10)

What pupils believe they learn

The sense of learning because this is what they are there for rather than for pleasure is ubiquitous and a central part of the school experience. The need to keep up with the rest of the class, without standing out, either for being clever or for being slow, means that the sense of the individual achievement is always a matter of comparison with others. It becomes a part of a necessary routine. One of the tensions in school is between competition and collaboration, between individual achievement and the pleasures and dangers of group work. The pupils like to work together, but realise that it is only in marginal subjects that they can do so. They see a distinction between what they ought to learn and what they actually do. When they expand on those skills that they have found most useful to have learned in school, they never mention Maths and English but focus on learning how to deal with other people, the social skills of working in groups and how to deal with teachers

> sort of how to stay calm...yeah. when teachers aggravate you. And how to communicate with others. And teachers that you don't like, stuff like that...
>
> (female)

Many of the most significant insights into the school experience lie below the surface of small differences. The routines are essentially the same. Thus the attitude towards the given subjects is that there is no choice but trying to work out how best to cope, how best to avoid drawing attention to yourself. Knowing when to talk and when not to is essential. Pupils might like group work and collaboration but official opportunities for conversation are few. The danger is that they might go against the central individual competition of school, pupils ranked against each other, schools ranked in league tables and teachers ranked by pupils and by OFSTED.

Schools as sites for teachers and discipline

The sense of uniformity is enshrined in the rules and regulations of school, the explicit and assumed etiquettes of behaviour. What happens privately, as in bullying and intense secret relationships, is one thing, but schools depend on the simplicities of boundaries.

> Its like you've got to be in boundaries. You're not allowed over that side of the school or down there . . . we're not allowed in the field and we're not allowed in the form rooms a lot of breaks . . .
>
> (female, year 10)

Rules mean what you are not allowed to do. There is little emphasis on good behaviour. Pupils do not report being asked to think out the consequences of actions. It is the boundaries that count, both physically and in terms of the curriculum, and it is these boundaries that they have to understand. Pupils feel they are expected to wait for orders – to sit and do nothing until the signal is given. They queue and are taught collective patience; all this is a matter of submitting to the rules, and understanding the implications and the boundaries.

The most important aspect of pupils guessing what is wanted is directed at individual teachers. What mood will they be in? How far can they go? Teachers are closely scrutinised not just for their vagaries but their differing expectations of discipline. Whilst they vary they also are seen to play a role. This is a matter of regret for pupils. They long to strike up a more personal relationship, to share knowledge or even a joke. They long for those moments that were afforded to them on school trips, when the imbalance of numbers and the constraints of time were no longer there. One of the regrets that pupils have when they think back on school is not getting to know teachers as people. At the same time, this is a regret that recognises that in the ways that schools operate there would be no time. Many of the comments that pupils make of their teachers are negative, because they find teachers negative or inconsistent.

> Now the teachers say that we should have respect for them teaching us and we should be listening to them. . . . they usually boss us around and when we do ask for help they don't tend to give you the help you need.
>
> (female, year 11)

The essential regret, rather than the criticism, is the fact that teachers do not really have time. They might either use humiliation and be very strict or, just as bad, be unable to keep control. The pupils see that this is not just a matter of personality but an aspect of the role. Whilst critical, they also understand teachers difficulties. They wish things could be different whilst complying to the realities.

This view of the teacher as carrying out a role which makes anonymous the individual and renders relationships strictly routine is part of the broadly simplified view of the experience of school in which conformity, acceptance of routine and the careful scrutiny of other people's behaviour makes every day's experience a familiar background to the minor excitements and tribulations of relationships with peers. This sense of the routine, however, also has important consequences. It gives an insight into the way in which society as a whole operates. It is a pattern of a social system that perpetuates itself, whether the consequences are beneficial or not.

The deep experience of school

There are three distinct aspects of the social system as presented through the experience of school that pupils detect. The first is the view of teachers and themselves as being in a distinct hierarchy. Pupils are well aware of who has power and sometimes this can be in unexpected places as when a particular pupil knows how to get the better of a teacher who is a little frightened or at a loss. Usually, however, the teachers are observed as having a deferential attitude towards the heads of department and through them, the head teacher. But it goes further than this. Pupils observe the power of governors and, most significant, if more occasional, the impact of inspectors. Pupils learn the way in which power is dealt and authority distributed, especially as it is directed against them. At the same time they live out the hierarchies of age and influence amongst themselves.

The second message that is acquired by pupils is about the importance of the individual looking after him or her self. The perpetual cries of unfairness are a manifestation of this. Schools are places where the individual is constantly competing, for success or for recognition. Far from the pleasure of collaboration, schools teach the importance of each one being 'on your own'. The tests constantly remind the pupils of the higher purpose of the curriculum, not to acquire understanding but prove you are better than others. All leads towards the ultimate examinations. The official part of school contrasts with the pleasures of relationships.

> sometimes I'm not alright and I can't be bothered to come because of all the tests that we are doing and that. Waste of time. My friends, I get on with my friends.
>
> (female, year 10)

The school as a social centre is juxtaposed to the concentration on the exposure of the individual.

The pupils learn that there is a balance between all the indulgences and loyalties of ties of friendship and the sharing of events, and the need to get ahead, to be quite strict about whom it is profitable to know and who might distract too much time from work, or who might give you a bad reputation. The pleasure of friendship is mitigated by the utility of networking, again reflecting a view of society.

The third influential part of school lies in the experience of bullying, in the realisation that people can be hurtful. The word 'bullying' here is used in its broadest sense, including the inadvertent, in being teased. It is the sense of the individuals being 'picked on'. Even the simple exclusion from activity can be felt as a form of bullying. Such feelings routinely involve the teachers. Being 'picked on' includes the imposing of discipline and the exposure of not being clever, for not getting the right answer in class.

> because you can't do anything without being tagged by anyone. If you go one way you get done. If you go around the front of the school you get done. If you go around the back you get done ...
>
> (male, year 10)

There are many opportunities for the feeling of humiliation in class. Simply not knowing the right answer to the closed question can be embarrassing. Such scenes that produce these outcomes can be purely inadvertent as often as they are deliberate, but the pupils' feelings are similar.

School and society: inclusion and exclusion

Schools therefore give the feeling that despite the occasional pleasures, gatherings of people will inevitably lead to difficulties, to teasing, to arguments, to incipient cruelty. One of the reasons for this is the pressure to conform. Anyone who stands out as different, more difficult, less clever, physically noticeable, is liable to be 'picked on'.

> Anybody that is different, really just because ... don't know, I'm not a swot, not like that at all really ... just because I'll sit down and I'll get on with my work 'Oh. You're a swot'. I'm, like 'Get lost: leave me alone.' They call me 'freak and I'm not a freak at all ...
>
> (female, year 11)

In these circumstances inclusion becomes much more difficult, and means the concerted effort by a school to convey different attitudes. The problem is that these consistent voices of pupils expressing what it is like for them are rarely listened to.

The three aspects of school that mould a sense of the way in which society works are those of hierarchy and power, the need to look after yourself by being astute in conformity and the sense of a constant threat of being hurt. The messages of school go beyond the ways in which pupils adapt to the immediate circumstances and form a more profound impression of life. The way in which the pedagogy works creates a distinct view both of the curriculum and of inclusion. Pupils' forensic analysis puts together a number of insights and draws inevitable conclusions.

These conclusions might be inadvertent but they are also very different from the official view of schooling, and the basis of policy. We know the rhetoric of skills and employability, of targets and outcomes. The pupils hear this but interpret it somewhat differently. The skills they know they are supposed to acquire are core skills, and they know they are important because they are told that employers demand them and they must have qualifications. Privately they find other skills for more relevant, like social skills. They realise that employability is significant; it is for that reason that they continue with school, seeing jobs as the whole purpose of school, as if there were nothing else, apart from 'standing up for your self'. They know targets, but presume these are for the purpose of government and competition, and that they, as pupils, are just ciphers.

Pupils' perceptions of policy

The difference between the official view of the curriculum and the purpose of school and the pupils' experience can be summarised through the example of inspection. Accountability, the close scrutiny of schools and teachers, 'named and shamed', is a central tenet of educational policy. Ofsted inspections are carried out at regular intervals to ensure that standards are improved and that the pupils acquire their entitlement to the national curriculum, and achieve the targets that will enable them to prosper. The idea of the school in this vision is clear; to maintain discipline, to check that teachers are working well with clear goals, that the curriculum content is delivered and that parents and governors are satisfied. Pupils know the policy and are assumed to have an understanding of what is going on when the inspectors arrive for their week of scrutiny. Indeed, the pupils have been prepared for the event.

What then do the pupils learn from this? Very little attention is normally paid to their point of view. Indeed, there have been moves recently to involve them even more deeply in inspections. They can make their views of individual teachers known. After all they do know what is going on. The question is whether this is really listening to pupils? We know that when involving pupils in any decision, like the appointment of a new teacher, they demonstrate penetrating acuity. What then do they learn from inspections?

Pupils glean three clear messages from their observation of the process of inspection. When one reflects on what they say then it appears obvious as well as profound. The first insight is into the effects on the teachers themselves. The moment that the inspection is announced there is a change in the demeanour of staff, which pupils quickly pick up. Even in the best-regulated, most practised of schools, the levels of stress rise. The cases of nervous breakdown and resignations are many, but the stress affects all and is well documented. This change, however, is accompanied by less emotional manifestations. There are changes to lessons, more time spent in tidying up documentation, refurbishing furniture, painting walls, re-mounting artwork and rehearsals. During the inspection there might even be a temporary change of staff.

From what is so far observed, pupils have learned from the anguish of teachers that bullying is not confined to the playground but official policy, unquestioned in its perceived necessity, whatever the consequences. They also realise that what matters is not what actually has been happening but the way it is presented; they see the value of 'spin'. All schools learn how to manipulate inspections and pupils learn that this too is part of public life. The third aspect of what is learned is even more disturbing. It is the power and centrality of inspection. They see the effect they have on their teachers. They begin to think that even if teachers are cajoling them to do well it is only because of their fear of inspection. When pupils are asked if their teachers care for them, a kind of trust, that bound teachers and pupils together, they say 'not really: they only care how well we do because of the league tables'. The professional authority and the personal care are undermined. We therefore hear a quite different line of thought.

> I can understand the point of view that they can't be bothered with it anymore, because like I say most of the people were just turning up at school because they had to. . . . Teachers basically weren't there to teach them; they were just to look after them . . .
>
> (male)

The saddest consequence of what pupils learn from inspection is the disenfranchisement of mutual trust. This is also the consequence of the routines that teachers have to follow, the set curriculum and the dictating of teaching styles. Whilst teachers might be uncomfortable with their lack of professional freedom, pupils are far more acerbic about it.

The purposes of school

The interplay between official policy, and its intentions on pedagogy and the curriculum, and the pupil's perception of school can be seen in the different interpretations of the purpose of schools. Sometimes they overlap, unintentionally, and sometimes they are profoundly different. On one matter there is agreement. Pupils assume right from the beginning that the purpose of schooling is to prepare themselves for employment. The idea of pleasure in learning, or in the moral or cultural benefits of education does not feature. Primary school children have a sense of constant preparation for the next more serious stages, and the outcome is explicit for them.

> If I don't go to school I'd know nothing and wouldn't be able to get a job or nothing . . . If you didn't go to school you wouldn't have no GCSEs and you wouldn't ever get a job nowhere.
>
> (boy, year 6)

> If you want to get a good job you've got to really work hard at the comp. that's the kind of second step to being an adult and just before you finish they tell you what job you're qualified for...
>
> (girl, year 6)

Whilst some of the details might not be accurate the sense that they are on a rite of passage leading to employability is a message that is close to that of the government, even if surprisingly deeply inculcated from the start.

If getting jobs is the underlying purpose of school, the skills of employability are not what pupils actually feel they are learning. They acknowledge that they have acquired a certain extra prowess at something like computing, even if they learn more at home, and they all have at least a favourite subject that they have enjoyed. The favourite subject is however almost never one of those deemed to be important. It is one that presents other aspects of school life, its pleasure in relationships. The two sides of school, formal learning and personal communication, are occasionally brought together. The subjects that are most enjoyed and most highly rated as giving them useful skills are those which allow a certain amount of collaboration or dialogue, like Art, or games, or music. Pupils point out that it is in these subjects that they learn to get on with others. Whilst the official purpose of school and the official curriculum is important, pupils actually say that what they learn is something different.

Social skills

The most significant skill is perceived to be social. The most testing social skill of all is deemed to be dealing with teachers. This might not be the official version of pedagogy but pupils are not only learning how to guess what teachers want and learning how to adapt but are imbibing insights into psychological behaviour. They might want to have more opportunities for personal dialogue than they get, but when the role itself becomes personal, this is another matter.

> He's always picking on other children in our class and its not fair on them, and you never know who he's going to pick on next. He did it to my friend the other day and she burst out crying 'cos she did her best, it took her half an hour to do her story the other day and he said that it really was horrible and she might have to do it again and she burst out crying and then in the end he tried to be all nice to her and as if he hadn't done it. I think he was trying to stop her telling people.
>
> (girl, year 6)

Examples such as this abound, even if this particular one is more extreme. Pupils observe the teachers' styles and react to them. They do not need such large-scale changes of mood to feel that they are 'picked on' or their work criticised as not meeting requirements. They learn, however, to adapt.

Social learning, including relationships with teachers, is a key element in the experience of school, adapting to different groups, both formal and informal. What is to teachers a style of organising, or the most efficient use of available resources for the sake of clear outcomes is, for pupils, the heart of the matter itself. What they are ostensibly doing seems to them of less importance. The formal curriculum is for pupils very often a matter of routine and nothing is more readily associated with the demands of school – 'do it again' – than Maths and English. When pupils are asked what they are learning they do not readily extract anything new, exciting or profound because what they are conscious of are the work sheets, the exercises and the repetitive tasks. The central concern is to do these set tasks neatly, efficiently and quickly.

> I get fed up with English sometimes because we do English exercises and they are mostly all the same because they give you a paragraph of writing and you have to answer questions on it and we do that twice a week and it's just because it's a bit boring.
>
> (girl, year 6)

Pupils do not easily see the purpose of many of the tasks that they undergo. They are very aware of the differences between the pleasures of experiment and creativity – again a case of discussion and group work – and the routines of set tasks. These can be boring and meaningless and, if difficult, cause barriers to learning

> I'm just getting a bit worried at the Maths. It's the only subject I worry about. It's my long division I get stuck on. I have to sit there and get worried and then I start shaking all over.
>
> (boy, year 6)

Schools are not associated with hours of pleasure. There are times during the course of the day when there are moments of excitement, a conversation or a breakthrough in understanding. For the most part school is an experience of vast tracts of time in which very little happens, interspersed with occasions of trauma.

What pupils would like from teachers

From the point of view of teachers, such a sense of routine might seem disappointing but it is an inevitable consequence of keeping order in such circumstances. Routine and its effects are a necessity and accepted as such. The way in which pupils interpret school as something imposed on them, to which they have to submit, causes problems for teachers. The fact that the way in which the national curriculum and the inspection system operates causes a rift between pupils and teachers is also unhelpful, especially as the pupils as well as the teachers would really appreciate having closer personal relationships. The regrets that pupils express about school are partly to do with the inevitably late realisation that they missed opportunities. This says something about the way the curriculum is presented. It is only later that pupils realise that if they had taken things more seriously or with more enthusiasm they could have learned more, and with greater pleasure. But this is not part of the ethos of school, either in terms of organisation, the core curriculum, or the attitudes of children and young people. There is a great sense of regret, but not as great as that which surrounds pupils' attitudes to their teachers. They are critical but they are critical of the circumstances and the role. They long for the opportunity to share knowledge rather than have it imposed on them.

Such a learning relationship, the sharing of curiosity, is at the heart of ideas of inclusion. Unfortunately the experience pupils have of school is of a series of complex exclusions: which works at two levels. The first is exclusion from knowledge. This is ironic, since the curriculum is supposed to cover everything. The way it is presented, however, is as a series of exclusions. The pupils see it as a guessing game, as trying to work out what is wanted. They associate it as knowledge on which they will be tested, as knowledge for the sake of testing. If the formal part of schooling is not inclusive, the various relationships and groups, with herd instincts and the imposition of hierarchies, also lends itself to the experience of a constant series of exclusions, from secrets and games as well as from knowledge. Those who do not conform to the most common of standards are vulnerable.

Conclusions

The curriculum, as presented, is a monumental edifice, imposing, arcane and impersonal. Seen as having an underlying purpose of preparation for jobs, and experienced as a series of tests, it is associated with routine. If pupils had their way the curriculum would be very different. They come to school well primed with curiosity and asking the most important questions that surround the puzzlement of life; why do people behave as they do? For some reason, this thirst for answers is denied and ignored. As teachers we are always puzzled by people and institutions, by individual and collective behaviour but we forget that curiosity is what drives children. If they had their way the curriculum would start with the 'big questions – why are people as they are – since these are the ones that are asked from birth, and explore the way that people have tried to answer it. In the broadest sense the idea of 'citizenship' would come first rather than being a reluctant afterthought. Thus stories and their meanings, rather than the skills of reading, would be central, together with art, music and history, all those subjects that people continue secretly to prefer.

If we understood the pupil's point of view we could construct a curriculum which would be very successful in developing all necessary skills as well as understanding. It would relate to the real world and therefore embrace science, engineering and maths. And yet, for some reason, we start with a misconception about young children. We have not yet learned to listen to their voices, let alone hear them. Perhaps we do not like the implications of what they are trying to tell us.

Further reading

See Cullingford, C. The Inner World of the School, Cassell and Cullingford, C. *The Best Years of Their Lives? Pupils' Experience of School.* Kogan Page.

Chapter 17

One teacher and a class of school students

The culture of the mathematics classroom and its construction

Corinne Angier and Hilary Povey

Introduction

Our story here is of the attempt by one teacher (Corinne) and a class of school students to reflect on the culture of their mathematics classroom and its construction. By studying one context in some detail and by listening carefully to the participants within it, our intention is to offer a contribution to an understanding of some of the ways in which the culture of mathematics classrooms may be poorly articulated with the views and needs of young people and with their locations within the wider cultures of contemporary life. In doing this, we seek to hold together curriculum, pedagogy, epistemology and classroom practices and relationships.

By the term culture, we signify the set of knowledges, subjectivities, conceptions and views of the world, values and social practices that constitute a particular social space. We understand the culture of a classroom not as fixed but as shifting, contested and problematic: it will vary, perhaps considerably, over time, from day to day and even from moment to moment. Equally, each participant will experience that culture differently, reflecting each individual's identities and positioning. We do not offer this story as a 'typical' or 'representative' case (Stake, 1972) but rather have 'shifted the locus of responsibility for generalisations' (Macdonald, 1977, p. 196) to the reader: the account is tested by the extent to which it is 'recognised' (Walkerdine, 1990, p. 196) and can be used by the reader to re-inspect experience.

A subsidiary aim of this chapter and the research upon which it is based is to contribute to the development of a more democratic research paradigm and of democratic praxis. This includes trying to renegotiate both the boundaries between participants and the sites where theory is developed. Further, we seek to join a developing tradition (e.g. Kinder *et al.*, 1996) in which an attempt is made to listen carefully to what school students have to say about their views and experiences and explicitly to invite them to share in the construction of knowledge about schooling. We believe that 'what pupils say about teaching and schooling is not only worth listening to but provides an important – perhaps the most important – foundation for thinking about ways of improving schools' (Rudduck *et al.*, 1996, p. 1). There are pragmatic, equity related and philosophical reasons for such research. Naturally, students, phenomenologically speaking, have privileged access to their own interpretations of their lives in school: it seems likely to be profitable therefore for educators to listen to 'students' critical perspectives, which might cause [us] to modify how [we] approach curriculum, pedagogy, and other school practices' (Nieto, 1994, p. 397f).

> What researchers – and teachers who have ventured down this route – have found ... is that young people are observant, are often capable of analytic and constructive comment, and usually respond well to the responsibility, seriously entrusted to them, of helping to identify aspects of schooling that get in the way of their learning.
>
> (Rudduck et al., 1996, p. 8)

Moreover, it conforms to the demands of social justice in both educational practice and in educational research that the students' voices are awarded a key status in school-based enquiry.

As we listened to the accumulating evidence from the class, we became convinced that the mathematics curriculum as mediated by the texts used (on the one hand) and the educational relationships lived out in the mathematics classroom on the other are fundamentally intertwined in forming and framing that cultural space. We have employed the metaphor of *spaciousness* to evoke a classroom culture which the students' responses give reason to believe was attractive to them and adapted to their needs. What we mean by *spacious* mathematics and *spacious* classroom relationships will become clear as the story of the classroom develops. The students' perspectives reported upon in this chapter provide the basis for a reappraisal and renegotiation of what it means to be a 'proper teacher'.

> Pupils are part of society, and attitudes change as the social climate changes. Some current deviant behaviour may simply be an expression of their impacting against an outmoded role – that of the 'proper teacher' – founded on a system of honour and allegiance to inhuman structures and traditions. Teachers who resist this role ... recognise the dignity of pupils, rather than seeing them as faceless occupants of roles themselves.
>
> (Sikes et al., 1985, p. 242f)

We offer evidence that these school students wished for different and more democratic classrooms. They linked (mis)behaviour with teacher–student relationships and valued the informal and the personal. Equally, in the context of the classroom relationships they valued, their talk about the nature of mathematics is democratic in tone: they speak about the subject as though they own it.

The research context

The classroom upon which we draw contained a 'top set' of about 30 students during their ninth, tenth and eleventh years of schooling (beginning when the students were thirteen and finishing as they became 16 years old). In writing this chapter we draw on the students' responses to their experiences using five sources of data:

- questionnaires completed by the whole class during year 10;
- group interviews, partially transcribed, with Hilary during their last full term in school: three separate groups were interviewed comprising one group of boys, one group of girls and one mixed group and including 18 students altogether;
- conversations with Corinne in the last weeks of schooling including at a residential revision weekend;
- written responses to questions from Corinne produced just after they had left;
- and interviews with Corinne in the month that followed.

Some of the comments are anonymous because students were given the option of naming themselves on written feedback. The students, almost entirely, come from white, working-class backgrounds, they live in a northern conurbation in England and are not closely affiliated with dominant groups. The school has no post-16 provision and students' academic aspirations rarely extend to higher education.

During year 9, Corinne had a given syllabus in the form of a list of topics to be covered but was able to work with the students in the ways and using the materials that she deemed appropriate. In the following year, the teaching in the department was severely constrained and they were required to implement a specific textbook-based curriculum. The textbook was accompanied by written lesson plans and statements of pedagogy: all the resources were provided and the teacher was conceptualised as simply required to deliver the predetermined curriculum package. As this tenth year drew to a close, although she was not following the new approach as closely as had been intended, Corinne became concerned about the effect that this was having on the students' relationship to mathematics and to each other: for the rest of her time with the class, during year 11, she reverted as much as she dared to the approach she had used in year 9. The interviews and writing at the end of year 11 indicated that for the students the curriculum they followed was much less dichotomous than it was for the teacher.

Spacious mathematics

[...] Over the last two decades at least, much has been written about the need for mathematics teaching to address meaning making by students rather than the proficient acquisition of procedural knowledge. Nevertheless, the dominant style in mathematics teaching continues to reinforce a procedural approach (Gregg, 1995; Brown, 1996, p. 206) and this can be seen reflected in the mathematics texts most commonly used in secondary schools in England and Wales.

When the emphasis is on procedural acquisition, students are presented with large numbers of closed questions, each similarly styled to the one before. The students' task is to reproduce set procedures just delineated. Each topic is split into its constituent parts and then split again and again so that it is presented in very small pieces. The exercises reinforce each small piece and gradually build them back together. The assumption is that students gradually build an understanding by mastering each constituent bit. The writer of the book decides what a bit is and in what order they should be digested. But, whereas for the textbook writer and the mathematics teacher those little bits can be reassembled into a coherent whole or, indeed, may never really depart from their place within that mathematical framework, typically for the mathematics student they remain isolated fragments. In her extended case study of two secondary schools, Jo Boaler (1997) found that 'It was the transmission of closed pieces of knowledge that formed the basis of the students' disaffection, misunderstandings and underachievement' (p. 145). In such a regime, given a larger problem requiring mathematical decision making and problem solving, the teacher will narrow the scope of the question and refocus attention down until no mathematical thinking is required, the final question often simply being a choice between (few) alternatives. The teachers 'seem to fracture the problems in order to help the students get answers' (Boaler, 1996, p. 23) and even then may either invoke memory or point to extraneous clues in pursuit of the right answer. Corinne found worry amongst her students about the procedural approach where simply achieving right answers is regarded as success.

Kathryn: All the time [when] I'm doing it out of the textbooks, I'm trying to... I know I should be doing it and the answers all right so I'll write it but never mind I'll revise it when it comes... but you never get round to it.

Frances: You don't know why you're doing it sometimes.

Spacious mathematics on the other hand is concerned to embrace large problems. Activities that are mathematically rich are more likely to generate the temporal and intellectual space within which students and teachers can make links both within mathematics and between mathematics and other experiences. In making such links mathematical meaning is constructed. Mathematics then has the room to grow as an open and creative subject not restricted to a rule-bound set of procedures.

Responses indicated that for this group of students the mathematics teachers' choice for the classroom also needs to have room to carry the students' interests if it is going to be a vehicle for effective learning. About a quarter of the students interviewed referred to what they felt to be the use value of mathematics. They felt that what happened in the classroom should relate to their present and future needs outside but they were prepared to give this a wide interpretation.

If you are learning something which is real there is a point in learning it... She makes all maths relevant... when we were doing statistics we used political stuff... to understand not only the data but the relevance it had... and how you could manipulate it... and that were much better than doing just made up statistics... it gives you an understanding of the world as well as maths.

(James)

The curriculum also needs to be large enough to carry the teacher's enthusiasms. All the students interviewed knew that Corinne found passionate enjoyment in the subject:

> She loves doing triangles!   (Dan)

> She loves it ... she's right interested in it   (Frances)

and although they smiled and indicated that they found this strange, they knew it was a key element in their own learning.

> ... you made learning very fun and enjoyable for me ... your mad method of teaching its brilliant! You bring maths to life.   (Dean)

> Our maths classes were fun and fantastic and they made you learn better.   (Sue)

> She makes it a lot more enjoyable. She makes it right funny. You don't actually dread going to a maths lesson.   (Rebecca)

Spacious teaching and learning

We now want to extend our metaphor to connect spacious mathematics to spacious educational relationships. We have called them spacious because we believe they need to be large enough to include more of the person than classroom relationships have traditionally allowed. They also offer the 'space' to be naughty, to make mistakes and to recognise and rectify them, to move one's elbows.

When asked to write about or discuss their mathematical learning, the students referred again and again to the social element in their learning. It mattered who the teacher was, it mattered who was in the group, it mattered how the classes was organised. These were the factors that they felt determined how they got on in lessons.

> I worked well because of the specialist care given to me by you. For example if I was not getting many questions correct, my confidence was boosted by you which helps. You learn if you are confident.
>
> (John)

This was a high-achieving, hard-working boy. It is interesting that he did not write 'when I got it wrong you showed me how to do it'. Instead he suggested that there was a very personal element in learning; how he felt about himself would determine whether he sorted out the mathematics. Corinne spent a great deal of time talking with these students. Her approach was usually the same: she tried to give them a sense of how important they were and how much it mattered that they came to school and got as much as they could out of it. They perceived their difficulties as always springing from the same source: difficult relationships, either at home or with peers or with teachers. What they wanted was some space to air their concerns without being judged or derided.

Consider the case of Katrina. Katrina was very unsettled at the beginning of year 9 and her work was really poor. Corinne had been told that she was one of the strongest mathematicians in the year and should be aiming for the highest tier of the school leaving examination. After lots of lessons in which Corinne chivvied her whilst she resolutely wasted time and after lots of moans about incomplete home-work and so on, Corinne finally sat down to talk with her. Corinne suggested that Katrina did not like the way Corinne taught and that she was disappointed that Corinne was taking the 'top set'. Katrina was so relieved that she went on to explain how much she had liked her previous teachers and how hard she had worked for her. They agreed that Katrina had every right to be angry. Mathematics was clearly an important subject for her. Corinne said she hoped Katrina would not take her anger out on herself: Corinne could cope with her not liking the way the lessons were run but could not accept her underachievement. It was a tuning point.

Corinne talked to her about this after she had left.

Corinne: Do you remember back now to the beginning of year 9 when you first came into my class...Do you remember how you felt...?
Katrina: ...different...different people as well...when you first start working with someone you've got to learn how they work rather than how you've been taught before but...you get used to it it's all right
Corinne: I remember you being fed up...disappointed...
Katrina: I'd got used to [working with the old teacher]...but after three years of being taught by you I got used to you as well...It's not just the teacher, it's the room as well...if you are sat in a room which is bright and lively, where you can talk...

She explained that you needed to be allowed to talk so that you could get to know people and hence work with them. She wrote:

> It took a long time to get everyone situated so the class worked efficiently. We all got on with you because you were sympathetic about what we were all going through.

Katrina also provided us with a powerful metaphor of the family:

> We all felt like a family in maths. Does that make sense? Even if we weren't always sending out brotherly/sisterly vibes. Well we got used to each other... so we all worked...We all knew how to work with each other...if like there were a new person come into the group they wouldn't know what we were like...because we were in groups we worked together...it was a big group... more like a neighbourhood with loads of different houses.

Jere Confrey (1995) has argued for a reconsideration of the role of emotion in cognitive development (p. 38), urging the need for a reproductive model which draws on the metaphor of parent–child communication: then 'the emotional character of these exchanges would not be stripped away nor be judged secondary to cognitive development' (p. 39). There is a need to recognise that within 'mathematics education...both facilitating and debilitating emotions play a significant role in learning, and...the emotional qualities of classroom interactions will exert a significant influence on what is learned' (p. 39).

We have termed the relationships which Corinne and her students were striving towards as spacious because we believe there needs to be room for students to conduct experiments in the process of becoming the persons they are going to be, to behave at times in ways that are problematic. Spacious educational relationships permit this because they are open rather than tightly controlled.

> I think when everyone is strict and sort of tense in a way it just puts you off because it gets you all psyched up...I always remember with the sewing group with Miss Taylor that was always a really strict atmosphere and I'd panic and do things wrong all the time...I don't think it really matters just so long as everybody's working...and I think there were always an element of people messing around but everyone were working at the same time and it was more relaxed so everyone went off and did their work and there was always someone coming up with a joke which sort of made you continue because you'd had a tiny break in a way. If it's ordered the classroom then no one really wants to work, they are just doing it because they have to and then they are not learning anything.
>
> (Sue)

This need for informality and the willingness to tolerate minor misdemeanours was expressed by several of the students and provoked no dissent from the other. We have heard it said that students like strict teachers: we did not find this echoed by these students.

Connecting the metaphor

In the previous section, we have sketched out spacious mathematics and spacious educational relationships: we now attempt to show how they are connected. The textbook curriculum which was imposed on Corinne's classes was both tightly controlled and exemplified an atomised approach to learning being based on small steps reinforced by large numbers of essentially similar examples. After the students had spent some time working from the textbooks, Corinne invited comment.

> [The worst thing is] when I find it hard understanding something and everybody else seems to understand. Or when people sit there reading their answer to questions and I'm sitting there confused.
>
> (Sally)

> I might not understanding something and everybody may be miles ahead. [With the textbooks there's] too much to do especially if you're doing them wrong but think you're correct.
>
> (John)

These particular response made Corinne aware that a number of the students were convinced that everybody else was finding the work easy. The use of the textbooks was resulting in a separation of the class into isolated individuals. Each pupils was becoming unware of the rest of the room except for the purposes of negative comparison and anyone having difficulty automatically assumed they were the only one. The algorithmic style of teaching was chopping mathematics into pieces that made no sense and the classroom into a place of isolation and poor communication.

When the content of the curriculum is atomised, there is pressure for social relationships within the classroom to become atomised too. Only two situations were identified by Corinne's students as being times when they would work on their own. The first was if they had lots of little questions to do. (The second was if the work was 'one of their strengths' and they didn't need to seek help.) The suggestions is that if the task involves working non-contextualised algorithms, or if it is routine, the tendency is for the students to work alone. Lots of short questions promoted insecurity as the students lacked confidence in what they were doing. When these students were presented with a longer, harder problem, their response was to work together.

Many pupils referred to working in groups, all of them positively. Some of the comments related directly to the issue of confidence.

> Factors which helped me in maths were working through questions with the other people on my table ... because I felt more confident, if we were all doing the same it was probably right!
>
> (Amy)

Others focused on mutual support

> If you are helping each other you get more done.   (Matt)
>
> It's better working in a small group ... you make up for each other's faults.   (James)
>
> If you are working round a table you can get ... the best part of every-body ... you can get the work done ... because one person's good at something and they are not as good at something else one of the other people on the table might be stronger ... your strengths are put together.
>
> (Neil)

and the development of understanding.

> You get it explained more clearly [to each other].
> In maths I always liked to work in a group, you can try and work it out yourself and then compare answers and just talk about the problems.
>
> (Dean)
>
> Talking to other people helped me understanding.   (Louise)

It is worth pausing for a moment to reflect on the remarks made here by working-class boys: they do not conform to the current discourse of boys wanting and valuing an individualistic and competitive classroom environment (Grant, 1998, p. 6). Is this because that discourse is privileging the voices of some boys over others?

These students were making a connection between the organisation of the curriculum and classroom relationships: if the work is challenging and spacious, the students will work together and communicate their mathematical understanding.

> It's better working on a big problem...in a table, something that requires you to think...you can check it.   (James)

> One big problem you need a group but lots of little problems you can just do on your own.   (Neil)

The students described how they worked with Corinne and their shared purpose with her.

Matt: [Corinne thinks a good maths lesson is] when all the class is working together to try to solve a hard question and stuff.
Donna: She likes to get everybody involved.

What the students were experiencing had something in common with a 'local community of mathematical practice' (Winbourne and Watson, 1998, p. 183): the learners were seeing themselves as working together: functioning mathematically; and as engaged in a common activity with the teacher. One student, impervious to the teases he received, asked publicly if he could move back to sit with another boy 'because we've got this mathematical thing going between us'.

Epistemology

Spacious mathematics is an open and creative subject. [...]

Corinne had tried to make space to offer them a wide range of experiences and talked to them in all kinds of ways, allowing them as individuals to take what made sense to them and attempting to inculcate a recognition of and respect for diversity.

> In science you mix chemicals and get one result. In maths you use the same things a lot but always get different answers.   (Jane)

> Maths is also about understanding about how other people think and appreciating opinions.   (Katrina)

Katrina expanded on this later.

Katrina: Everyone's got a different...So everyone's got a different way of working. People might get to the same answer in the end but there are loads of ways you could do it.

Corinne: And that doesn't worry you?...I asked some of the year 11s who I haven't taught to write down what they found difficult about maths and some of them wrote that they didn't like the fact that there was more than one way of doing something, they found it unsettling.

Katrina: No it's interesting. Maths is about understanding methods, sequences and getting your head around different ways of thinking. I believe maths is different for every person. Mathematics is the strangest and probably one of the most important and interesting subjects I will ever learn.

Such understandings of the nature of mathematics impinge on ways of knowing (Ernest, 1991; Jungwirth, 1993; Povey, 1995; Johnston and Dunne, 1996). In a spacious classroom, there is room for students to have insights that the teacher doesn't have. Teachers can afford to make silly mistakes on the board and to encourage students to understand the human errors in published material too. When their answers did not match the textbook, the students became increasingly confident that they were right. One pupil even spotted an error in her trial examination. It must have taken a tremendous amount of personal authority to believe in her own mathematics under examination conditions. Teachers can seek out topics (probability is one such) where it is possible for the teacher to find herself saying 'Wow! I would not have done it your way, that is lovely, thank you for explaining it to me'. Algebraic manipulation can often be done in a variety of ways and it is wonderful to rub the teacher's working off the board and replace it with someone else's. Other times it may be a matter of communication and the teacher can stop the class and say, 'Someone has just expressed this idea really well. Listen.' In such an open and easy space, students can begin to build a sense of their own mathematical authority.

> She treats you as though you are like...not just a kid. If you say look this is wrong she'll listen to you. If you challenge her she will try and see it your way.   (Donna)

> She doesn't regard herself as higher.   (Neil)

> She's not bothered about being proven wrong. Most teachers hate being wrong...being proven wrong by students.   (Neil)

> It's more like a discussion...you can give answers and say what you think.   (Frances)

To be willing to stand corrected, what message does this give the pupils? It helps to validate an inclusive epistemology of mathematics which is person-related and nurturing of intuition and insight (Burton, 1995). It contains the message that the students' contributions are essential to the class, and that the mathematics is not wholly predetermined in a book or lesson plan but it happens then and there.

> If one enters the educational enterprise with arrogance one's own views of knowledge quickly overpower the insights of the children. When the classroom

norms are developed in such a way as to promote the exchange of student methods with mutual tolerance and respect, the children themselves become increasingly confident of their contributions and the system becomes self-reinforcing. In both peer relations and in adult-child interactions, the roles of expert, teacher, learner, and novice, are flexibly drawn.

(Confrey, 1995, p. 41)

This suggest an equality between teacher and learner, not an identity: it confronts us directly again with what it means to be a teacher.

Conclusion

We have attempted in this chapter to draw mathematics, classroom relationships and ways of knowing in an interactive circle, each dependent on each other and each mutually constructing and framing each other. We have used the words of students to indicate how mathematics, mathematics lessons and educational relationships might change better to meet their needs. We find, with others, that:

> . . . the conditions of learning that are common across secondary schools do not adequately take account of the social maturity of young people, nor of the tensions and pressures they feel as they struggle to reconcile the demands of their social and personal lives with the development of their identity as learners.

(Rudduck et al., 1996, p. 1)

Perhaps we need a very different model both for teachers and classroom dynamics. There is evidence that work out of school hours is more successful than work done during the normal school day. Many of the education action zones, the result of a recent UK initiative intended to combat underachievement, intend to focus on work in this penumbra around school rather than directly on the classroom. Is this a tacit admission that the traditional structure of the classroom is no longer viable? Many teachers will have often wondered why pupils can be so lovely and interesting at break or when you meet them out of a lesson but in the lesson they become difficult and unmanageable. A student in Corinne's school recently commented that he was fed up with the way some *teachers* were so different outside lessons. What are the factors that constrain and limit classroom cultures in the school day but disappear out of hours?

Participants in the classroom need to renegotiate, in ways that acknowledge the need to shift the distribution of power, the relationships upon which their classroom is predicated.

The maths teacher was more normal and more down on our level.

> I think it depends what kind of teacher you start off being, like if you're a right nice teacher like not wanting to be just loud and horrible then I think the students are all right with you.

(Jaqui)

The students have to be close enough to see teachers struggle in just the same way as they do, to see them transgress, at times breaking or disregarding rules. The classroom needs to be a place where it is possible to model the process of looking honestly at things that are going wrong with a belief that there are strategies to redeem them. It needs to be a place in which both students and teacher can take risks and where it is possible for trust to be betrayed but given again or earned back.

What we have attempted to indicate is that the curriculum and the perspective on the nature of mathematics which is embodies are not separable from the nature of the relationships amongst classroom participants. We do not believe that all teachers need to act in identical ways nor are we offering a blue print. Rather we suggest that, by listening to this particular group of young people, the need to pay attention to some key aspects of the cultural spaces that are mathematics classrooms is highlighted. We have attempted to portray one teacher and a mathematics class severing some of the cords of tradition that bind them, cords of institutional structures and relationships and of the mathematics curriculum. In this portrait, we discern a spacious curriculum inseparably intertwined with spacious relationships; we suggest that both allow room in which to grow a more democratic mathematics.

References

Boaler, J. (1996) Learning to lose in the mathematics classroom: a critique of traditional schooling practices in the UK, *Qualitative Studies in Education*, 9(1), pp. 17–33.

Boaler, J. (1997) *Experiencing School Mathematics: Teaching Styles, Sex and Setting* (Buckingham, Open University Press).

Brown, M. (1996) FIMS and SIMS: the first two IEA International Mathematics Surveys, *Assessment in Education,* 3(2), pp. 193–212.

Burton, L. (1995) Moving towards a feminist epistemology of mathematics, in: P. Rogers and G. Kaiser (Eds) (1995) *Equity in Mathematics Education: Influences of Feminism and Culture* (London, Falmer).

Confrey, J. (1995) A theory of intellectual development: part III, *For the Learning of Mathematics*, 15(2), pp. 36–45.

Ernest, P. (1991) *The Philosophy of Mathematics Education* (London, Falmer).

Grant, L. (1998) Girls on top form, *The Guardian*, 6 January 1998.

Gregg, J. (1995) The tensions and contradictions of the school mathematics tradition, *Journal for Research in Mathematics Education*, 26(5), pp. 442–466.

Johnston, J. and Dunne, M. (1996) Revealing assumptions: problematising research on gender and mathematics and science education, in: L.Y. Parker, L.E. Rennie and B. Fraser (Eds) *Gender, Science and Mathematics: Shortening the Shadow* (Dordrecht, Kluwer).

Jungwirth, H. (1993) Reflections on the formulations of research on women and mathematics, in: S. Restivo, J.P. Van Bendegem and R. Fischer (Eds) *Math Worlds: Philosophical and Social Studies of Mathematics and Mathematics Education* (Albany, SUNY Press).

Kinder, K., Wakefield, A. and Wilkin, A. (1996) *Talking Back: Pupil Views on Disaffection* (Slough, NFER).

Macdonald, B. (1977) The portrayal of persons as evaluation data, in: N. Norris (Ed.) *Safari Occassional Publications 4: Theory in Practice 2* (Norwich, Centre for Applied Research in Education, University of East Anglia).

Nieto, S. (1994) Lessons from students on creating a chance to dream, *Harvard Educational Review*, 64(4), pp. 392–426.

Povey, H. (1995) Ways of knowing of student and beginning mathematics teachers and their relevance to becoming a teacher working for change, unpublished PhD Thesis, Birmingham University.

Rudduck, J., Chaplain, R. and Wallace, G. (Eds) (1996) *School Improvement: What Can Pupils Tell Us?* (London, David Fulton).

Sikes, P., Measor, L. and Woods, P. (1985) *Teacher Careers: Crises and Continuities* (Lewes, Falmer).

Stake, R. (1972) The seven principal cardinals of educational evaluation, in: D. Hamilton, D. Jenkins, C. King, B. Macdonald and M. Parlett (Eds) (1977) *Beyond the Numbers Game: A Reader in Educational Evaluation* (London, Macmillan).

Walkerdine, V. (1990) *Schoolgirl Fictions* (London, Verso).

WinBourne, P. and Watson, A. (1998) Participating in learning mathematics through shared local practice. *Proceedings of 22nd Psychology of Mathematics Education (PME) Conference*, Stellenbosch, South Africa, July.

Chapter 18

Living and learning

The school experience of some young people with disabilities

Máirín Kenny, Eileen McNeela and Michael Shevlin

Introduction

The 'Hidden Voices' project was designed as a small-scale exploratory qualitative research survey. The key objective was 'to register the experience of young people with disabilities in second-level schools; so that it shapes developments in system policy and practice' (Kenny *et al.*, 2000). Particular attention was devoted to adopting research procedures that respected and validated the experiences of young people with disabilities (Atkinson and Williams, 1990; Beresford, 1997). The survey was conducted by means of semi-structured audio-taped group interviews with young disabled people. Potential participants were contacted via involved agencies, and sixteen young people agreed to participate. They were interviewed in three groups.

Group composition

Statistical information on people with physical and sensory disabilities in Ireland is not available (Department of Equality and Law Reform, 1996), but the population is known to be small, scattered and diverse in relation to criteria such as range of disabilities, socio-economic status, ethnic status, family factors, gender and urban/rural locational continuum. Therefore the concept of a 'representative' sample was considered to be problematic. For this reason, and given the scale of the project, the researchers opted for cluster sampling. Invitations to participate were issued via agencies involved with young disabled people.

A few points relating to the participants warrant consideration. All participants in this project were either already in or intended to enter third level or further education. Female participants outnumbered males by two to one – the reverse of the gender balance in the general population of people with disabilities. This may have been circumstantial, given the small scale of the survey. There were five rural and eleven urban participants. Participants' disabilities included significant and minor physical disabilities, sensory disabilities and specific learning difficulties.

Interview procedure

In order to maximise participants' involvement in the research, the interview process was conducted in two phases. The first-phase sessions were designed to gather participants' initial accounts of their experience; the second-phase sessions gave them an opportunity to reflect on their accounts and to critique the researchers' interim analysis of them. For the first-phase interviews, the researchers devised a topic checklist to ensure that issues identified in current literature would get aired at some stage in the group discussion; other issues were added in the course of the interview discussions. From initial analysis of transcripts of these discussions, an interim statement of findings and a modified checklist were drawn up, and these formed the framework for the second-phase interviews.

Interviews were taped, and tape transcripts were analysed using discourse analytic methods (Potter and Wetherell, 1989; van Dijk, 1998). Potter and Wetherell note that the essential criteria for discourse analysis procedures can be observed, whatever the level of detail. Discourse analysis focuses on.

> what is actually said or written, not some general idea that seems to be intended... Analysis is made up of two closely related phases. First the search for pattern in the data... Second, concern with function and consequence... [and] forming hypotheses about these.
>
> (Potter and Wetherell, 1989, p. 168)

Close textual readings of data yielded the findings presented here; review of the full data body in the light of these findings indicates that more detailed analysis would probably not generate further insights.

Official texts (Department of Education and Science documents on provision for students with disabilities) were examined in the light of participants' accounts, and the role of system context in shaping their experience was identified.

This study validates the argument for consulting students regarding their own education (Lewis and Lindsay, 2000). More importantly, the issue of returning findings to research participants is of ethical significance. An interview experience, and processing it, is part of the life of the participant and can have diverse knock-on effects. Each interview provided participants with a context wherein they could reflect on their experience, place it in a wider context, and develop their thinking about issues that affected them. The two-phase structure offered participants a chance to push their thinking further. They valued their role as research partners, and wanted to know if the report would promote effective inclusion policy and practice in the school system. That in turn highlights the ethical imperative of disseminating research findings, and promoting change in policy and provision to reflect these findings.

Data presentation

Where quotations are presented in sequence without intervening commentary, it should be assumed that each paragraph comes from a different speaker and a separate location in the discussion. Where a paragraph series is a string of conversational interactions, it is stated in the commentary, and speaker-labels S1, S2, etc. are used.

Key elements of participants' experience, particularly with regards to their school experience, were shared by all, whatever their disability/difficulty, gender or location. When a participant is speaking about how her/his experience is specifically related to one of these factors, this is named in the commentary, but otherwise quotations will not be 'tagged' with disability, gender or locational labels, in order to respect and highlight the commonality of experiences.

Curriculum access: a social and personal experience

In the following review of elements from participants' discussions of their experience in second-level schools, it will be clear that accessing the curriculum is at once a social and an academic achievement, that students' social lives intersect with, shape and are shaped by, 'school work'.

Students with disabilities are entitled to a normal school carrer – to real opportunities for full access to the curriculum, and full involvement in the social life of the school. A fundamental prerequisite for such access is the achievement of being present and engaged where the curriculum is being delivered and wider activities are being pursued. This physical presence and engagement prerequisite has a number of levels, the most obvious of which are choosing a school; accessing classrooms; using equipment; using transport. This sounds too obvious to need stating, but the experience of participants in this study revealed that the need to be present and engaged is far from fully appreciated in the delivery of school services.

School entry

For participants, social considerations were foremost in the first and most basic step involved in accessing any curriculum: choosing a second-level school to attend. The following speaker considered enrolling in a 'designated' school (a mainstream school resourced to support students with disabilities):

> I had one look at that [designated school] and I said no, that's no the school for me – I don't know, I didn't like the look of it. I had two cousins [and] all my friends going to my local school so basically I'd know everyone going there. It was only across the road from the primary school. No one was going [to the designated school], it would be like making new friends all over again. That's why I said no.

He named two grounds for opting for what might be termed 'complete normality': he disliked the distinctive 'look' of the designated school, and he far more lengthily depicted flow of his peers to the local school. As the next speaker said about her mainstream school:

> It was different, you know it was nice like, it was nice being with the normal crowd. Like to see what everybody else was doing.

Not all participants shunned support issues in their choice of school. The next speaker needed support to access the curriculum, and she valued it:

> I thought it was a good school, it catered for disabled people and it had two resource teachers and if you needed help with any subject they'd give you special tuition on a one to one basis.

But in some schools, dominant perceptions of disability could intervene to inhibit the struggle to maintain a discourse of normality:

> I was going to go to the carry-on from primary [second level school], but the headmistress wouldn't allow me to do home economics because I might spill something on someone, or biology because it was on the top floor. So I instantly removed myself from that school and went to another that would allow me to do the subjects I wanted.

This participant's ambitions collided with perceptions of her in the 'carry-on' school, where she found herself categorised entirely in terms of her disability. No one else mentioned point-of-entry barriers of this type, but as will be seen, many encountered them within the school.

It should be noted that school choice issues are engaged with during a transition between levels of formal education provision. So they can usually be kept private to the young person making the transition and to her/his guardians and chosen confidants. In this study, the transition in question is from primary to second level, but the same considerations pertained to experiences of transition to third level.

Getting around

However, once a participant was enrolled in a school, he or she encountered levels two and three of fundamental access to the curriculum. Level two is the achievement of getting into the classrooms or other physical spaces where the curriculum is delivered. Virtually all the participants with physical disabilities encountered difficulties accessing at least some teaching spaces: as one said, if classmates didn't carry him up to second-floor subject classrooms, he 'just didn't go to that class'. As his comment shows, social considerations were now embedded in peer relations, the struggle was engaged with under the gaze of classmates:

> The first year or so took me a while to settle in – there was one other person I think with a disability in the school so it was kind of difficult just to basically get around. And asking for help – I found that difficult, I didn't like asking the same person all the time and you know it was difficult finding somebody different every day or you know some people would make a fus over me and other people wouldn't think. It was a mixture of reactions.

In the absence of physical facilities to enable her to move independently around the school, this participant's disability became an omnipresent identity marker, skewing her social interactions. She cringes at the memory of its 'difficult...difficult...difficult' impact on her peer relations. The next speaker's comments show just how much some people with disabilities must bring their personal needs into the public domain:

> If I wanted to go to the toilet, the cubicles were very small; I had to go to the teachers' room. They knew and I had someone outside the door just in case they'd come. It wasn't too bad.

There may be a level of comfort with the facts of human biology in this image, but it primary depicts dependency-driven personal exposure, and as such it again indicates skewed peer relationships. The cumbersome arrangement must also limit access to classrooms and curricular activities. But as will be seen, this speaker's stoicism ('It wasn't too bad') was a feature of several participants' management strategies.

Happily, some participants went to schools that were well prepared to offer inclusion: flexibility in the built environment is possible, and as is clear in the next excerpt, access to the built environment and to be the built environment and to the academic process were often almost synonymous:

> There were girls in wheelchairs and they got round easily and everything was at a level where they could do everything.

The note of social independence is also clear: students who can 'get around easily' and 'do everything' are free to relate as equals with their peers, and can leave their disability in the background.

But the dominant experience was of oversight to the point of virtual denial of the disabled student's existence. The following statements are shocking indicators of how able-bodied students were learning to treat the variety of human capability.

> One girl had spina bifida. She couldn't handle the crowds; there were 1200 in the school. She left.
>
> I had to go up four flights of stairs to get to my classroom and I had to come down before the rest. If I came down at the same time as them they'd just push; once they basically knocked me down one flight.

In this physical/social context, it hardly needs saying that it would be hard for a disabled student to trust in the possibility of developing mutually respectful peer relations.

Actors or watchers

Level three in physical access is being able to use the 'tools' of school work, to the level of each student's personal competence. The diverse list of tools could be paralleled by an equally diverse list of supports and adaptations needed, so that students with disabilities have equitable access to use of home economics and science instruments, PE equipment and means of transport for field studies, as well as oral instructions (hearing aids or lip-reading) and written text (reading aids or substitutes) in almost all arenas. But focus on diversity of needs could distract from the commonality in the social impact of access difficulties. This level of access also became a disability-focused social issue, and talk of this impact was threaded through the accounts of all participants.

Teacher–student relations are not part of the topic of this chapter, but the following quote highlights the impact on peer relationships where supportive teachers are not resourced within overall school provision:

> A few teachers took me aside and went through things with me. But we had to work in the canteen; there was nowhere else. Classmates were astonished at me – spending time with a teacher! If they knew what they were talking about they'd know I needed the extra help.

The same pattern emerged often in their talk, of exclusion arising from lack of supports, and inclusion being only possible through friendly help. And in the following extracts from a participant with dyslexia, the helpful peer is an example of respectful discretion:

> She took the notes and I copied them. It was never discussed, it just happened. She was everything to me; she was a brilliant, brilliant friend.

She felt she could not turn to others in her class:

> I wouldn't ask for help. You might not be actually told you're stupid, but you're getting the hidden messages so you're not going to go 'I'm stupid, can I have help?' Like writing down homework from the blackboard was a nightmare for me – I always went home with half sentences or with the same sentences or with the same sentence down three times.

For people with physical disabilities, this struggle against slipping from actor to audience status in the learning situation is particularly clear in subjects that require physical work. Again, schools varied, as the following selection of remarks bears out:

> In science, using things on the bench, I just sat down and watched.
> We'd pair up and my partner used to do all the physical work. I just couldn't do it. I couldn't hold a glass of water.
> I think most of us were excluded especially in sports – the school wasn't equipped to cope. They tried, but the majority of times you had to stay out.
> I wasn't excluded from any sports. Actually they pushed me into things more than taking me out – 'you are going into this, no questions asked!'

But the dominant order can seem natural, even invisible, even to a student with a disability:

> The PE teacher let me watch. There was no discrimination.
> *[Q: Did they include exercises suited to you?]*
> Oh no, no. But he was very good.

Demonstrating how the two-phase interview structure opened possibilities for evaluation for participants, this speaker had come to a different viewpoint by the second interview:

> The nearest I got was inside the hall ... He could have let me referee, there's nothing wrong with my mouth.

So, school custom and practice could seem immutable, not just to able-bodied professionals and peers, but also to the very students who were disadvantaged by system rigidity. The hidden curriculum of the able-ist environment must be made visible and questionable to all, if the social fabric of the school is to become truly inclusive. This becomes even clearer in relation to extra-curricular outings.

> I would listen to them when they came back – 'You missed a great couple of days, we'd great fun'. Even sitting beside them hearing them laughing, it was laughing at something you didn't understand. I didn't like that.

This is a dramatic illustration of how true it is that 'to take no stand is to take a stand'. System oversight delivers a powerful lesson about the legitimacy of the status quo, to the included and the excluded alike.

The culture of silence about disabilities affected peer interactions: students with 'hidden' disabilities could encounter insensitivity born of general ignorance:

> [A] lad in my class said something about computers and I said I have a problem with remembering everything, I have to write them down ever since I got sick like. He said, 'Being sick wouldn't have anything to do with your brain', and I said, 'I think it might'. He didn't realise what is wrong with me. Which is hard to cope with in some ways. I feel like I have to put it out in the open when I see people.

It is difficult to see how this speaker could have avoided having to explain her disability, but the unthinking 'able-ist' social ethos of some second-level schools (as noted here) would both increase the need for her to explain, and discourage her from doing so.

To conclude this section, a return to what is generally assumed to be the core work of the school will serve to highlight what participants wanted from their second-level experience. System oversight and priorities lead to escalating stress:

> In second level it was stress just to get the academic first, to be the same as everyone else. Then it started to be the stress – to stop you being different, in social life and academic.

In this compacted statement, the speaker depicts herself moving from a common assumption that second-level school is about academics, to the realisation that the social is also significant. At the same time she moved from trying to be 'the same as everybody else', to the greater struggle to 'stop you being [made] different'. She had had to struggle hard to get ability-matched placement in a streamed school. The key to freedom from such escalating stress and exclusion is an inclusive school environment and ethos, one that recognises the student right to have what he or she needs to fly free, as the next speaker did in college:

> I have the technology now, which is my wings, that's the biggest difference. I can overcome people's attitudes now, I can, I'm independent, I can read on my own, I can type on my own. I haven't come up against exams yet so I will see how that goes.

Participants wanted normality, but the school system reflects and endorses the 'normal' exclusionary ethos of society unless the issues involved in making normality inclusive are specifically addressed.

Life after school: social and personal

This section expands on how participants' unsupported struggle distorted their general social relations with their peers, in and out of school. In effect, the topic of socialising was opened up in their talk about events like school trips. The curriculum and broader social life feather off into each other: socialising during school activities and socialising in and out of school are marked in similar ways by thoughtlessness born of ignorance, and by lack of supports.

In the previous section, the ignorance of able-bodied peers was highlighted. The next remark suggests that this ignorance may well be born of unfamiliarity:

> If one of my friends walked in here [centre for further education for people with disabilities], they would be frightened to talk to someone and that is horrible to say, I think ... They would be frightened of the unknown really, like I was when I first got sick.

The majority 'suffer' from ignorance, the minority with disabilities pay the price. Given their de facto marginalisation in putatively integrated education and work settings, it is not surprising that many young people with disabilities have skewed peer group relationships. Participants expressed anger and depression as their efforts not to be 'different' were frustrated. As noted in the talk of school earlier, many of them were developing stoic acceptance of the status quo ('it was alright', 'there was no discrimination'). Given the absence of emancipatory supports in mainstream schools, it is not surprising that many of them welcomed the 'level playing pitch' of specialised provision and were happy to work with disabled people while at the same time holding on to other able-bodied friends. Not surprisingly also, de facto exclusion resulted for many in a thin and erratic presence in the social scene. Participants' talk about socialising (a heartfelt need in adolescence) was so powerfully clear, it requires little comment. The following excerpts illustrate how the wider social environment and the classroom realities intertwine:

> I have a very select few friends. It takes me a long time before I'd trust them with certain aspects of my life, and I think the fact that I couldn't do as much as other people meant I was excluded from going out with the class – I think they were nearly afraid I would hurt myself. It was unreal the slagging and it can be at disabled people. They're just doing it for a joke; they don't know what the person feels.

The following interaction shows how damaging the outcomes of inappropriate school provision can be:

> *S1:*   I suppose I excluded myself. I didn't feel I was worth anything. I wasn't the type of child that would burst into a room bubbly. I was just too caught up, I hated school, I hated everything about it. I spent my whole life trying to be sick – you know, the ear aches and stomach aches, that was me. I just went in and tried to survive the day. I wasn't bullied or picked on, I just switched off for an awful lot of years.
>
> *S2:*   It happened to me for a year as well... there was no purpose in transition year, it's just bang in the middle and they give you work and they don't care if you do it or not and I got depressed for the whole year. And you're going through puberty whatever it is and I was drinking. I had a major drinking problem... ah, I don't know why, I just lost all my confidence. I just didn't know how to find a friend. It was all going through my head, OK, these people they weren't paying enough attention.

In an environment that didn't 'expect' them, they became invisible. This continued on into wider social activities. The following account shows how a young woman's friends learned, but not before they had unthinkingly left her in deepest personal isolation:

> [When] I got sick all my friends were just starting to go out to night clubs... I told them I didn't want to hang around with them anymore... I just put the phone down and cried because none of them had a clue... Three and a half years later, I went out with them a couple of weeks ago and I remember

thinking to myself they were really looking out for me. Everyone was upstairs, all the young people dancing away and one of my friends [said] 'We'll go downstairs, there are no seats'. She was thinking of me and that never happened before . . . They are only realising now. Better late than never.

One young man tentatively identified the rejection he encountered as akin to racism:

> If someone talks to me and I go sorry, I'm deaf, I lip-read, and if they walk away, fine, but I'm not going to talk to them again. I don't know, 'racist' might be the word, it might be too strong. But I'm in a club and some people don't accept it. They might think I'm talking very loud and drunk out of my head and I'm talking a load of rubbish. Girls stand back, they seem to have really big problems with my being there. I don't know why. If they have a problem it's not my problem. I have to be straightforward, I can't hide it, can't go saying 'I'm not deaf, I know exactly what you're saying'. I *don't* know.

It hardly needs saying that these extracts pose a challenge to schools: how to prepare majority and minority to build an inclusive society. The next speaker expands on the school agenda:

> Underlying the school really in second level it is the exam in the end. But it is also how you relate to each other . . . you know life does not go kindly, life just throws bad deals at some people and I think there should be a support group in every school and college to deal with it – specialised people, their job should be to help people . . . and teachers should be trained to spot these signs at their early stage.

This young man was speaking about second-level provision for all. When it comes to building a social life, many if not most adolescents experience insecurity and feelings of isolation. What is significant about the experience of young people with disabilities is that their pain could so clearly be reduced if they could engage in their adolescent struggles within an inclusive society that supplied them as a matter of course with the resources they need for independent living and learning. Obviously, in such a society, in which diversity of capabilities was accepted as normal, life for all young people would be vastly improved.

Concluding comments

Access to the curriculum is a social achievement. Participants' opinions about the 'work' of school, about attending classes, doing assignments, participating in activities relating to areas such as home economics, PE, science and school trips – all this talk was saturated with how the struggle to engage, conducted under the gaze of their peers and without appropriate supports, was also a struggle against skewing their social self-presentation and peer relations towards an omnipresent disability focus.

Underpinning inadequate educational responses is a simplistic perception of students with disabilities. The system lacks ambition for them; indeed at times it is even suspicious of their right to recognition as young people with highly varied potential and needs. Often, in the absence of system commitment to providing adequate and appropriate supports, participants had to rely on the kindness of individual peers and teachers.

It is worth noting what happened when participants negotiated the two 'moments' of entrance and exit (choice of school, and – though it was not strictly part of the topic of this chapter – applications for supports for examinations). These moments are relatively private, in that they need involve only the student, guardians and professionals. At this point, system unpreparedness and even suspicion culminated for many of them in a struggle to access examination supports. In both these moments, many students with disabilities start all over again to reach for normality, to push open the doors of academic ambition and social involvement for themselves. This is probably true for all young people, but it has particular significance in relation to those with disabilities. Thus, the restrictions of primary level are shed in transition to second level, and likewise, ambition for normal life informs many students' approaches to third level, despite their struggles and failures, and ensuing chronic focus on their disability and how to surmount it, during their years in second level. Such resilience and ambition demand an equally ambitious response from the system.

Happily, most of the participants had at some time met good teachers; some of them were fortunate enough to have found good schools. However, *ad hoc* responses are grossly inadequate. Development of an inclusive ethos and provision of adequate supports are ethical imperatives above all because they are a human right and necessity – as is proven by the drastic impact of their absence on the social lives of these young people. Whatever their academic status, people with disabilities live in society and are entitled to be full members of it, especially of their peer group.

In their engagement with learning and living within any level, most participants continued to display great resilience. For instance, the young woman with dyslexia persisted until she found her technology, then flew joyfully into her course reading and could look the world right in the eye. There was some bitterness, as in the case of a participant who perceived the whole world as being opposed to her (she summarised college as 'me against 799'). It is surprising that far more of them were not bitter, especially given the intense pain in their social experiences. Rather, there was a lot of talk about how people are basically decent. But in the accounts of depression, anger and defeated struggles there is a clear indicator of the need for counselling supports as well as learning aids and physical needs assistance. Those who opted for specialised provision were undoubtedly most articulate about their disabilities, most actively engaged in identifying their rights, and critiquing the able-ist agenda informing all our social structures. One measure of truly inclusive education will be when such reflection can be engaged with openly in mainstream.

This focus on the social dimension of the participants' experience powerfully highlights the ethical urgency of the task of transforming our overall education system, schools ethos, built environment, and pedagogic resources and procedures to ensure inclusive education, informed by ambition for all students. Young people with disabilities want normality, and in school terms this means the freedom to spread their wings academically and socially, in the company of their peers, in an educational context that expects them all to aim for the stars.

References

Atkinson, D. and Williams, F. (eds) (1990) *Know Me as I am: An Anthology of Prose, Poetry and Art by People with Learning Difficulties.* London: Hodder and Stoughton.

Beresford, B. (1997) *Personal Accounts: Involving Disabled Children in Research.* Norwich: Social Policy Research Unit.

Department of Justice, Equality and Law Reform (1996) *A Strategy for Equality: Report of the Commission on the Status of people with Disabilities.* Dublin: Stationery Office.

Kenny, M., McNeela, E., Shevlin, M. and Daly, T. (2000) *Hidden Voices: Young People with Disabilities Speak about their Second-level Schooling.* Cork: Bradshaw Books.

Lewis, A. and Lindsay, G. (2000) 'Emerging issues'. In A. Lewis and G. Lindsay (eds), *Researching Children's Perspectives.* Buckingham: Open University Press.

Potter, J. and Wetherell, M. (1989) *Discourse and Social Psychology.* London: Sage Publications.

van Dijk, T.A. (1998) 'Critical discourse analysis'. Second draft, January 1998. In D. Tannen, D. Schiffrin and H. Hamilton (eds) (2003) *Handbook of Discourse Analysis.* Oxford: Blackwell. http://www.hum.uva.nl/~teun/cda.htm.

Chapter 19

Inclusive learning experiences

Learning from children and young people

Julie Allan

Introduction

Children and young people are increasingly being recognised as actors and citizens (Moss and Petrie, 2002), with rights to express views on matters such as their education, health and care (Alderson, 1995). These rights are enshrined in law and in codes of practice, placing an obligation on local authorities and schools to seek the views of children (DfES, 2001; Lewis, 2003). But what insights do children and young people offer into inclusion? How can they help to make curricula and pedagogy more inclusive? In this chapter, I consider the emergence of children's voices within policy and practice and examine how their closely circumscribed function and role has limited their effects. I then explore some of the ways in which children could make a difference to the understanding and practice of inclusive education and consider the kinds of changes necessary to enable the views of children and young people to be acted upon. This chapter draws on research with children and young people in which I have been involved over several years and include a study of children with special needs in mainstream schools (Allan, 1999) research on children's learning (Allan *et al.*, 1998; Duffield *et al.*, 2000); a study of children's rights (Allan and I'Anson, 2003) and a Scottish Parliament Inquiry into special needs (Scottish Parliament, 2001a,b). Children and young people have, in each case, offered some profound insights, which could help us to shape inclusive learning experiences for them.

The emergence of children's voices

The UN Convention on the rights of the child, signed by 111 countries and ratified by 52 has placed children's rights high on public and political agendas. The Convention has attracted some criticism, largely because of the 'chasm between Convention and practice' (Freeman, 2000a, p. 279). Communitarians have argued that the strident and absolutist nature of rights generates selfishness, whilst the 'right' have suggested that the family is undermined by the rights agenda (Freeman, 2000b). Whilst the children's rights legislation arising from the UN Convention represents a considerable step forward, children are still constructed in law and in educational policy as 'aliens' (Van Bueren, 1995, p. 141) or as 'serfs' (Beck, 1997, p. 161). Professionals assume a position of acting in the best interests of the child and adopt the role of protector.

Relationships between children and adults within school envelop them within rigid stratifications (Roy, 2003) which firmly establish the territories of teacher and taught; knowledge and knower:

> The view of the teacher as expert also tends to reinforce the image of the teacher as autonomous individual. As a possession, knowledge also implies territorial rights, which become naturalized by the compartmentalization of curriculum. The cultural myth of teachers as experts, then, contributes to the reification of both knowledge and the knower.
>
> (Britzman, 1986, pp. 450–451)

Furthermore, conventional thinking about children as 'in need' or 'at risk' and professional approaches to supporting learners construct children as recipients of provision and incapable of negotiating its form and content.

School councils and representation on committees have been the most common way in which schools have encouraged children to voice their opinions. These have, however, tended to restrict children's involvement to matters such as playgrounds and uniforms, and have avoided issues of teaching and learning. At the same time, children are subjected to increasing levels of surveillance through the compliance models of children's services that are in operation (Moss and Petrie, 2002). It has been argued that for the rights agenda to succeed, there needs to be a re-examination of conceptual frameworks of children's representation (James and Prout, 1990; Christensen and James, 2001) and of childhood more generally (Moss and Petrie, 2002). Dahlberg et al. (1999) have suggested that this could be done through a form of pedagogical documentation, enabling us to question the images and discourses of the child we have embodied and produced and to ascertain what voice, rights and position the child has in our institutions.

My own interest in the views of children and young people emerged early in my career as an educational researcher. In externally funded research, the perspectives of children and young people were often of greater intrinsic interest than those of practitioners and policymakers; increasingly, I became convinced that their stories had an important role, not just sitting alongside other accounts, but often challenging and subverting them. In each of the four projects discussed here the voices of children and young people are central. Actively Seeking Inclusion (Allan, 1999) is concerned with the experiences of eleven young people with a 'special needs' label and their mainstream peers. Parents, teachers and headteachers also provide their views, but it is the children and young people who give the book its title and who generated new understandings about inclusion.

In a study of children's learning, carried out for a local authority (Allan et al., 1998; Duffield et al., 2000), we interviewed children about their experiences of learning and teaching several times and although they had initially found the discussions difficult, they became more fluent and articulate and pronounced themselves pleased, but surprised, to have been involved in this way:

> the questions were easy but good answers were difficult... [it was] complicated to think what you really mean.
>   You don't usually talk about these things
>
>   (Allan, 1998)

The children described their experiences of learning and teaching and identified the features of effective practice that they felt they were entitled to.

In one primary school in Scotland, a headteacher has attempted to take the children's rights agenda as far as possible and, together with Save the Children, we have been researching the impact of this 'experiment' on the children's relationships with each other and with the adults in the school (Allan and I'Anson, 2003). A disability consultation group was established in the school by a parent who has two disabled children. Seven 11-year olds joined the group and named it the Special Needs Consultation Group (SNOG). They set about investigating the experience of disability within their school, finding out how to make inclusion work for all children in the school and educating their peers about disability. The children's insights have shaped practice throughout the school and they are seeking to expand their work to include other schools.

The final piece of work referred to in this chapter concerns an Inquiry into special needs in Scotland, undertaken by the Scottish Parliament Committee on Education, Culture and Sport and to which I acted as adviser. Evidence was obtained from a wide constituency of professionals, parents and children and young people and some of the young people who provided written submissions were invited to visit Parliament to offer more detailed 'advice'. What they had to say influenced the politicians to the extent that it was asserted that 'parents and children are the key to the solution of special educational needs – not the vested interests of one profession or another, or one party-political interest or another' (Scottish Parliament, 2001b, Col. 822).

Learning from children and young people: new takes on the 'problem' of inclusion

To children and young people, the justification of, and the means to, inclusion can seem incredibly clear, as this letter to Tony Blair illustrates:

> Dear Mr Blair,
> We are a group of disabled and non-disabled young people and supporters who believe we should all have the right to go to our local mainstream school. We feel that children in special schools miss out on a decent academic and social education and those in mainstream schools, who hardly ever see disabled people, miss out on the opportunity to learn about and appreciate differences,

rather than only seeing disabled people through the patronising view of the media.

We feel we deserve each other's friendship and that the segregated education system denies us the chance to be together and see each other for what we really are. We are asking you to put an end to compulsory segregation by changing the law. We want to be together!

Yours sincerely, the Young People of Great Britain, c/o Young and Powerful

(Shaw, 2002)

Children and young people also have a highly nuanced understanding of inclusion and learning, in spite of an often patronising regard for them from adults and a discouragement from thinking and discussing these processes. The individuals involved in the four studies featured here offer new insights which could reframe our understanding of inclusion and exclusion and help us to imagine new possibilities for practice. First they reveal what it is like to experience inclusion and exclusion; second, they identify where some of the barriers to inclusion lie within schools, through their own practical engagement with these and their ability to see what adults may miss; third, children and young people are able to invent new selves through the experimentation with and the experience of inclusion. These are considered, in turn, here.

How was it for you? Experiencing inclusion and exclusion

Inclusion policies and practices have been developed with scant regard for what it means for the lives of children and young people and their families. The experiences of inclusion and exclusion by the children and young people in the four projects challenge how these processes are understood.

Inclusion, according to the children identified with special educational needs and their mainstream peers in *Actively Seeking Inclusion*, was not some static, once and for all, event concerned with placement and resources. Rather, the students regarded both inclusion and exclusion as much more unstable processes, occurring in 'moments' and often switching them between being included and excluded. The research also revealed a clash of discourses between, on the one hand, the children's desires (e.g. to be seated beside their friends, or treated 'normally') and, on the other, the teachers' articulation of what they saw as the children's needs (for support). Tensions from these competing discourses of desires and needs often arose within the classroom but usually led to the silencing of the students' desires by the more voluble professionally based needs discourse.

The mainstream students in *Actively Seeking Inclusion* demonstrated highly nuanced understandings of disability and of the conditions required for justice and equality. They also revealed how they played a key role as inclusion *gatekeepers*. This was read as operating as within a micro-regime of governmentality (Foucault, 1991), which functioned as a set of unwritten rules of conduct and sanctioned or prohibited particular actions. Foucault's use of the term governmentality combines the power to direct conduct with a particular mentality or presumption that 'everything can, should, must be managed, administered by authority' (Allen, 1998, p. 179). The mainstream students' governmentality, appeared, for the most part, to support inclusion, for example, by sanctioning strategies which were pastoral or pedagogic in their orientation. At the same time, however, these students also revealed some ambivalences and uncertainties, for example, where they felt anxious about, or sorry for, individuals, and these had disabling effects.

In the children's learning project, there was evidence of teachers teaching to the middle and those at either end of the ability spectrum being disadvantaged and excluded. Pupils characterised by their teachers as 'low ability' described feeling 'rushed' and causing impatience when they asked questions:

> The teacher just rushes on, and people who get [grade] ones were putting their hand up. If you went out to ask for help he would give you a row . . . We didn't understand it, we asked and he never even heard you – you keep putting your hand up – that's when we get punishments.
>
> Ask the teacher and they'll help you . . . [but] some teachers crack up on you and say you've not been listening.
>
> (Duffield et al., 2000, p. 270)

One pupil described how 'sometimes when I'm stuck I just kid on I'm writing because the teacher gives you a row if you're not [writing]' (ibid.). Pupils labelled as 'high ability' talked of being bored and insufficiently challenged. They also found that their attempts to challenge themselves were responded to with frustration by their teachers, in this case because they were perceived as being 'off task' or as challenging the teacher's authority.

The children in the SNOG group saw inclusion as an insurmountable right for all children and had formed the group to ensure this was achieved in practice. One of the members, Alistair, commented:

> I just felt good cos I liked helping them and I learned that everyone should be treated the same not differently even if they have a different colour of skin or they look different.

Their motives for forming the group included a desire to make a difference, 'to see how it feels' and the fact that they 'care'. They understood that inclusion was denied to some people as a consequence of barriers. These are explored in the next section.

The Scottish Parliament Inquiry heard from children and young people who had experienced exclusion, in both special and mainstream schools. One individual described herself as having 'escaped' from special school with her dignity just about intact; another young person used the same phrase, but was referring to his escape from the mainstream. For this student, mainstream schooling amounted to a refusal of his deaf identity and an attempt to assimilate him, which led to his exclusion

> At breaks and lunch time, all my hearing friends would go into groups. They would listen to music and talk about pop records, so I felt very isolated. I went through some depression. It was also extremely difficult to communicate with the teachers who could not sign. How was I supposed to ask questions? I had an interpreter, but I did not have the interpreter for all classes – only for English or maths. For classes such as physical education, there was no interpreter. Therefore, I would have to write things down. I felt embarrassed about that ... During my time at mainstream school, my confidence had deteriorated and I decided that I could not go back. I stayed at home for six months.
>
> (Scottish Parliament, 2000a, Cols 1141–1142)

This youngster had moved to a special school for the Deaf and had been astonished at the contrast:

> I was shocked; the college was so different from mainstream schooling. I had not realised how good it would be for me. I thought that it was just the equivalent of mainstream school, but in fact it was the opposite. At the mainstream school I was bullied, but that never happened to me at Donaldson's College. Now, looking back, I feel that I made the right decision in going to Donaldson's College ... the communication is there and it is very easy. Everyone can sign – the teachers, children, cleaners and gardeners – communication is vital and it is very easy.

For this young person, the effortless communication that was possible in his new school, but denied in the mainstream, made the difference between inclusion and exclusion. Further evidence from children and young people alerted the MSPs to the need to move beyond distributive calculus (Slee, 1993) and to recognise the potentially highly exclusionary nature of some mainstream settings:

> Inclusion is about more than being in the same building; it is about being with others, sharing experiences, building lasting friendships, being recognised for making a valued contribution and being missed when you are not there. Inclusion is not an issue of geography. Yes, we need buildings to be made accessible, but change can happen only if people have accessible minds. We need to realise that it is a fundamental right of all children to be educated together. We all need to realise that today's children are tomorrow's future. We need to work together in partnership to secure that future.
>
> (Scottish Parliament, 2000b, Col. 1190)

Barrier-spotting

Coffield (2002) has suggested that young people function well in the role of citizens and bullshit detectors. They also appear to have a highly sophisticated ability to identify barriers to inclusion and the means of removing them.

The disabled and non-disabled students in *Actively Seeking Inclusion* identified an abundance of barriers to inclusion in their schools. The most significant of these were attitudes and these were not blatantly negative, but were more subtle, usually caused by a difficulty in dealing with an individual's impairment and more common among teachers than pupils. This is illustrated by one visually impaired student, describing a particular teacher:

> She's really nice, but she never says 'see' to me – she says 'I'll give you this and you can listen to it' and it's a sheet of paper and she never likes to use the work 'see', or anything to do with the eyes and you can tell when people are trying to avoid that. It puts you off
>
> (in Allan, 1999, p. 62)

This was coupled with some misunderstandings about the nature of her impairment and its effects and some crass behaviour:

> They always ask you to come down to the front, in front of the whole class and things like that and I don't really need to be at the front because I can't see the board in the first place anyway and if it's television, I prefer sitting at the back because I've got tunnel vision and I can see it better.
>
> (Raschida, in Allan, ibid.)

Mainstream students were equally derisive about teachers' inability to cope with particular impairments without making a fuss. A mainstream student described one teacher's behaviour as 'patronising':

> [The teacher] was going on about the fact that they couldn't see properly, she just kept going on and on, and just wouldn't stop ... She was being really really bad ... She was being really really horrible to [two visually impaired students]
>
> (in Allan, 1999, p. 63)

The mainstream students also accused the teachers of giving 'special treatment' which was unnecessary and unwelcome to disabled students:

> I think they sometimes go out of their way to help [the disabled student] but she doesn't like that, she likes to be treated normally ... She doesn't like any special treatment ... If anybody makes a fuss of her she gets really embarrassed and she just doesn't like it. She's always complaining if people make a fuss of her. She'll say, 'Oh God, I wish they hadn't done that'. She just likes to be treated like everyone else.
>
> (Ibid.)

One of the visually impaired students was praised for challenging the 'special treatment' she had received:

> For instance, there was one time, people were talking in class, it was, like, a group of us, just girls in my group and one of them was talking to Laura [visually impaired student] and so one of them got a punishment exercise and Laura didn't, because she's visually impaired, So Laura spoke up and said, 'I'd like one too – there's no point in treating me differently, because I don't like that, I just want to be treated normally'.
>
> (Ibid.)

The mainstream students recognised that being around disabled people could be uncomfortable, because of a fear of doing or saying the wrong thing. However, they described how they overcame their own uneasiness through dialogue with disabled students and by focusing on their desires rather than their needs.

According to the participants in the children's learning project, teachers represented the most significant barriers to their learning. These mostly arose from the teachers' failure to provide adequate feedback on how they were progressing. One 11-year-old girl commented:

> The teachers give us good or bad. I can't understand why I get bad when I have worked well... Teachers never give us any help at all.
>
> (Allan et al., 1998)

The failure to provide good explanations was also identified as a barrier to learning and one group commented wryly on how, if they asked for an alternative explanation, teachers would often just repeat the explanation more loudly.

The parent leader of the SNOG group set up a simulation exercise, in which the pupils had to pretend to be a wheelchair-user, blind or without communication and to attempt to participate in 'normal' activities both in and out of the school. In spite of the potential essentialist problems associated with simulation exercises of this kind, their experience was salutary. The social model of disability, developed by disabled people (Oliver, 1996), focuses on the barriers – environmental, structural and attitudinal – to participation. Despite its obvious relevance to schools in identifying the changes necessary to be inclusive, this model has proved elusive to many professionals, who have clung tenaciously to deficit-oriented approaches of special educational needs. The children, however, adopted a social model analysis very quickly and with apparent ease. After some initial essentialist observations, for example, about whether it was harder to go to the toilet in a wheelchair as a boy or a girl, the pupils began to spot barriers to participation. These included awkward doors, a fire escape door which didn't work, inaccessible steps, dining room tables and computers at the 'wrong' height for the wheelchair and a telephone for calling for help in the toilet which would be unreachable by a child. The most significant barriers to participation, according to the children, came from the attitudes of their peers and the teachers. The students were highly critical of the spectacularisation of their presence in the wheelchair: 'When we were in the wheelchair everyone looked at us in a way', and found teachers just as guilty as their peers in this respect. The pupils also identified pity as a major barrier to inclusion and participation and one boy described how the group members set about challenging this within the school:

> I think everyone that's got a disability feels better when you treat them the same ... I think that's how they feel – they just like to get on with their life ... Cos they don't like being felt sorry for – just because they have disabilities doesn't mean they should be treated differently. That's what the group's all about – to make sure people don't treat each other differently because they look different. So that's what we've been doing.

In their evidence to the Scottish Parliament inquiry, children and young people described the most significant barrier as being negative attitudes towards them and low expectations of what they could achieve:

> Often kids get stuck in a cycle of diminished expectation because of social perceptions and beliefs. I wish there could be a shift in perception.
>
> (2000b, Col. 1201)

One respondent described barriers which were placed in his way by professionals and which almost denied him a mainstream placement:

> Both my parents were adamant that I should have the same rights, opportunities and life experiences as other kids ... After many months of fighting with doctors, psychologists and local authorities, I was finally given the green light to begin my schooling in a mainstream class.
>
> (Ibid., Col. 1188)

Although this individual had overcome these barriers, he had encountered further obstacles within school, for example, by being denied the opportunity to go on a foreign exchange trip with his peers or participate in after-school activities.

New selves, new practices

> Never interpret: experience, experiment
>
> (Deleuze, 1995, p. 87)

The insider perspective provided by the children and young people have provided new insights into the processes of inclusion and exclusion. They have also indicated how the practical experience of, and experimentation with, inclusion has had an impact on their identities.

The accounts provided by the disabled students in *Actively Seeking Inclusion* revealed highly sophisticated forms of transgression against the disabled identities and experiences imposed upon them by their peers, teachers and parents (Foucault, 1977). Transgression is a form of resistance involving the crossing of limits or boundaries. It is not antagonistic or aggressive, nor does it involve a contest in which there is a victor; rather, transgression is playful and creative. Also described by Foucault as 'technologies of the self' (1988, p. 11) are acts of resistance which

> Permit individuals to effect by their own means or with the help of others a certain number of operations on their own bodies and souls, thoughts, conduct, and a way of being, so as to transform themselves in order to attain a state of happiness, purity, wisdom, perfection or immortality.
>
> (Ibid., p. 18)

Among disabled people, transgression has been a significant means of challenging limits and disabling barriers. Whereas disability activists have been involved in a long campaign of direct action against disabling barriers, transgression has been a more indirect and subtle form of challenge by disabled people. Transgression enabled the disabled students in this study to gain some control over their lives and their relationships with others and they described ways in which they either transgressed in or out of disability. Transgressive strategies which moved the students away from a disabled identity included using humour to put peers at ease, pretending to be 'blind drunk' rather than drunk or avoiding going to the toilet; acts of transgression towards disability included claiming a more disabled label and requiring peers to provide help. Teachers were generally unsympathetic to, and critical of, the students' transgressive practices, tending to read these as evidence of students' failure to accept the 'fact' that they were disabled. The practice of transgression at least enabled disabled students to challenge some of the barriers created by teachers, based on what they perceived them to *need*, and to assert some of their own desires.

The children who participated in the children's learning project were clear about the need for teachers to reshape themselves in such a way as to enable them to function well as learners. They identified a number of features of good teaching that enabled them to participate and learn effectively:

- Being made to do class work and homework;
- Being made to write down an example, not just watch it;
- The teacher goes over work done, marks work, checks jotters;
- New material is explained;
- Questions about understanding are taken seriously and answered clearly;
- The teacher grasps which point is not understood;
- There are opportunities to experience 'real' activities;
- Practical activities are balanced with writing;
- Enough time is given together with a deadline for finishing.

(Allan *et al.*, 1998)

The children also articulated a number of rights in relation to their learning in which they saw themselves as having the following:

- Having high expectations of what they can achieve, as a result of praise and encouragement, along with guidance on how to do better.
- Gaining confidence about learning, through teacher encouragement, good explanations and feedback and having their views listened to.
- Having a say on a wide range of matters affecting them as learners and making decisions about what they learn and how.
- Working in group/paired activities, enabling them to benefit from sharing ideas with peers and developing social and citizenship skills, whilst minimising the possibilities of arguments arising within groups or individuals dominating or being isolated.
- Receiving detailed and individualised feedback to enable them to improve their work.

(Ibid.)

These rights placed the children in an active role as learners, allowing them to take some responsibility for their own learning and requiring a greater level of respect and trust from teachers.

Involvement in the SNOG group represented a chance for one young person to acquire a new self. This student, Alistair, had been labelled as having severe behavioural problems and according to his headteacher, he was destined for permanent exclusion because of his violent behaviour against other students and staff. Alistair described his transformation:

A: I used to be, like, really really bad. I used to fight everybody, but now I've calmed down because I've got a responsibility to look after them.
J: Can you say more about that?
A: Well, when I started to know them I was, like, I need to show them I want to be good, cos I used to get into fights and stupid things like that but when I started to get to know them and got into the SNOG group I started my behaviour; I wanted to start again and be good.
J: Is that right?
A: Yeah, cos I didn't want everybody to know me as Alistair the bad boy. I want to be good now. So that's what I was trying to do when I went into the SNOG group.
J: Wow. So, before you used to get into lots of fights?
A: yeah. Now I get into them not that much . . . but sometimes I'm amazing and no-one thinks that I used to fight and that, but I just kick it off again. I just want to be good but I cannae sometimes. I think I've really improved my behaviour. I used to be really bad but now I'm not that bad. I'm quite good now.

His lapses had become infrequent and seemed to be beyond his control, but he was able to repair the damage:

A: I get into a fight or I get angry because it didn't happen. If I didn't get to sit beside my friends I start to get angry. I just want to be a good boy now. As everybody says 'good boy'. That's what I want to be – I want to prove them all wrong. They all think I cannae behave but I want to prove them all wrong that I can behave. . . some people just know me as 'there's Alistair – stay away from him'. But I'm to prove them all wrong – that I'm good. I'm going to be good. I just want to be good now. But I was bad a couple of weeks ago.

J: Were you? So what happened then?

A: I was shouting at a teacher. I said something to him really bad and I had to get taken home . . . At the time I was all angry and I just shouted, but afterwards I regretted it cos I knew I'd done wrong, but you can't change the past but you can make sure the future's better.

Alistair spoke of how his involvement in the disability group was initially motivated by a desire to get closer to disabled people, but that he had quickly realised that such sentimentality was misplaced:

I just wanted to have them 'cos I thought they looked amazing. I just wanted to be with them . . . I thought they looked so cute and things like that. But everybody feels sorry for them but they're just the same as us so they should just be treated the same.

During the group discussions, Alistair appeared to be the most comfortable with the social model of disability and when the others, including the parent leader, drifted towards essentialist analyses, he guided their focus back onto exclusionary barriers. Alistair appeared to have found within the space of the disability group an opportunity to create a new assemblage of the self. Alistair the bad boy was not eradicated entirely, but at least he could be deflected by the Alistair who had responsibilities, as someone who cared and who was, in his own words, 'amazing'.

In her evidence to the Scottish Parliament, one young person, reflecting on her success as a 'product of inclusive education' (Scottish Parliament, 2000b, Col. 1184), described how she had taken a long time to acquire confidence about her identity:

This is the first time in my academic career . . . that I have not felt that if I do not get it right I will be sent back to special school.

(Ibid.)

Another individual argued that inclusion was not just a fundamental right for everyone, but could help shape the identities and experiences of mainstream pupils:

It is frequently thought to be a good thing for a disabled child to go to a mainstream school. However, it is equally good for the non-disabled kids. I received a lot of positive feedback from people in similar situations to mine. The classmates learn much from the disabled child – it has been a very positive thing for them throughout. The challenge is what makes it interesting.

(Scottish Parliament, 2000b, Col. 1193)

Creating inclusive learning experiences is indeed a challenge, but these children and young people have provided some hints as to the possibilities for change.

Seen and heard: reworking adult/child relationships

The students' accounts offer a sanguine view of inclusion which does not hold to a utopian 'vision' (Barton, 1997, p. 239); rather, their view of inclusion recognises the place of 'struggle' (ibid.) and highlights the importance of relationships within the school. Their accounts suggest that inclusion can realistically be achieved, but only if the exclusionary nature of existing practices and adult/child relationships is acknowledged and altered.

The UN Convention provides a valuable framework for shifting practice, providing, as Cairns (2001) asserts, adults recognise that they have responsibilities to recognise these rights. This means establishing 'dialogue, not consultation' (ibid., p. 355) with young people, giving them 'opportunities to ask why of public services' (ibid.) and challenging the assumption that adults always know best.

A reworking of child/adult relationships might involve blurring the boundaries between the two binarisms. Teachers might also be invited to ask two pedagogical questions: first of all, how do we, as 'pupal and forgetful learners, listen to others' narratives?' (Gregouriou, 2001, p. 134). Secondly, how do we, as teachers, 'become messengers, to ventriloquize, transfer and recite others' narratives in the context of our classrooms?' (ibid.).

A more positive construction of the teaching relationship might be as 'contact zones,' (Pratt, 1992), spaces of engagement with the other. These are

> Social spaces where disparate cultures meet, clash and grapple with each other, often in highly asymmetrical relations of domination and subordination . . . the spatial and temporal copresence of subjects.
>
> (Pratt, 1992, pp. 4–7)

These relations between individuals could be treated as spaces in which trading of modes of representation and the negotiation could take place within a space of contestation:

> Trading and engaging in each other's idioms leaves neither the metropolis's nor the periphery's modes of representation untouched. Rather, it corrupts, distorts and hybridizes both of them.
>
> (Gregouriou, 2001, p. 139)

Gregoriou, drawing on Plato's *Timaeus*, suggests that teachers may themselves become displaced receptacles for others' narratives, acting as travelling mediators or sophists. This requires cultivation of teachers, not through self-reflective critique, tolerance of, respect for, or celebration of, difference, but through an invitation to inhabit new spaces:

> It is a place we *create* when in hosting others we change, hybridize our discourses and identities, and let others teach us, from the beginning, how we are different and multiple *within ourselves*.
>
> (Ibid. p.146; original emphasis)

Such engagement may enable determinate categories of teacher, student or curriculum to be discarded, looking instead for encounters which create 'fluctuating fields of habits, affects and ideas that are in continual flux' (Roy, 2003, p. 151). These encounters could also encourage an altered sensitivity to difference and lack' (Conway, 1997, p. 82). In Deleuze and Guattari's (1987) terms, student teachers could become 'sorcerers' (p. 241), engaged in the production of affect:

> thus initiated, we turn the tables on lack and move from passive consumerism to active production . . . it can open us toward affirming the unknown which, in a sense, is pure difference.
>
> (Roy, 2003, p. 102)

A more succinct rendering of the necessary changes was provided by a teacher, who suggested that the teacher had to shift from being the 'sage on the stage' to being the 'guide on the side'.

Slee (2003) has argued that educational disablement and exclusion should be reframed as cultural politics and that the various parties involved should be brought out of the 'trenches and bunkers' and encouraged to 'treat each other with dignity and respect' (p. 217). Children and young people should also be afforded this dignity and respect and a key way of doing this is ensuring that they 'play a key part in shaping inclusive education' (ibid.) This implies not just listening to their voices, but also being open to the new possibilities for action they reveal:

> As soon as you address the other, as soon as you are open to the future, as soon as you have a temporal experience of waiting for the future, of waiting for someone to come: that is the opening of experience. Someone is to come, is *now* to come. Justice and peace will have to do with this coming of the other, with the promise.
>
> (Derrida, 1997, p. 23)

References

Alderson, P. (1995) *Listening to Children: Children, Ethics and Social Research*, Barkingside: Barnardos.

Allan, J. (1999) *Actively Seeking Inclusion: Pupils with Special needs in Mainstream Schools*, London: Falmer.

Allan, J. and I'Anson, J. (2003) Children's rights in school: assemblies and assemblages. Paper presented to the European Conference on Educational Research, 17–20 September, Hamburg.

Allan, J., Duffield, J., Morris, B. and Turner, E. (1998) Raising achievement in S1 and S2. Report to Stirling Council Education Services, University of Stirling.

Allen, B. (1998) Foucault and modern philosophy, in *The Later Foucault* (ed. J. Moss) London: Sage Publications.

Barton, L. (1997) Inclusive education: romantic, subversive or realistic? *International Journal of Inclusive Education*, 1(3), pp. 231–242.

Beck, U. (1997) Democratisation of the family, *Childhood*, 4, pp. 151–168.

Boyne, R. (1990) *Foucault and Derrida: The Other Side of Reason*, London/New York: Routledge.

Britzman, D. (1986) Cultural myths in the making of a teacher, *Harvard Educational Review*, 56 (40) pp. 442–455.

Cairns, L. (2001) Investing in children: learning how to promote the rights of all children, *Children and Society*, 15 (5), pp. 347–360.

Christensen, P. and James, A. (2001) Researching children and childhood: cultures of communication, in P. Christensen and A. James (eds) *Research with Children: Perspectives and Practices*, London: RoutledgeFalmer.

Coffield, F. (2002) A *New Strategy for Learning and Skills: Beyond IOI Initiatives*, Newcastle: Department of Education, University of Newcastle.

Conway, D. (1997) Tumbling dice: Gilles Deleuze and the economy of repetition, in K. Pearson (ed.) *Deleuze and Philosophy: The difference Engineer*, London: Routledge.

Dahlberg, G., Moss, P. and Pence, A. (1999) *Beyond Quality in Early Childhood Education and Care: Postmodern Perspectives*, London: Falmer Books.

Deleuze, G. (1995) *Negotiations*, New York: Columbia University Press.

Deleuze, G. and Guattari, F. (1987) *A Thousand Plateaus: Capitalism and Schizophrenia*, Minneapolis: University of Minnesota Press.

Department for Education and Science (2001) *Code of Practice on the Identification and Assessment of Pupils with Special Educational Needs*, London: DfES.

Derrida, J. (1997) The Villanova roundtable: a conversation with Jacques Derrida, in J. Caputo (ed.) *Deconstruction in a Nutshell*, New York: Fordham.

Duffield, J., Allan, J., Turner, E. and Morris, B. (2000) Pupils' voices on achievement: an alternative to the standards agenda, *Cambridge Journal of Education*, 20 (2), pp. 263–274.

Foucault, M. (1977) A preface to transgression, in D. Bouchard(ed.) *Language, Counter-memory, Practice: Selected Essays and Interviews by Michel Foucault*, Oxford: Basil Blackwell.

Foucault, M. (1988) Technologies of the self, in L. Martin, H. Gutman and P. Hutton (eds) *Technologies of the Self: A Seminar with Michel Foucault*, London: Tavistock.

Foucault, M. (1991) Governmentality, in G. Burchell, G. Gordon and P. Miller (eds) *The Foucault Effect: Studies in Governmentality*, Hemel Hempsted: Harvester Wheatsheaf.

Freeman, M. (2000a) The future of childen's rights, *Children and Society*, 14 (4) pp. 277–293.

Freeman (2000b) The end of the century of the child, *Current Legal Problems*, 50 pp. 505–558.

Gregoriou, Z. (2001) Does speaking of others involve receiving the 'other'? A postcolonial reading of receptivity in Derrida's deconstruction of Timaeus, in G. Biesta and D. Egéa-Kuehne (eds) *Derrida and Education*, London: Routledge.

James, A. and Prout, A. (eds) (1990) *Constructing and Reconstructing Childhood*, London: Falmer Press.

Lewis, A. (2003) Accessing, through interviews, the views of children with difficulties in learning, in M. Nind, J. Rix, K. Sheehy and K. Simmons (eds) *Inclusive Education: Diverse Perspectives*, London: David Fulton.

Moss, P. and Petrie, P. (2002) *From Children's Services to Children's Spaces: Public policy, Children and Childhood*, London: RoutledgeFalmer.

Oliver, M. (1996) *Understanding Disability: From Theory to Practice*, Basingstoke: Macmillan.

Pratt, M. (1992) *Imperial Eyes: Travel Writing and Transculturation*, New York: Routledge.

Roy, K. (2003) *Teachers in Nomadic Spaces: Deleuze and Curriculum*, New York: Peter Lang.

Scottish Parliament (2000a) Official Report: Education, Culture and Sport Committee, Wednesday 14 June.

Scottish Parliament (2000b) Official Report: Education, Culture and Sport Committee, Wednesday 21 June.

Scottish Parliament (2001a) Official Report of special needs Inquiry. Retrieved on February 18, 2002, from http://www.scottish.Parliament.uk/official_report/session-01/sor0517–02.htm

Scottish Parliament (2001b) Official report of debate on motion S1M-1931: special educational needs. Retrieved on February 18, 2002, from http://www.scottish.Parliament.uk/official_report/session-01/sor0517–02.htm

Shaw, L. (2002) '*We want to be together*'. Retrieved 22 July, 2003, from http://inclusion.uwe.ac.uk/inclusionweek/articles/together.htm

Slee, R. (1993) The politics of integration: new sites for old practices? *Disability, Handicap and Society*, 8 (4), pp. 351–360.

Slee, R. (2003) Teacher education, government and inclusive schooling: the politics of the Faustian waltz, in J. Allan (ed.) *Inclusion, Participation and Democracy: What is the Purpose?* Dordrecht: Kluwer.

Van Bueren, G. (1995) *The International Law on the Rights of the Child*, Dordrech, Martinus Nijhoft Publishers.

Index